# The Junior Headmaster's Daughter

*Stepping from the shadows of sexual assault on the journey to recovery.*

## Joanna Mary

Cover and internal design by Coven Press

www.covenpress.com.au

Images in this book are copyright approved for use by author

First printing: March 2026

Paperback ISBN 978-1-7645159-0-0

eBook ISBN 978-1-7645159-1-7

Hardback ISBN 978-1-7645159-2-4


www.joannamaryauthor.com

A catalogue record for this work is available from the National Library of Australia

Distributed by Lightning Source Global

# CONTENTS

# PROLOGUE

It was because of my father's employment at an elite school in Australia, that I exposed to a world of sexual predators. Sexual predators that had been highly active for many years. Sexual predators that had also gone unnoticed for many years. Or, perhaps they had been noticed but not properly seen and deliberately never reported.

It was with some of these predators that I became a child sexual abuse victim too. Some of these abusers were my parents' so-called friends. These friends included, not only Geelong Grammar School staff, but one of their friends that was a Geelong Grammar School parent.

The itinerary for my life dramatically changed because of this abuse and I started to head down a road which turned out to be totally the wrong way. A no-through road. I am definitely sure I was stuck in this whirlwind vortex because I was the daughter of the Junior Headmaster at Geelong Grammar School.

My story paints a pictured environment for institutional child abuse. A closed isolated community, that was set up ideally to protect and educate children but rather, became a community to harm them. A community where people could move and behave in, that carefully hidden from the outside world. A community where unethical behaviours could also be obscured. It resembled a cult or sect. It completely shut, private and strictly regimented environment.

My story typifies my vulnerabilities, from being an innocent and ignorant little girl who has always struggled to become an independent and confident adult human being. My intentions are extremely far from wanting to hurt anybody by authoring this book. But I want to explain how my life has progressed because of my institutional child sexual abuse.

Another one of my objectives is to hopefully help other people navigate their way through similar experiences. Especially those, who have suffered any sort of sexual abuse and are possibly still trying to recover from it. Hopefully, anyone reading this book will try to understand what it is like to have lived a life as a sexually abused victim. For those who have been the victim of child sexual abuse, I would hope that it enables them to progress from being the victim, to becoming a survivor. I completely understand how hard it is to recover from abuse and how, unfortunately, victims tend historically to gravitate towards further abuse.

I also would love to help those people around the abused, to try and consider, understand and believe that this experience is never erased from our beings. It cannot be erased. It permanently taints and disfigures an individual's emotional growth and maturity. This is one of the hardest concepts for me to grasp and I have struggled with this for most of my life.

People from good and bad stages of my life, have been included, mostly to epitomise my way of thinking at certain times. These people have all been part of my journey.

There are stories of the nasty Jo and stories of the messed up Jo. By putting these pieces of my life together, I have found ways to forgive myself and importantly apologise to others that I have hurt. I now have found better ways to deal with the Post Traumatic Stress disorder that followed because of these life changing events.

I have always been truthful and, unfortunately at times, because of my honesty, I have suffered the consequences. I hate lies and I do not really like people who lie. So, this is my entire truth. I am never going to be, or never want to be, labelled as someone who is not honest. The good thing about liars is they nearly always get found out, and it comes back to bite them. It always pays to be honest.

Every person mentioned in this book, reflects a true memory of what happened and how it happened. There are other people who have also facilitated the way I have learned to heal. There may be other times when things seem cruel and I am unfeeling. There are other stages of anger and rage. My abuse has made me put up a front at times and enabled me to truly guard myself. Every survivor of sexual abuse goes into survival mode to protect themselves. Although historically, victims will often still attract more abuse and will not know how to protect themselves before it is too late. It is about learning and living how to become a survivor. A survivor of child sexual abuse.

We all learn through experiences, no matter how awful. But sometimes it takes too long to learn. That is where the torment, hatred, guilt, and depression can come into our lives. If only we could have found love for ourselves, without being on a path of inner self destruction.

The method of my explaining certain incidences may horrify some, but that is the way I reacted to things. The events that happened to me and how I behaved during my darker times. Things were bad. Things were desperate. I was totally confused about how I felt about so many things. I was also unaware of some of my terrible behaviour.

I have really hated myself. It took me years and a few great people, to enjoy who I am and finally like myself again. I am articulate and intelligent and people do like me. I never thought that I was like that and never believed it at all during these darker times.

In my life, I have been sexually abused as a child, I have been a bulimic, I have been bullied, I have been a drug user, I have been an alcoholic and I have been raped on a number of occasions.

I am deeply sorry for the way I have behaved but I am not sorry at all that I couldn't really help it. I didn't like me and the best way not to like yourself, is to take other people with you. I chose to try suicide a few times because I really wanted to die. Bulimia is a slow suicide and so is alcoholism. People can also die mentally, without dying physically.

Child sexual abuse is like a cancer that never goes into remission. It just continuously bleeds into your mind and leaves permanent bruises in your memory. But fortunately, things can get better.

In a few chapters, I have included my writings and letters written. They are an important part of my story. They are also important in helping you understand how I felt and how I feel, when I was in that time as well as reflecting on that time. Some pieces were written when I was sober and lucid, and some pieces were written when I was drunk. Some when I was emotionally moved and some writings when I was in the midst of a panic attack or recovering from one.

This is my story. For those who want to read it. It is especially for those that want to read and hear my words and try to understand.

I have been inspired by so many to author this book. I have engaged in factual books about other people's lives, who have been sexually abused, and it has helped me to express myself and, importantly, teach me how to heal myself.

There have been many people who either did this entire or some of the journey with me. Some, who are associated with Geelong Grammar School and some of whom I have worked for. Some are simply good friends. These good friends are my beautiful family. There are also others who I came in to contact with during the Royal Commission into Institutional Child Sexual Abuse and the committal hearings against Dr David Brian Mackey. There was the fantastic support work of the Victims Assistance Program in Victoria and the incredible support of the Victorian police.

Another inspiration was something that has always been on my mind. I remember telling my mother once, that I wanted to write a book about my life. Her answer to me was "Who would want to read a book about you?"

It still causes me much confusion and hurts about why my mother never thought my story would be worth reading. Probably because she saw me in so much emotional turmoil. She also never even tried once to find out why, how, and what to do about my abuse. I have always been totally miffed about this.

So, here it finally is and I am glad I have achieved such a task. I hope it may help every person, in some way, to heal if they need to. Find comfort that you are not the only one who has had a totally messed up time. Unfortunately, there is no manual for a lovely life and there is no manual for an abused child to survive either easily.

I have come in to contact with so many survivors of child sexual abuse, both males and females. Some of whom I knew at Geelong Grammar School and other institutions in the Geelong area. There are so many more out there as well, tied into the church.

I know of others, who have never been able to get back on track. And, unfortunately, I have known some people who have taken their own lives. This includes a few people from Geelong Grammar School. This has happened because of the institutional child sexual abuse.

For those of you who have suffered any sort of abuse, you can live through it, and there is someone out there always, to help you find your way. By finding you, you can find your way.

I remember a piece of graffiti written on the walls of a station on my daily trip to Melbourne for work. It said, "If you are not looking for the solution, you are part of the problem."

At the time, I didn't know which way to go because I was in my early twenties and I was the problem. But if I had read it, without my soul being deeply engraved in pain and horrible experiences, it would have made a lot more sense.

We all are the creators of our own destinies but there are always, and always will be, major detours. Trust me, my detours took me places I would not have chosen to be, but they are all now the little chapters that make me the person that I am.

And finally, now I am not too bad.

# CHAPTER 1

## *WHERE IT STARTED*

My name is Joanna Mary Herbert.

I was born at the Western General hospital in Edinburgh, Scotland on 16th September 1965. I was the second-born daughter to English parents. My father at the time, was a young schoolteacher. He was employed at a well-known boy boarding school in Edinburgh, Scotland. The school was the Fettes College.

As well as being a teacher, my father was also an international rugby player. On the day I was born, he was overseas playing rugby union for England, in the Argentine. My father was 32 when I was born and was physically approaching the end of his international sporting career. Also, with an expanding family, he decided things needed to change, for all our futures.

After my next sibling, Lisa, was born, my father applied for teaching jobs at a school in South Africa and a school in Australia. The school in Australia was the prestigious and elite, Geelong Grammar School.

In 1968, my father accepted the position of employment at Geelong. Very delighted with the opportunities that this position would create, he accepted a job as an English and History teacher.

We flew into Australia in January 1969. This enabled us to have some time to settle into a house that was provided by the school. The first school term began in early February. My father's first campus at the school was at Corio, which is situated on the northern side of Geelong. There were four campuses and Corio was for students in the secondary level. It was the main campus and about an hour's drive from Melbourne.

Other campuses included the Glamorgan campus, which is situated in the suburb of Toorak in Melbourne and caters for primary school students. The Bostock house campus, which is on the south-west side of Geelong, catered for primary school levels and years 7-8 in secondary levels. Bostock became Geelong Grammar School Highton in the seventies, when there were amalgamations with other private girls' schools. The Timbertop campus has students in Year 9 only.

The Timbertop campus has become well known, because his Royal Majesty, King Charles III, formerly Prince Charles, attended the school for two terms, in 1966. It is situated in north-eastern Victoria, near a town called Mansfield and the region is called the Victorian high country. The Mansfield district is a beautiful mountainous area, with ski fields and a large human-made lake called Lake Eildon.

I don't really remember much of my life as a four-year-old at Corio. But I do know that my sisters and I made friends with other children, who also lived at the school. My parents also made lifetime friends with some of the other members of the school. It was an extremely close-knit community. This community became our parents' entire social life. Everyone associated with Geelong Grammar School were all a huge part of the school community.

My parents had a house provided for them on the school grounds. Most full-time teachers were provided with a house on the school premises. This was so they were always available to the day and boarding students. Teachers also had to be available for sports activities, after school tuition had finished for the day. Other teachers were in charge of day houses and others did evening duties in the boarding houses. This included supervising evening studies and then making sure students were getting a good night's sleep. A housemaster normally lived in a house connected to a boarding house for obvious reasons.

Our first house was in a little court called Cameron Close. We had a few other families living nearby and our direct neighbours were the Crole family. There were four Crole children. Hugh was a lot older than me, then there was Kitty, who was my older sister's age, Claire, who was my age and then Christopher, who I can only remember as always being naughty and getting in to trouble. I think that he was about the same age as my closest sister, Lisa.

There was another family close by and across the field from Cameron close. They were the Mackeys. Dr Mackey was the general practitioner at Geelong Grammar School. His wife, Sue, who I think may have been a nurse, became particularly good friends with my mother. The Mackeys had three children at this stage, two boys and a daughter who became a good friend of Lisa's. Their youngest daughter came along later.

At some stage we would all end up playing together, because our parents socialised with their parents. Other school resident children were the only friends that we had to play with. Our parents only went out of the school grounds to go shopping. Or if we were holidaying somewhere.

After a year at Corio, in early 1970, my father was transferred to the Timbertop campus and continued to teach History and English. I believe he was also head of a group of boys' units or dormitories. This was quite normal practice at Geelong Grammar. Most teachers and schoolhouse masters had extra responsibilities outside of the classroom.

Attendance at Timbertop was an incredibly special year at GGS and still is. The campus was established in 1953 by the headmaster at the time, James Darling. It was an outdoor experience of many challenges, as well as education. You could say, at the time, it was set up so boys would become better and stronger charactered men. The Timbertop campus is situated about half an hour's drive from Mansfield.

# TIMBERTOP

The year at Timbertop, was really the one I remember well. We lived in a little house on the campus. There were two or three other houses, all in a row on our road. Everything was walking distance, so my father didn't need to drive a car very often, during term time. It was a nice existence for all of us and very community orientated.

A few things do come to mind that I remember well. We had a washing line outside, which underneath it was a Jumping Jack ant nest and my mother was often bitten in the summer, when she was putting our clothes on the line. You would hear screams coming from the washing line on a regular basis.

A Jumping Jack ant has a potent venom, and the sting would last for around 15 minutes. An extremely painful sort of experience and quite a nasty ant, alongside bull ants, that are found in bushy areas in Australia. Not deadly but pretty close to death pain. They were something my English mother had never been exposed to. And quite frankly, her experiences with them at Timbertop, were truly memorable occasions.

During the winter, it would sometimes snow. The school campus is set high enough above sea level for snow to settle on the ground. It was great fun for us and we would all rug up and play outside. Sometimes for a treat, my parents would pack us into their station wagon, and we would go up to Mount Stirling. There was always a lot more snow when you went higher into the mountains. We would toboggan on plastic sheets and play for hours until we were sopping wet. We, also at that time, had a German Shepherd called Katie, and my sisters and I would delight in throwing her snowballs to catch.

My father was very busy during term time at Timbertop because extra duties were expected from the teaching staff. But he was free to do other things in school holidays. We tended to do things more as a family then. Mum and dad would visit friends for a meal, normally those they had made through contacts at Geelong Grammar. My parents also met local Mansfield people through my older sister and myself, as we attended school and kindergarten.

One family were the Yenckens and, to this day, my parents are still incredibly good friends with them. We would spend time with them in the school holidays. We stayed with them at many Easters, even when we had left the campus at Timbertop.

Easter was aways great fun at the Yenckens. We would have an Easter egg hunt around their large garden. In the evenings, whilst our parents were having a relaxing drink or wind down, we would watch a music program called Count Down on television before we ate dinner. We would all hang out together and play on their farm. It was a lot of fun and the memories are still so vivid.

Those were also the days when we were still living at Timbertop where we would be put to bed in the back of the station wagon to sleep. And when the night was over, our parents would drive us home, without any harness or seat belts on us, for about half an hour. There were no such things as harnesses and seatbelts in the 1970s. One of my younger sisters, who was born whilst we were living at Timbertop, used to travel in a cane basket on the back seat of the car. Not strapped in at all.

Apart from our cat and dog, my father had some pet kookaburras that he would feed daily with mince. I remember the kookaburras showed up on one occasion, to show off their new family to us. It was just an enjoyable time as a young family, reflecting on it all.

Whilst we were at Timbertop, my eldest sister was attending the local primary school in Mansfield and I was enrolled at the Mansfield kindergarten for three days a week. On the mornings I went into Mansfield kindergarten, we would catch the school bus into town with Old Meggsie Hogarth. He would drop the Timbertop community kids at school and kindergarten then also pick up any supplies for the Timbertop campus.

On the days I went to kindergarten he would sometimes pick me up on the way home in the school bus. I sat up in the front of the bus because I was the only one coming home at that time. We would chat away about things together and we liked each other's company. Well, as much as you can say, for a four-year-old. There was something that stuck out for me at my age and that was, I can always remember old Meggsie never had any tissues in the bus. On a day that I had a snotty nose, he would get the roll of toilet paper out of the glove box and say it was also for blowing your nose. I didn't really like using the toilet roll and found it quite rough. Funny how you remember these simple things.

I was very fond of Meggsie and would go back to his house, where he lived with his wife Betty, and have a drink or a snack before I went home. Betty was a heavy smoker and always had a cigarette in her hand. She also always had very funny coloured hair. It changed quite regularly.

Old Meggsie quite often visited the Hunt Club Hotel in Merrijig on our way back to Timbertop. It was there he would pick up the mail and, of course, grab a few coldies to have at home. I learned later in life that Meggsie was a bit of a drinker. I think he eventually lost his job because of the booze, but to me, he was a famous character. When I was a little girl, I thought he was just great.

Merrijig is a little community, about 15 minutes from Mansfield, on the way to Mount Buller. The Hunt Club Hotel also known as Merrijig pub, was the one stop shop for post and the local watering hole. Back in those days, it was probably the only commercial property in Merrijig.

Whilst we were at Timbertop, my mother was pregnant. Because it was her fourth child, my mother would quite often have an afternoon nap. Lisa and I would also snuggle up and have a sleep too. Life was so lovely as a four-year-old, whilst living at Geelong Grammar School.

When the days were warmer in late spring and in the summer, my mother would pick me up from kindergarten and we would stop at the bridge over the Delatite River in Merrijig and have a dip. By this time, my next sister was born as well. She would set up the baby bouncing frame with her feet in the water to cool her down.

There were other families at the Timbertop campus, and we would play with the other children when our parents got together. The Thomsons and the Hogans. They were mainly boys, but Peter and Helen Thomson did have a daughter called Serena, who was a little older than my older sister. My parents, my three sisters and I all made friends with our community. There were always big family gathering photos of us together at Timbertop.

We hung out during school holidays and always had a few adventures. I remember getting into trouble one day, as a group of us had gone down under the bridge on Timbertop creek. The bridge was on the Timbertop driveway, and we had made a cubby house and lit a fire. The cubby consisted of towels for the walls, and I think we may have even taken pillows down as well. We all had intentions of staying the night. The bridge gave our fire away because there was smoke coming up through the decking. We didn't end up spending the night down there, but it was another one of our great childhood adventures at Timbertop.

My parents also made other lifetime friends in Mansfield. Apart from the Yenckens, mentioned above, there were other families like the Ritchies, who we would spend time with. We also had holidays with these friends when we had moved away from Timbertop.

Other families in the district were also friends and, to this day, are still friends. Most of their children went away to school in their secondary years and a lot of them attended private schools, including Geelong Grammar School. Most of my parents' close friends' children attended Geelong Grammar.

## BOSTOCK HOUSE AND GGS HIGHTON

We left Timbertop at the end of 1970. My father, at this stage, was offered and accepted the junior school headmaster's position at the school's Bostock House campus. We moved there straight from Timbertop.

Bostock House was situated at Highton, a suburb on the southwestern outskirts of Geelong. At the time, this area was rural and there were farms nearby. We lived below Marcus Oldham Agricultural College and next to, what was known as the Hermitage School. The Hermitage was a private girls' school.

We had masses of space to play, with a 25-metre swimming pool, playgrounds, tennis courts, and sports fields to roam on. Life was great fun. We made new friends with our neighbours' children. The new neighbours were the Wades and the Weigalls. My parents also made long term friends with our neighbours.

Our house was attached to the boarding house. The school boarders' dining room had a door that could be accessed from our sitting room. This was so my father was always accessible to the young boarders if he was needed.

We spent a lot of time hanging out with the boarders, who at the time, were all boys. I was definitely a tomboy anyway and loved playing football and cricket, rather than doing girly things. My older sister was more interested in music and helping mum. When I wasn't spending time together with the boys, I would visit the two ladies that used to work and live in a flat in the boarding house. Their flat was attached to the boarders' dining room and the kitchen.

Josie and Marie were a couple of spinsters that lived next door to our family. They were old fashioned but were life mentors for the boarders of the day. They fed, cared for, and mothered the boys in the boarding house. Really hard to describe their role but they fit in as important people in a young developing boy's life, without being too influential. Maybe nurturing without committing. Incidentally, Josie had begun working at Geelong Grammar School at the age of 14 and was employed as a cook. Josie was a fantastic cook. I loved them so much and I described them as my fairy godmothers.

Life was just like a fairytale.

I spent a lot of time, especially with Josie, in the kitchen. She taught me how to make scones, biscuits, and sponges. I would go over every day after school and eat two or three fresh pieces of crusty bread with jam and butter. I remember they used to get the big tins of apricot and raspberry jam. This was mostly to cater for hungry boys, so there was always enough.

My family used to have Sunday lunch or dinner in the boarding house with the boarders. It was a great part of our growing up at Geelong Grammar School, Bostock House.

My older sister and I both started school in Geelong at Morongo Girls College. This was because at this time, Geelong Grammar was not coeducational. My younger sister, Lisa, started preparatory school at the Hermitage school a few years later. My older sister and I did three years at Morongo, before Geelong Grammar went coeducational.

The transition to coeducation was when Geelong Grammar amalgamated with the Clyde School. Clyde had more senior girls than primary girls, so they attended the grammar school's Corio campus. None of the girls from The Clyde came to Bostock.

Up until the amalgamation, there were only boy boarders at Bostock but, as the school was enrolling more girls, there soon came more female boarders. The old boarding house was only set up for boys. We had the first junior schoolgirl boarding at our house. Her name was Dawn Sharp and she was from Castlemaine, in Victoria. There was a separate room with ensuite at the front of our house and that was the room made available for Dawn.

During the first year after amalgamation, at eight years old I was the only girl in a classroom of about 20 boys at Bostock House. It was here the existence of sexual predation started, with two of the boys in my class having fathers that were found out to be sexual predators. Two other children in my class were physically abused daily by a teacher at the school in grade six. Myself and another boy were also sexually abused. Six of us in one classroom, were caught up in some way, in the child abuse ring.

There were girls in other classes that had at least two of them in the same number of pupils. I really didn't mind because I accustomed to and always had hung out with the boys. Boys were all we had to hang out with anyway, being the junior headmaster's daughters.

The Hermitage school was the sister school to Bostock House and was only just starting off with female primary school students. An amalgamation took place with the Hermitage School in 1976, and, because of the amalgamation, the school was now known as Geelong Grammar School, Highton.

As the years progressed, there were more girls at the school and there was enough room at the old Hermitage boarding house to accommodate both girls and boys.

It was at Highton boarding house that other horrible sexual abuse started in the nineties. The perpetrator was Philipe Trutman. Philipe was a boy student I remember in the boarding house at Bostock house. When we were younger girls, my sister and I used to sit with him and watch TV.

When the boarders moved to the Hermitage boarding house the old Bostock boarding house became a music school. Josie and Marie moved into Geelong and retired. And we continued to live in the same house for about 10 years.

One more thing that comes to mind about our younger days at Highton and at Bostock house, was that my parents would often entertain parents of other students. They would have them over for a coffee or a drink or have a dinner party with them. It was a Geelong Grammar School thing to have good relationships with parents. There was even a parents and friends committee that would bring parents together with the school staff.

My parents also spent a great deal of time with the well-to-do of Geelong. More than likely, because school fees at Geelong Grammar were always higher than most private schools in Victoria.

Dad was also invited out to many other important or prestigious events, including sporting opportunities, such as VFL finals series etc with his connections to the school. Bob Davis, a former Geelong football player, had invited my father to many football finals series in the seventies and had also enrolled his son at Geelong Grammar School's Highton campus.

My father had the opportunity of meeting other famous people, including Australian prime ministers, senior politicians, and business tycoons through his career at Geelong.

Being the father of four daughters at the time, my father was always very protective of us. He warned us about not getting into strangers' cars. There was an occasion I remember when an ex-Geelong football player named Bob Davis, came to Bostock for the first time. He had asked me where my father lived. And I said that I would take him there. He offered me a lift in his car. I declined the invitation because of what my father had told me about getting into strangers' cars. I just ran ahead of him.

Interestingly, there was never any warning about friends of my parents being dangerous. They trusted their friends and did not think they would behave inappropriately with any of us. Parents and friends of the school were also definitely off any radar as predators. It would have never been discussed or considered because of the Geelong Grammar School name. The other conception I had was, I think my parents thought, for someone to abuse you, they would have to be a complete stranger. Or someone on drugs. How wrong were they?

From the days of Bostock House, many wonderful family friendships started. Our parents' friends' children became our friends. One special family were the Dawsons. Cam Dawson was the owner of a Ford dealership in Geelong. The Dawsons had their children enrolled at Bostock House and the Hermitage. My parents became very friendly with Cam and Jill. As a result of this friendship, we started to spend more and more time with their children too. Tony was a little older than me and, in the year, above at school. Their daughter Penny was fondly known by Cam as PJ, because she farted a lot when she was a baby. She was a little younger than me and, in the year, below at school. Tom was the youngest. Tom was a chronic asthmatic and spent many a night in intensive care in hospital, struggling to breathe. Tom was also chronically allergic to horses. One sniff of horsehair could potentially be a medical disaster.

I became incredibly good friends with Penny. We are still remarkably close friends, some fifty plus years later. Because of my growing love of horses, I would often be invited to go out to Penny's place for the weekend. In the school holidays, we would go to riding camps for weeks on end at a local horse-riding facility, Koombahla Park. Cam had some involvement with the centre of which I am unsure of. The equestrian centre was near to Ocean Grove and close to where the Dawsons had lived.

Cam and Jill and all their children loved horses. Penny and Tony had their own ponies. But because of Tom's chronic asthma, he had to settle for a donkey.

Whenever I stayed with the Dawsons, there was always a ritual that had to be strictly adhered to. It was put in place if we had been either riding or had any contact at all with horses, saddles etc. All our clothes had to be removed and put in the washing machine and then, we all had to either shower or have a bath and put fresh, clean, and unhorsed clothes on. This was because we could not contaminate anything that could possibly come into contact with Tom.

When Cam built his dream home, next door to Koombahla Park, he designed it so that coming in from horse riding was a breeze for all of us and medically sound for Tom. Over the years, I spent more time with the Dawsons than any of my sisters. However, my youngest sister is Jill's goddaughter.

The Dawsons were like family to me. They took me to Mount Buller in the winters of 1977, 1978 and in 1979 to go skiing. Cam and Jill also took my younger sister and myself for a three-week trip to New Zealand in 1979. During that same year, I had been at Timbertop and an extra two weeks of amazing snow skiing had been such a bonus.

Mum and dad had gone overseas to Britain to catch up with family and friends and the Dawson's as usual, had taken us under their wing. When Cam and Jill needed to go overseas, my parents were guardians for Tony, Penny, and Tom. This was how close-knit the Geelong Grammar School community was, especially in the seventies.

## OTHER FAMILY HOLIDAYS

My parents bought a block of land at a quiet little coastal town called Aireys Inlet. The block of land bought specifically to be built on, and this would be our first house ever in Australia. This is because we had always had a house provided for our family by Geelong Grammar School.

Aireys Inlet was the place we would go to in school holidays. My father still worked during the school holidays but did have some time off out of his office. We managed to go there quite regularly when the house had been built. A week here and there in the school term holidays and for an extended time during the summer holidays. We all loved the beach, and we also lived on a creek. My sisters and I would spend the holidays in our Canadian canoe, fishing or just rowing up and down the creek to the beach. We often had other families visit and we would all bunk down in the downstairs playroom.

My parents quite often had visits from other parents that were involved with the school. The Yenckens, the Mackeys and our cousins came to visit, as well as other old family friends.

We sometimes spent other holidays at other people's places. They were normally people that my parents had met through Geelong Grammar School. Either as teachers, or people who had enrolled their children at Highton. My father also knew a few people from his days of playing international rugby for England.

One particular family dad was in contact with from his rugby years were the Hines family. Dad had played rugby against Geoff Hines. He and his wife Sandra had touched base with my parents when they moved to Australia from the United Kingdom. They had three children. Andrew, fondly known as Bugsy Hines, because he had buck teeth, then there was Nicolas, who had amazing red hair with beautiful olive skin and Alison, who was the youngest.

The Hines had bought a small farm-let at Howlong in New South Wales and built a lovely house. They chose to live there so that Mr Hines could work nearby in Wodonga. Howlong is about four and a half hours drive from the Highton campus in Geelong. It was because of the distance from Howlong, the children were enrolled at the school as boarders. The farm-let was on a few acres and had a swimming pool. It was an exciting place for kids. Lots of places to ride horses, go shooting for rabbits and just plenty of space.

In September school holidays in 1977, our entire family was invited to stay there for a week. Then, because I was great friends with Bugsy, I was invited to stay on another week. Mr Hines had an appointment in Geelong at some stage after the second week, so he offered to deliver me to my parents, when he went back down to Geelong. That worked well with all, and my parents were happy with that arrangement. Great, more horse riding and shooting with Bugsy. For an entire week. I could not have been happier.

Dad packed all seven of us into the car and we headed up from Geelong. A good five-hour trip with stops for wees etc, probably making it more like seven hours. Dad has always joked about the occurrence of wee stops, with five daughters and a wife with a Chinese bladder. We had done quite a lot of travelling long distances in the car since we had been in Australia. And stopping for nose powdering was always on the list.

The day after we arrived at the Hines farm-let, we went out shooting rabbits. It was such great fun and we all learned how to gut them etc. We also learned how shoot a rabbit in the right area, which was also important. This was because you could make a good mess of a rabbit if you shot it in the intestines. It would be not only messy but smelly if you had a bad shot.

My sister, Lisa, and I also just loved horses and ponies. The Hines children were lucky to have them, so we did a bit of riding as well. There were lots of riding trails close by to ride on. It was a great family holiday and we all enjoyed ourselves.

In our family, when we were younger children, we had always kissed our parents' good night before retiring to bed. I remember one particular night, when my parents had finished dinner and they were having a few drinks, I went to my parents and kissed them goodnight. Geoff Hines then asked, where was his kiss? I didn't really want to kiss him, but both my parents insisted I did. It took a bit of pushing by all, but I did it in the end and it was just a short peck on the cheek.

That was more than likely the beginning of him trying to sexually groom me. You could call it a test of my vulnerability. But because I was so young and immature, I couldn't recognise any form of grooming and certainly did not understand it. My family stayed for a few more days and yes, every night I would have to kiss Geoff Hines goodnight. This was always after I had kissed my parents' good night.

I did not really feel very comfortable with this ritual at all, but I was so young and immature that it never occurred to me it was not right. I am also sure it never occurred to my parents either. Geoff Hines was definitely sexually grooming me, and it was right in front of my parents' eyes. I was nearly 12 years old and just starting to change as a girl to a physically maturing young woman. With these gradual changes I also became more modest. I did not have any understanding of the act of kissing, and definitely no understanding of any sort of sexual advances.

Mr Hines became more and more touchy with me, even when my parents were about. In hindsight, this touching would have progressed from the first night that I was made to kiss him goodnight. Because I had kissed him, he would have seen it as an invitation to touch me.

He would find an opportunity to just brush close by me or touch me on a few occasions, but I never really understood what he was doing. I certainly did not like it and found it a little creepy but would fob it off. Ignore it. I didn't really know what it was anyway and I definitely wouldn't have mentioned it at the time to my parents. Their reaction would be that I was making things up and I would have been in trouble for even mentioning it. They would never have believed me anyway. That is because this was one of their friends who just happened to be a Geelong Grammar School parent.

There was one day in particular I remember vividly. We were all in the swimming pool. He came up behind me and was groping my body by the edge of the pool, everywhere that he could. I had a hole in my one-piece bathers in the crotch, and I remember he put his finger in there. He even told me there was a hole. It was right near my vagina and as he came in from behind, he groped near my anus. (This is probably why for years as a teenager and even as an adult, I hated anyone ever touching my bottom) I was still, obviously too frightened or confused to know what was happening. More like immaturity for my ripe age of 11.

When my parents had gone back to Geelong, I managed to try and avoid Geoff Hines as much as possible. He had finished his holiday and, thankfully, gone back to his job in Wodonga. He worked at a dog food factory and did a lot of travelling each day. There were some instances where he was late home or away for a night. I did, however, have to give him a kiss each night when he was at home.

Another memory that comes to mind was once my parents had gone, I was moved into the bedroom that they had been sleeping in. I often wonder, on who's recommendation? I was definitely more accessible to him in that room, and it was also more private. Prior to my parents going home, I had been sleeping previously with all the other girls.

On the last night that I stayed at the Hines, I had gone to the bathroom and had a shower before going into to my room to get ready for bed. On returning, Mr Hines had walked into the room and I was completely naked. Because of my modesty, I raced around to the bed and put on a dress to cover myself up. Mr Hines had said, "Don't worry, I have seen a lot of little naked girls before."

Then, the next thing I knew, the hundred or so kilogram man was lying on top of me, with his tongue down my throat and his hands groping me between my legs.

I was in complete shock. I froze in horror. Time just froze and this didn't seem real, because it should not have been happening with a 40-year-old man and a young girl who wasn't even a teenager. From my frozen reaction, he must have realised what he had just done, was not at all right. He then got up off me and left the room. I remember being so frightened and shocked I couldn't sleep. I just couldn't wait to go home.

I remember having to fly down from Albury to Melbourne, sitting next to him and trying not to even look at him, let alone allow him to touch me. The thought of what he had done made me feel so dirty and he was so repulsive to look at.

When we landed in Melbourne, Mr Hines had hired a car, so he could drive us both back to my parents' house at Geelong. The plane flight and the drive to Geelong were excruciating. I just couldn't get far enough away from him, even on the aeroplane.

I felt the need to escape from him and I am sure the body language told all. I wore a horrible baggy dress that covered every inch of me and went right down to my feet. I hated him so much for what he had done.

In hindsight, this was probably the start of my self-image problems that later led to anorexia nervosa. The timing of Geoff Hines' abuse was during my initial stages of puberty.

I couldn't understand or reason about what had happened. Was this a normal thing to happen to young girls? Did this happen to most young girls? There was complete confusion. The silly thing is, after it happened, I completely blocked the entire experience. It just dropped right out of my conscious mind.

The only thing that ever came close to me recalling it, was in my dreams. Nightmares was probably a better word. I would be naked and being touched in my private parts and just couldn't get away. My entire body would become a dead weight and I couldn't move. Like trying to run in sand, with lead weights on your feet.

My mother had noticed that I didn't really like Mr Hines. She never asked me why but whenever that horrible man turned up, I always went out or down to my bedroom. Because of my behaviour whenever he was about, she began warning me when he was visiting our house. This went on for a few years and, even when we had moved out to the campus at Corio, he would still turn up to visit. I would just make myself scarce until he had left. He never had the opportunity to interfere with me again. Let alone see me.

I really don't think it ever occurred to my mother something sinister may have happened. And she never really asked. And even if I had remembered at this time, my parents would have probably got angry, not believed me and I would have been told to get over it and stop making things up.

As daughters of the junior headmaster and then senior administrative person at Geelong Grammar School, we were expected to be seen and not heard. We could also never be in trouble because it would be extremely embarrassing for my parents. It also meant, we couldn't go to anyone with a problem, because we wouldn't be believed. We were always told to get over whatever it was because it just was not that important. Silly little girls and petty little stories. We were regularly told, it was totally about our wonderful education, and we should relish in it. Apparently, all my sisters did, except for me.

There was a considerable amount of fringe benefits that came with working at Geelong Grammar School. So, anything that could jeopardise these living conditions, was also prevented. We all just knew that we had to be seen and definitely not heard. Even if there was something terribly wrong, we had to keep it to ourselves.

There were also some very memorable experiences that occurred whilst we lived at Highton. One being my father's very explosive temper. Whenever dad was cross, or even to this day, when he is cross, he is definitely a person to avoid. He can be frightening.

There are a few occasions so vivid in my mind when his temper got the better of him. In this day and age, it would be child abuse. Me, being the number two of five girls, the tomboy and black sheep, I had a great knack of really testing my father's anger temperature gauge. It was always a test to the limit.

On one occasion at school, I had been given a hideous pair of red clogs. I have no idea what tempted me to do it but, instead of my polished black school shoes, I put them on and went off to school without a care in the world. Of course, I was summoned to the school headmaster's office. My father tore shreds off me verbally and told me to go home and change at once before anyone had seen me. He had even threatened to give me the cane.

Teachers used to cane children at school before it became child abuse. Old school discipline, I guess, but normally for boys only.

On another occasion, where I really tested my father's temper, was one night after dinner. Mum had gone to the ballet with a friend, and my youngest sister was asleep in her bed. She was only about one or two years old at the time. As usual, I was stirring up my two younger sisters in the television room, and they had woken my youngest sister up. My father really blew up. I was standing in front of the television, and he was bent over with his eyes level with mine. Then he slapped me, so hard across the face, that he knocked me clean out. I only avoided hitting the television because he grabbed me as I fell. I became conscious after a while, and I was sitting on his knee. My sister Lisa remembers this occasion vividly.

There was also another incidence at Aireys inlet, where he hit me again. Our living area was upstairs and the playroom and bedrooms were downstairs. On occasion, we were told not to go upstairs if my parents were to sleep in. The noise from someone walking around on the deck upstairs was loud and it was also directly above my parents' bedroom. Of course, I wanted to go upstairs and, without thinking, upset my parents' sleep in. It may have something to do with stirring up Lisa and my other sister too. That was a common occurrence.

I was summoned to their bedroom. I sat on their bed, and my father slapped me across the face once, then backhanded me with another hit and then slapped my face again. My mother just sat there. I could feel myself swaying and my cheeks went from a burning feeling to numbness. Fortunately, on this occasion, he didn't knock me unconscious.

Since then, I avoided being hit by not being around my father when he was angry. I was always referred to as Jojo when dad was angry. Fortunately, when Jojo was used, I knew what might have been coming. So, I soon learned to make myself scarce.

There was a time a few years ago, he wasn't particularly well and, because of his discomfort, he was incredibly nasty to my mother. On one occasion, when I had made a visit to them, dad started his nasty talk. Within a few minutes, I announced to my mother that I was not staying to have a cup of coffee because I could not stand how dad was treating her. I was possibly very anxious and on the verge of a panic attack and it was an horrible, uncomfortable premeditated feeling. When she had said, "Why don't you say something?" my answer was, "Because I don't want to get hit." She had absolutely no answer to that.

I was sure she remembered the incident at Aireys Inlet but was too gutless to say anything. Or too frightened to. Dad has never hurt my mother physically but had certainly been vocally nasty.

Around the same time, I also remembered going to the supermarket before I had visited on another occasion. The visit was for a Father's Day present. I walked up the biscuit aisle, grabbed a packet of NICE biscuits, wrapped them up and produced them to dad, saying Happy Father's Day with a grin on my face. Mum and I were both amused and dad was a little confused. I should have really bought the entire box full.

Later on, in my school years at Corio, my father was a little more lenient and would simply say, "Get up to as much mischief as you want to but just don't get caught."

It was always about saving my parents face. Keeping up appearances sort of stuff.

## MY YEAR AT TIMBERTOP
## TIMBERTOP AND BULLYING

All the girls in my family were involved in sport, were good at sport and were always in the teams picked for competition. Some of my sisters and I won back-to-back championships every year. I remember winning four in a row and my sisters won their fair share too.

At times, there were jealous kids at school who would say I only won a championship because my father had rigged it. This happened on numerous occasions.

After my assault by Geoff Hines, I was at GGS Highton for another year and then I went to Timbertop. This was one of the hardest years I ever had at school. Because Timbertop was Year 9, it meant that students from both the Highton and Corio campuses were together for the first time. Another reason it was difficult was, I was also incredibly young for my school years. I lacked the maturity the other girls had physically and mentally. I hadn't even had my period yet and was only 13 years old. Most students in my year were 14 or about to turn 14 at the beginning of Timbertop.

Because of the increase in the number of girl students, this meant double bullying, from two lots of jealous girls. There were cliquey groups that formed in the three girls' units at Timbertop. We each had 12 girls in a unit and there was a mix of new girls to the school - Corio girls and Highton girls. As you can imagine, not only with the hormone changes taking place and our brain cortexes developing independently, but there was also an incredible mix of personality. There was also a social caste.

There was the 'in' group of popular girls with the boys, the group that were in the middle and the drop kicks. There was also a development of a group called the mean girls. These girls were rarely achievers and were nasty out of jealousy. The girls who always looked to be having a great fake fun time, just so they would be noticed.

Another thing I had great difficulty with was, I found it extremely hard to be in hiking groups with the people I wanted to be with. I was quite often on the list of girls who didn't have a hiking group and you ended up in a group with other girls like yourself. People that did not have a regular group.

I really thrived on hiking, running and all the other activities and I do believe there was again a lot of jealousy amongst my peers. Stories were made up about me and most of the time it was to put me down, so they would feel like they were better.

There was one bullying incident at Timbertop I remember happened on the murderball court. Murderball was a game we played in physical education. However, no murders were ever committed.

A couple of the boys in my class had always picked on me and, on this particular day, I was being called a slut. This sort of bullying was not uncommon at Timbertop and there were other girls and boys that really did it hard that year because of the constant nastiness.

At this immature age, I had never even kissed a boy, let alone had sex with one. I told the boys to go and truly get fucked. The master in charge on the court, then sent me to see the principal to explain my behaviour.

The head of Timbertop at the time was a priest and it just happened be Peter Thomson. He was still working at Timbertop from when we had lived there in 1970. I proceeded to tell him what had happened and what was said to me. We talked about it and he sent me back to school. He then dealt with it accordingly. Incidentally, one of the bullies also happened to be his own son. The boys were spoken to about the incident and they never really bothered me again.

The only other bad time at Timbertop was getting my arm bashed on my birthday by two boys. The swelling was so big that my sleeve was tight. One of boys just happened to be the son of a successful truck businessman in Victoria. Just goes to show all people are capable of bullying, even if they are wealthy. These sorts of events would happen from time to time at Timbertop and you really could not say anything about it because you would be bullied even more, especially if you dobbed.

There was one very notable time for me at Timbertop. This was when the hiking master, Ian Stapleton, also known as Choko, had asked me up to the hiking master's residence for a chat about things. He had noticed I was having difficulty in third term, getting set up with a regular hiking group. I was one of last people picked on a few occasions and he wanted to know if I was okay. It was really quite amazing to have someone who had some sympathy and was generally concerned about me, as I was not really fitting in with the group. Unfortunately, during this era, this was a rare occurrence at Geelong Grammar School. I was just lucky, I guess, that someone had perceived something was not quite right with this little black sheep.

My confidence was starting to dwindle, and I was, understandably, getting left behind by my peers. Not sure, but this could have possibly been the beginnings of my mental melting down after the Hines sexual abuse.

I really wasn't very happy when I left Timbertop but was glad that it was over and hoped things would improve. Another interesting fact: all the exercise in the Timbertop year made most girls put on weight. We were fed carbohydrate-fuelled food and also gained weight through extra muscle from all the activities. I had put on a fair bit of weight and decided to go on a diet in the summer holidays. This would be the beginnings of my eating disorder, and I started to be obsessed with the way my body looked. I was very careful and controlled when it came to my weight. I was obsessive with weighing myself and also exercising more.

# SCHOOL AT CORIO YEAR 10, 1980

By the time school had gone back in February, I had lost a stack of weight. I was extremely fit as I had been training during the school holidays. Dad had always encouraged us to keep fit and in great shape, so when we competed in sports at school, we were one step ahead of everyone else. I had spent time in the pool, so I was swimming well. I was nicely tanned and loving how I looked. I had always previously piled my plate up with food and now I was eating less. My father used to refer to me as the dustbin, because I always ate so much. I would quite often eat some of the food my sisters had left on their plates. My appetite was enormous because of all the sporting activities I did.

We had spent a few weeks at Aireys Inlet at the beach house and had run on the beach most days. We also kept up with our swimming training at Geelong Swimming Club.

I had never really had boyfriends in my early secondary years at school. I was always a year younger than nearly everyone else and I guess I was immature as well. I was also more interested in sport than boys and that's when everything changed at Corio.

There were older boys and I was also looking particularly good in a pair of bathers. I even had photos taken of my bum in bathers once. They circulated around the school for quite some time. This was a confidence builder in some ways, but I also became obsessed in keeping my appearance the same. Probably to the pound in weight.

I received a fair bit of attention from the boys for a while but never really liked anyone enough or was interested, until the last term of school. I also had doubts about the nice things that people said from time to time. Meaning I could not see it myself. It was as if I felt I didn't deserve it.

It was late in 1980 and during the athletics season, that an older guy in Lindon (the Year 12 repeater house), took a liking to me. He was going out with a girl from Clyde House, who he finished with, as we got to know each other. I was a little scared because he was nearly 18 and I had only just turned 15. His name was John. It was absolutely the most amazing feeling to be kissed for the first time. I just couldn't believe how wonderful it was. He walked me back to the day house Allen and kissed me in front of the path that led to my study room. I even think one of my feet left the ground. It was that wonderful a kiss.

Because it was late in the year and he was finishing school for good, we really didn't get up to much more than a little heavy petting. He asked me down to his room at Lindon one afternoon and we began kissing. Then, to my absolute shock, he proceeded to put his hand down my pants. I just froze. This had never happened to me with a boy before and I guess my reaction was to go into survival mode. I was numb. Apart from the incident with Hines that I had completely blocked out at the time, I had never before been exposed to this sort of petting. Because of my reaction, he gave me a doubtful sort of look and asked me, "This has never happened to you before, has it?" My answer was a definite, "No."

There had been rumours for years about me having sex with boys. And, of course, they were not true. Because I had grown up with and played sport with boys for most of my life, people would assume that for a girl at the age of 15, I would more than likely be sexually active. I also guessed that John thought I was active sexually and decided it would be just the normal thing to do. It never happened again after that. With the school year finishing, so did the relationship.

The next summer was spent swimming training again and also spending more time at the beach. We used to go down there as a family and meet up with other friends. We often spent time with another family called the Galloways, whose kids were of similar age and also went to Geelong Grammar School. There was no life outside the school. Everything revolved around the school.

# THE DIRTY DOCTOR

In 1981, I was in Year 11. I was 15 years old and really becoming obsessed with my weight. The year before, I had gradually cut down my food so much that lived on an apple a day, a salad with truly little protein for lunch and lollies from the tuck shop. I skipped dinner altogether.

I continued to play plenty of sport and tried to run every day. On top of that, I was training with whichever sport we were doing at the time of year. My weight had plummeted to under 50 kilograms.

I had become totally obsessed. I weighed myself twice daily and if I ate too much, I would exercise even more, so I wouldn't put any weight on. I remember eating something at our house in Highton and then strenuously exercising. I kept weighing myself until I weighed the same that I did that morning.

In the summer holidays, my mother had a discussion about my weight with her dear friend, Sue Mackey. They were sitting at the school pool and my mother asked for her advice. Sue said to make an appointment with her husband, Dr Mackey, and that he surely would be able to help. My mother was very naive about mental health and eating disorders. She was extremely worried about me and not knowing what to do. She decided to make an appointment with him, to discuss my loss of weight.

The first appointment was absolutely awful. The first thing he asked me when I walked into the surgery was, "Are you still screwing around with boys in the bushes?"

I was shocked by that comment and also felt extremely uncomfortable. The comment made me feel really dirty. I had never been with a boy like that before and thought it was a very strange thing to say to one of his close friend's daughters. I did not know or understand why it had that effect on me.

He weighed me and we talked truly little about anything and that was all that happened in the first appointment. Then, I was to have another appointment with him in a month or so. I was supposed to gain some of the weight that I had lost and he was going to weigh me and we would discuss it further.

I only went to him that second time and then never went back about my weight. It wasn't doing my mental health any good at all. In fact, his smutty comments were horrible and all he did was exaggerate my problems. I didn't like him anyway; he was always extremely creepy. He made me feel extremely uncomfortable. In hindsight, I could see Mackey displayed the attributes of a groomer and his behaviour, when I went to him, was the same.

The other matter I know now, is that eating disorders are better referred to a clinical psychologist or psychiatrist. Unfortunately, Mackey was too arrogant for that and never referred me. My mother was totally in the dark and possibly drawing at straws when she engaged him. If anything, he probably did more damage to me than good. Just like rubbing salt into an open wound. Feeding me to the lions!

Early in 1981, things started to become more social for me, and I became more interested in boys. I was also allowed to attend my first formal dance. The Boat Race Dance was an annual event held every year for form five and six students. The dance was normally held at a fairly reputable place in the city of Melbourne. Dinner was served, along with beer and wine. The alcohol was not regulated or supervised either. I ended up that evening, sitting under the table with a guy called Chappo and we drank beers until it was time to go home.

Because this was my first formal event, my parents were not happy about me staying with friends in a hotel in Melbourne. So that they could take me home, they had gone out in the city. After the dance, they picked me up and took me home to our house at the school campus at Highton. It was on the way home and at the Ford Motor Company in Geelong, that I asked my father to pull over. I had an uncomfortable urge to vomit. I had mixed beer and wine, and it really didn't agree with me. My mother happened to confirm that to me at the time, just when I was throwing up the contents of my stomach. I don't think mixing any drinks on your first try is recommended.

The following day, I felt fine. Then I missed school on the Monday because I had a delayed hangover and an incredibly upset stomach. Chappo had looked out for me that day and asked what had happened, the following day at school. Within a couple of weeks, he had ditched his old girlfriend and had started seeing me. He was my first serious boyfriend.

In the second term of that year, I was put into Clyde house as a boarder because my parents were going on long service leave. They were away for three months and my youngest sister, who would have been about five or six years old, went with them. When my parents returned from long service leave, the school had built a new house at the Corio campus which was right next to a boy's boarding house. The house was called Cuthbertson house, Cuthy for short. And it just so happened that Chappo was in Cuthy.

Boarding in the Clyde house was great fun but I looked forward to going back to my parents' new place. By this stage, it was school holidays. Lisa was home from Timbertop. We spent our school holidays riding our pony and just hanging out.

Due to my eating disorder, my health was really suffering and I was extremely malnourished. Because I was so unhealthy I kept getting cysts and boils on a regular basis. Then I discovered one day, mainly because it was extremely painful, a boil on my Labia Majora. A Labia Majora are the outer lips on a woman's anatomy, that are normally fleshy and covered with pubic hair.

Incidentally, the Labia Minora are inside the outer lips. They begin at a woman's clitoris and end under the opening to a woman's vagina. The reason why I have included this will become apparent as you read on.

I was never allowed to go to a doctor of my choice, because my mother had always trusted Dr Mackey with all of us. That, of course, was because he was a so-called long term family friend. So, I really had no choice but to make an appointment with him. Also, because he was based at the school, it was easy to just go to the medical centre. I was also too embarrassed to show or to discuss it with my mother, so I made an appointment to see him. I went to the medical centre. He had kept the centre open that day especially to see me, as it was during school holiday time.

This would be one of the biggest life changing experiences I would ever have. I entered his small office and surgery. There was a high window at the side and a larger window looking out with sheer blinds. I removed my clothing as requested, so that I could show him the painful cyst on the outside of my Labia Majora.

Instead of focusing on my cyst, Dr Mackey proceeded to focus straight away on my Labia Minora and began to stimulate my clitoris. This continued for at least a minute with a dirty smirk on his face. He smiled because he definitely knew what he was doing to me. He was relishing in the fact he was sexually turning me on. I stared at the high window behind him and went into survival mode until he was finished. I really didn't know what to do. I was in such inexplicable shock when he had finished, that I put my clothes back on and just left. I don't remember what was even discussed regarding my cyst. I just had to escape.

What had just happened? Was that normal? Is this supposed to happen? Is this supposed to have felt the way it did? Why did he do that to me? Why did he enjoy seeing me feel good? Is that normal?

I remember getting out of there as quickly as I could and running away to be on my own for a while. In hindsight, I am sure I had a panic attack. I didn't tell anyone. I couldn't tell anyone. I felt so ashamed. There was absolutely no way my mother would have believed me. And I certainly would never tell my parents because I might have gotten into trouble for even talking about it. Again, it would have been something I had made up.

The only thing I ever did after the assault, was to warn my sister Lisa to be incredibly careful if she goes to see Dr Mackey. I didn't tell her why.

But she took heed from my warning and wore a one-piece bathing suit to an appointment when she had to go and see him.

Geelong Grammar School had seemed a wonderful childhood place to exist in those younger years. A fairytale to a young girl. At this stage of my schooling and existence, it had now gradually turned into a living hell. A living hell that seemed to last an eternity.

# CHAPTER 2

## *DISCOVERING DRUGS*

I can't remember the year exactly but in the very early eighties, a big decision changed with our family's holiday house arrangements. My parents decided to sell our Aireys Inlet house. I remember that me and my younger sisters and I were devastated.

We were all at the age where we would hang out with girlfriends and their families and head down to the beach for hours. My parents also trusted us to go and hang out at Fairhaven. At Fairhaven there was a surf club, and we had a rather good social life. No boyfriends, but just fun hanging out, as teenagers do.

As a result of the sale of Aireys Inlet, my parents decided to build a house that could return some income. It made a lot of sense because Aireys Inlet would sit empty through most of the school year. Dad was always busy working in school holidays, and we really only spent the majority of our time there in the long summer school holidays. We would often go to Aireys just after Christmas and spend about four weeks there. Dad always needed to return to Geelong Grammar Highton a week prior to school recommencing for the new school year.

My parents chose to look at a house block at Point Lonsdale. Point Lonsdale is about the same distance from Geelong as Aireys Inlet. At Point

Lonsdale, there is a large base of the Australian military. And because of this, there was the opportunity to rent the house out to the army during the year to pay the mortgage, and we would still be able to have the use of it over the summer holidays.

My parents had other friends at Point Lonsdale, some being Geelong Grammar School associates, including the Mackey family. We had visited the Mackey family as younger children at Point Lonsdale, and they had visited us also at Aireys Inlet.

So, because it made sense, my parents built a house at Point Lonsdale. The house was nothing like Aireys Inlet and I never really liked going there. It was a brick veneer house, which wasn't beachy and just never had a good vibe for me. I also did not like the beach at Point Lonsdale. Or some of my parents' friends who lived there.

At Aireys Inlet we had an enormous stretch of beach that went from the lighthouse all the way down to a beautiful beach called Eastern View. When we were madly exercising as young girls, my parents dropped us off at the first beach at Fairhaven and would run alongside the water to Eastern View.

We would only go down to Point Lonsdale during the Christmas holidays. And I think I only spent a couple of holidays there. I really didn't like it as much at Aireys Inlet where the beaches were ocean beaches with great waves. Point Lonsdale was a dirty shipyard in my eyes. Like the bayside beaches in Melbourne. Smelly and dirty.

It was the second summer we spent in Point Lonsdale that I met a guy called Chris. He was a smoker, liked smoking dope and was from Ballarat. He was my boyfriend down there for a few weeks during that summer. We just hung out, smoked dope, and went to the beach. We had fires on the beach at night and walked around with other friends during the day.

We had other friends staying at Point Lonsdale at the time. They were the Robins, who were our next-door neighbours at Corio. I usually hung out with Charlotte, who was also a chronic bulimic, and Catherine always hung out with Lisa at home. We caught up when were at the beach that summer and meet up to have a smoke etc and go to the beach together. Unfortunately, Chris dumped me for Catherine. I was upset that a friend had moved on in, but I guess that is the way it goes, when you're a teenager. That ended my time at Point Lonsdale.

# CHAPTER 3

## *BULIMIA*

After the Mackey experience, my obsession with my weight and total control, progressed to yet another level. Starving and over exercising were arduous work at times and I loved the taste of food. So, I decided I might try throwing up anything I consumed. There were also other girls at school that were doing it and they weren't putting on any weight. I had always loved all food, and this now meant I could stay slim and eat absolutely everything I wanted to. There was also never a lack of food during term time because we all helped ourselves in the dining hall. At Geelong Grammar School Corio, all day students are provided with two meals a day, including lunch and dinner.

Another bonus to me at the time was, because of the large population of students in the senior school, there were plenty of bathrooms to go and vomit. It was always easy to find somewhere, where no one would hear you. I became extremely secretive about it. When I ate too much, I would simply just stick my fingers down my throat, and it would all just come up. And so began, what was going to turn into 16 miserable and extremely lonely years as a chronic bulimic.

My relationship with Chappo went on until the school year finished. We mucked around with heavy petting and enjoyed each other's company.

Our relationship was only ever at school because he lived in the northern beaches area, just north of Sydney. Because he surfed so much, he was always tanned and really looked like a surfy with blonde bleached hair. He was also slim and not very tall, so I didn't feel physically threatened by him. He was the right sized guy for me.

We hung out after sport in the afternoons and smoked cigarettes down at the Plannie. The Plannie was a pine plantation on the edge of the hockey oval. It was a place where we could get up to whatever we wanted and be able to look out and see if a staff member or the school marshal was coming. The school marshal's name was Piggy Ross. His job was to maintain that students should be where they were supposed to be and not doing anything that they weren't supposed to. His mode of transport was a quiet bicycle, and he would sneak up on students. He had a famous line which was, "Don't run, I know your name." Of course we ran.

The Plannie was an extremely popular place for students to smoke. Heavy petting and other sexual activities amongst students were also done in the Plannie. Chappo would drink on the weekends with his friends at school and sometimes smoke a bit of dope. The first time I ever smelled marijuana was when I caught him smoking it one day and asked what it was. It smelled vastly different to cigarettes. I had never used drugs and was always frightened of them.

Chappo had wanted to go further sexually with me whilst we were at school. But because I was a virgin, I didn't want to have intercourse at school and so he respected that. I also didn't want to have sex because it was scary and I really didn't want to get caught at school. So instead, we just did a great deal of heavy petting.

At the end of the school year, Chappo left after his final exams but was going to meet up with me at an end of school year party. This was going to be when I consented to having intercourse with him for my first time. Just after he left school and before the party, there was one particular afternoon that I will never forget.

The boys from Cuthy would sometimes come over into our back yard from next door and smoke cigarettes if my parents at home. My sister, Lisa and I also had a few drinking parties in our back yard over the years. On this occasion, two of Chappo's friends came over for a smoke at our house. When we had finished smoking, they asked if they could come into the house and see my bedroom. With great naivety and without thinking too much about it at all, I let them in.

When we were in my bedroom, they both proceeded to take my pants off and started playing with my private parts. I went into that numb survival mode again and completely shut off what was happening to me. Through the assault part of the experience, I just focused on a mark on my bedroom wall. After a while, because they clearly weren't getting a reaction from me, they gave up and one of the boys left.

You could say they digitally raped me. I didn't say no but I didn't really verbally consent to them doing that either. I really didn't know what to do apart from switch off and just zone out. Survive!

Then, because of my bewilderment about the entire experience, I did something that was absolutely out of left field. After one of the boys had left, I proceeded to make the other guy feel good with Vaseline on my hand. I don't know why I did that. Was it because I thought that I would be accepted somehow? This acceptance was the most confusing thing I found that comes from being sexually abused. Why did I have to be accepted by someone sexually for them to like me?

The worst thing was they told Chappo about it. I couldn't explain why I had not just told them to go away. I really didn't know what to do. Maybe it was because of the freeze reaction and survival mode that I managed to find easy to do, just like I had before.

It wasn't until the end of year party that I saw Chappo again. The party was being held over near the South Australian border on a farm which was owned by the father of a guy called Nick Kentish. He was a boarder in Cuthy in the same year as Chappo. Quite often, end of year parties were held on farms all over Victoria. It meant there could be a lot of people and a lot of noise and no neighbours complaining. Nick's father grew potatoes, so Nick's nickname was Spud.

Chappo and I sorted out the incident that had happened at the end of the year with his two friends. So, everything was back to how it had been planned to happen at the party. It was there that I had my first ever sexual intercourse experience. It was at the age of 16 and not on school property. Boy, did it hurt and, of course, I couldn't understand why it was made out to be such a popular thing.

After that night, I was in a complete mess. It was also due to the emotional entanglement that comes from having sexual intercourse. Alongside it all, I knew I was never going to see Chappo again. He had no reason, apart from school, to return to Victoria. He had also applied for university in New South Wales.

To add fuel to the fire, I had decided not to eat all night. The next morning, I was so upset having to say goodbye that I stupidly consumed three quarters of a small bottle of Southern Comfort on an empty stomach. Probably not ideal, before a 10-hour bus trip back to Geelong.

I was so inebriated. Whilst on the bus, I sat next to a friend of Chappo's, Brod, who tried to get me to drink water. I was so hot and out of sorts that I poured most of the water all over me. Then everything was spinning so badly and I kept passing out. Consequently, I have never drunk Southern Comfort again and I certainly never will.

I remember my father picking me up at the railway station in Geelong where the buses pull in. He proceeded to drive to the pool to do swimming training. I can't remember if I just opted out and sat in the car. I had fortunately sobered up by then, but training was out for this little black duck.

It was in that same long school holidays at the end of the year, that my mother had gone over to England. She went over to see our relatives and was due to be away for about six weeks. I know that it wasn't her fault, but this is when my chronic bulimia really set in.

I missed Chappo so much and was so agonisingly lonely. I would cry myself to sleep cuddling his Cuthy school jumper, because it still smelled of him and his Blue Stratos aftershave.

The saddest thing about living at Geelong Grammar was during school holidays when we were stuck there. All our friends from school were at their own houses, in their own states. The only outing we would have was swimming training. That was every morning and every afternoon. Dad would wake us up and drive us in to the local pool at least five days a week. If we weren't being trained, we would be keeping fit in other ways. Because my father was so competitive, he would make you feel as if you had to win all the school championships.

It was a long summer of feeling abandoned and incredibly lonely. I became more and more depressed. My parents always said we were lucky to live at a school with all its facilities. But to me, by this time, it was like a hell or a prison for most of the time. A lonely empty place.

After we had settled back at Corio the previous year, Dad took on the role of administrator at the school and, nearly every day, he worked during the holidays. Dad's job was enormous and included enrolments, timetables and a lot of public relations work, so he was extremely busy. He worked very hard the entire time my mother was away. Except for when he was taking us to swimming training. My older sister was away overseas in Japan for a year and I was the oldest at home with my other sisters.

Every day was the same routine. We were up at 5.30am and down to the pool and for the next nearly two hours, we trained. Then dad went to work and we returned to the pool for the afternoon session. And trained for another two hours.

We were always starving. When we got back from the pool, we would eat copious amounts of food. There was always milk and cereal and heaps of bread. My mother had spent many days making beautiful jams from fruit she had purchased. She also used to go to the Sunicrust bakery in Geelong and buy an entire freezer full of day-old bread for a very cheap price. Ten cents a loaf.

This, of course, was a bulimic's delight. I would just keep eating bread, with lashings of butter and jam. A typical binge would include nearly an entire loaf of bread, plus all the trimmings. I would put butter on as thick as a slice of cheese and then heap the jam onto it. I ate anything else that I could find. Forbidden foods, like ice cream and biscuits, would be allowed. This was because I could just spew them up. Sometimes, I would eat so much I could hardly walk and it really hurt.

Then I would then go to the Beehive classrooms, that I knew had been left open during the holidays, and not far from our house. I would put three fingers down my throat and vomit it all up. I would vomit until I tasted the foul bile. Then I would go back to the house after a wash and try not to do it all over again. But most of the time, I would end up back in the kitchen again, finding something else to binge on.

I just passed my days with the same awful routine. It got to the stage sometimes that I would feel so weak from vomiting, I would shake. Then I would have something light to eat to start with and then another binge would start all over again. Other times, I would make a batch of biscuits for the family and eat most of the uncooked mixture. I just couldn't help it anymore. I just didn't have any idea of how to eat. I couldn't control myself around food at all. It was a horrible, lonely existence. Some days, I was bingeing and purging five times a day.

As a consequence, and also because I smoked by then, swimming became less important. Bingeing was my entire existence. I couldn't eat a normal meal anymore, without overeating. I ate from the rubbish bin, I ate from the compost bucket and I was also known to eat from the dog bowl. I was caught on this horrible merry-go-round and just couldn't get off.

By the time my mother had returned from England, I had eaten at least two dozen jars of jam, quite a few pounds of butter and the bread in the freezer was very low or gone. She was furious. She had known about my bingeing and vomiting. The big giveaway was because there were quite often ants in the toilet, around the bowl and on the floor.

This made me become more secretive and I soon learned to make sure the toilet and floor were clean after purging, so she didn't know when I had binged. This, of course, made me even worse. I was always hiding the existence that I was stuck in. Food was an addiction and like an addict there were lies, deceit and denial. It totally took control of me.

Unfortunately, it isn't a well understood mental disease and definitely wasn't in the eighties. Because of this naivety about bulimia, my mother was always more worried about waste and money. She was never worried about trying to understand why I was slowly killing myself. I didn't realise why I was doing it either but really couldn't help it anymore. Her hating my bingeing and my secretiveness also became a serious trigger. I found it very hard not to start on a bingeing frenzy. It happened nearly every time I walked through the front door of our house at Corio. I would head straight to the pantry and fridge. I would even plan binges in my spare study classes at school. My parents would be out of the house and it was the perfect amount of time to binge eat until I was full and then enough time to vomit and clean up.

I really could not control myself. There was a horrible, silent void that existed in me. I didn't understand it and a simple way to deal with it, was to quickly fill it up with food and then just get rid of it.

Another horror I experienced with being a bulimic was, sometimes I wasn't able to get the food out. This would almost send me into a panic. Some of the reasons I couldn't vomit were, I didn't have enough fluid whilst I was eating or I had eaten an entire jar of peanut butter. Sometimes I hardly chewed the food and it would be stuck together in gluggy chunks.

In order to make vomiting easier, I would drink a glass of warm water with a dessert spoon of bicarbonate of soda and then shake my body up and down. This would make the food break down into smaller bits and thus come up easily.

Then, if I didn't manage to get it all up, I would over exercise or take heaps of laxatives. I also came across a medicine that induced vomiting called Syrup of Ipecac. I was known to use that at times. It tasted absolutely disgusting but it worked. It got rid of the food. Getting the food out of my body without gaining weight was the ultimate goal.

Another thing that suffered were my teeth. I started having more and more fillings at the dentist. My gums would also really hurt. The acid from my stomach was stripping the enamel from my teeth and I was dealing with infected gums and the start of gum disease. Visits to the dentist became a scenario for panic attacks. I had adrenaline injections with fillings which gave me heart palpitations. The sound a diamond drill made used to send my nerves into spasms. I also detested the dentist. He was also a parent from the school. He had the breath of a man with severe halitosis. The entire experience was horrific.

My bulimia continued constantly throughout my Year 12. I was frequently very ill and my final exams were directly affected because of my constant sickness. I also spent more time bingeing and purging and less time studying. I was actually offered a compensation pass for one of my exams. This was because I had a bout of influenza and was delirious with a high body temperature.

The cost on my body from being a bulimic was intensifying. At around 16, I just simply stopped growing because of my bad health and malnutrition. Later on in life, I learned that I had suffered from Scheuermann's disease which caused my thoracic spine to stop growing. I always wondered why I never grew to the height that matched my size nine feet.

I failed quite miserably at my first attempt at Year 12. I really didn't care that much at the time. When I was offered another year at school, it felt safe for me to stay on. I wasn't ready or mature enough to get out of the institutionalised life yet. On top of all of that, I also had a dwindling confidence problem. I was actually scared to leave the few comforts of my school years.

I was keen on becoming a physical education teacher, so I had to repeat my final year. I had turned 17 in September, during my first attempt at the VCE. And because I was so young, I was not mature or confident enough to pass. Most students finishing school are 18 years old. I also had another massive problem and that was that I had a chronic eating disorder.

In my first year of doing Year 12, I went out with a guy called Smitty. He was 11 months younger than me, and we dated for about nine months. I am sure my relationship with him ended because of my depression, irrational behaviour, and total lack of self-confidence. Probably some of the main drivers of my bulimia. Or maybe bulimia was driving them? Relationships were always fucked up during this time. Relationships were fucked up every time. Probably not because of the bulimia but because of my parents' friend's abuse. Bulimia was only a by-product.

Along with my bulimia, there were also a few thoughts about how I hated myself so much and did not really want to live anymore. I thought about suicide and actually tried once when I was with Smitty. The attempt was unsuccessful, and the suicidal urge went after about 10 minutes. Also, in the back of my mind I remembered what my mother had always said. That suicide was a very selfish thing to do.

Let's get one thing straight before I go any further. A person who suicides really does not care about how selfish it is. It is a clear and precise statement of just not wanting to live anymore. And some people just cannot live with themselves anymore.

My feelings of dislike for myself, partnered with my slow death by malnutrition, was never really thought about at the time in depth. This was because I could not understand why I could not control these cravings or why I had horrible thoughts about living or not living. There was nothing to tie in any reasoning about the way I behaved or about the way I felt. I know now all this was to do with the sexual assaults.

Because I had suppressed the moments of the abuse in my subconscious mind, they couldn't be expressed in my conscious mind. This is what is known as selective amnesia. Selective amnesia refers to the loss of specific memories, while other memories are still intact. This is often linked to traumatic and stressful events. It is a protective process where the mind can cope with overwhelming or distressing situations. This is why I didn't remember, for such a long time, the trauma I unfortunately experienced as a child.

Unfortunately, back then, we couldn't talk about anything to do with such matters, and we also would not have been believed.

## MY WRITINGS ON DESCRIBING BULIMIA

When I was a bulimic, I was under an enormous panic to get the food into me and then out of me. Food was stuffed in and, quite often, not chewed. My eating slowed down and became more uncomfortable and then it was just not possible to fit another thing in.

*What's the time? When is mum home? Oh my god, I only have 15 minutes to spew and get back to school.*

*Three fingers and a gag and at least a kilo of food starts to spill out of my mouth. I am sweating profusely, and my heart is racing. I can feel my pulse. Back to the kitchen. Bicarbonate and warm water. Swallow. Jump up and down to shake it up. Back to the toilet and three fingers later, there is that horrid taste of bicarbonate of soda and then more food and then bile. I am shaking again and exhausted. Relieved that my stomach does not hurt from too much food and, yes, I can feel my hip bones sticking out. Wow, that was a hugely successful binge session. Clean up so there aren't any ants. Check the walls. Spray with smelly stuff.*

There were also times when I hadn't had access to a toilet and had to vomit elsewhere. A shower would come to mind. However, it was exceedingly difficult trying to push half-chewed food down a shower drain.

One of the hardest things was hiding it from people. Hiding the bingeing, hiding the vomiting, and hiding the smell afterwards. My breath was always okay. The food matter I brought up was nothing like when I was nauseous and vomiting. It basically tastes almost the same as when I first ate it.

I must have been so awful to live with. I really could not help it and normal people really do not understand the way a bulimic behaves. There is lying, stealing, and even breaking into houses to steal food to put away for the next binge.

My family were once given the use of a friend's place for a weekend, and I filled my bag up from their pantry with their food. This was so I could have extra food and have a binge. It also meant there wasn't a lot of food missing from our house. My mother, understandably, became very conscious of the amount of food going missing.

On another occasion, I stole food from Dr Mackey's house one school holidays and then proceeded to vomit in the toilet there. Quite possibly, it was a way of getting my own back subconsciously. I was exercising my control over a situation.

There were also the binges that started in Geelong, and I would eat my way through a huge $20 worth of really crappy food. I would continue my binge whilst on the train on the way home and then drink enough fluid so I could stop in at one of the school's toilets and purge before I got home.

Also, another thing about being a bulimic, it is not as noticeable to the eye as a person suffering from anorexia. A bulimic does, from time to time, get some nourishment from their food. It really depends on the time it takes to purge. Most bulimics keep their weight at a normal level and don't keep losing it like an anorexic.

This makes identifying a bulimic a great deal harder, unless of course you live with one. Tell-tale signs of a bulimic are puffy eyes from straining, ants in the toilet and masses of food disappearing, long term tooth decay, scars on knuckles, yo-yo weight loss, and secretive behaviour

My final year at Geelong Grammar School Corio, I returned to school in early February 1983 and was boarding in the repeaters boarding house called Linden. I shared a room with another girl who had also failed her first attempt. We had a small flat with a bathroom and lounge study area. The flat was tucked at the end of one of the other day student houses. It was ideal and a good place for me to study. The flat was also away from my parents' house and I was boarding. Being away from them, I had more control over what I was doing, which was something I really needed at this stage.

The other thing worth mentioning about my second attempt at Year 12, was there were new assessments developed in the Victorian education system. Previously, all scores were assessed in the final external examination at the end of the year. This assessment or exam was three hours in length, and everything relied on your performance. In my second attempt, the curriculum included a 30 percent internal assessment and only 70 percent of the total assessment was in the final external examination. This helped me with my confidence, and I also had fantastic support from teachers in my chosen subjects.

Year 12 English was one of my best subjects at Geelong Grammar School. I had an amazing English teacher, Mr Anthony Strazzera, who not only believed in my ability but thought my writing at the time was pretty good. He actually referred to my work with a phrase, "It was just smoking." A beautiful explanation of freedom momentarily through writing, with recognition and expression.

In my first year of Year 12, I had an awful English teacher. He had completely crushed me in the classroom verbally and I felt absolutely hopeless at English. Quite strangely, this same English teacher coached me at hockey and was incredibly supportive of me on the playing field. Unfortunately, never in the classroom. I was not a favourite there.

Incidentally, this same English teacher was yet another child sexual abuser at the school.

It was now so refreshing to have Straz. He helped me build my confidence and honestly believed in my ability. I even started to believe in my abilities. We were studying a book, called Sons and Lovers by D.H. Lawrence. It was quite a complex book to analyse, and I really enjoyed learning and understanding the emotional side of the story. It helped me to draw on some of my own feelings and emotions and enabled me to clearly express them. It also helped me to intuitively feel some of the pain that was emanating from the subjects in the book. Feeling empathy for the first time. Straz was amazed with how well I got a grip on the book and I ended up scoring very well at English in my second VCE year. In my internal assessment I received an A rating.

I spent a considerable amount of time in my study at school, even during the holidays. It was away from our house, and I could focus on swotting for exams. I was also without the temptation of the pantry and the uncomfortable feelings I always had in our house. Those uncomfortable feelings were also the triggers that used to send me off on a binge.

Straz, like Choko at Timbertop, had noticed something different about me. At class one day, he asked me to go to his office, which was located in one of the boys' boarding houses that evening. He must have sensed something about how I had responded in some of my English classes. Maybe he thought there was an underlying problem.

Unfortunately, he wasn't able to address anything and neither was I. He was an extremely perceptive man but, unfortunately, not a psychiatrist, which I definitely needed at the time. However, he did teach me how to express some of my emotions during that time. I do remember writing something to the effect that I was a wet, woollen blanket blowing in a hot north wind but I would never dry. Trying to escape but I just couldn't.

I always felt trapped and did not know why. Was I still trapped as that little girl in a body that was changing slowly? Or was I trapped and still wanting to be that little innocent girl?

My body changed but I could never grow mentally or emotionally into it. I guess that was something that came as result of being abused as a child. Or was it the bulimia? Or was bulimia the result? There were always so many unanswered questions.

Year 12 finished without a hitch and I made some new friends. One of these friends was Sherryn, Shez for short, and we became great friends and are still in close contact these days. I also managed to get my Year 12 Victorian certificate of education. Not brilliantly but I achieved good enough marks to get into Primary School Education at Ballarat College of Advanced Education.

We spent a few weeks at Point Lonsdale in the summer holidays at our horrible brick veneer house. Because I decided it would be more fun to hang out with Shez, the remainder of that summer was spent with her. We were either at her place in Highton, a suburb in Geelong, or down at her father's pub at Anglesea. Anglesea is a beach town on the west coast of Victoria and is about 40 minutes from Geelong.

Summer with Shez was great fun. I would catch the train and a bus to Sherryn's place in Highton most Fridays. Then Friday night we would go out dancing at a local night club and on Saturday we would head down to Anglesea. To earn our keep, we would do a little bit of work at the pub in the kitchen. We would then spend the remainder of the night at the disco until the pub closed.

For most of the time that we ever went out, Shez's father Ken used to pay for us. He always gave Shez money for us to both have a few drinks and then be able to catch a taxi home. It was great to be young and partying. And Ken was so generous to me. I can't imagine what my social life would have been like, if I had just stayed at home. This meant I could meet new people in a different place. I was also finally free from Geelong Grammar School, Corio.

In February, Shez went off to a secretarial college in Geelong, and I started college in Ballarat, where I commenced my primary school teacher course. Because my VCE results were just okay, I needed to do a year of primary school teaching first and then try and transfer into the physical education course.

Because Ballarat is too far from Geelong to commute, I ended up in a share house with some other students who were also attending tertiary education in Ballarat. We had a large, terraced house and inside, we had those amazing soaring ceilings. The bedrooms were large and divided by a long hallway that finished in the living area and kitchen with the bathroom found at the very end of the house.

I had a loan from my parents for paying the rent and there was another sum of money for food and other items. I remember that it wasn't very much. I was smoking by then, so I just stole cigarettes from large supermarkets because I couldn't afford them. I didn't drink alcohol except for the weekends I was in Anglesea with Shez.

I enjoyed my course to start with and was doing okay. I remember one particular day being at college and we were discussing elite schools. Of course, I piped up and said I had attended Geelong Grammar School. Interestingly, a group in my lecture completely stayed away from me for the next month. This was because they assumed I would be a stuck-up snob.

It's funny how people think. It was also worth noting there was a stigma about Geelong Grammar School being elitist and snobby. Especially to people who had been educated in the state public system. However, we all ended up hanging out together in the end. I enjoyed college when we were on campus but it was different when we started doing teaching rounds in the local Ballarat primary schools.

I did a few teaching rounds but my confidence was really lacking and I hated being up in front of a class. Even in front of small children. Confidence and the lack of it, always stemmed from my bulimia. In hindsight, my confidence had been lacking for years.

My mother kept a list of the money we borrowed and updated it regularly. It was enough to cover rent and food. In order to earn a little extra money, I had a casual job starting little kids swimming in the water at a local pool and that would pay for a few extra things from time to time. But I was still a poor student.

I was also very thin at this stage and my health continued to suffer. Another reason for being so thin was I couldn't afford to binge as much, so I wasn't even getting the minuscule amount of food I would retain if I didn't vomit it all up. I was suffering badly from malnutrition. With that, I suffered with the flu and colds on a regular basis.

I remember a weekend where Shez and I had gone to Anglesea and I had the flu. We had been to the pub and ended up at a 21st party in Point Roadknight. I was so sick I nearly collapsed and was escorted out of the party and told to go home. I think they thought I was severely drunk or under the influence of drugs. Instead, I was a skinny bulimic with influenza, who was actually sober and straight as a judge.

By this time, my teeth were bad and I constantly had gingivitis. Gingivitis is so painful and makes you feel very ordinary. The acid from my stomach from all the vomiting, combined with my thirty plus a day cigarette use, wasn't doing my gums or my teeth, any favours at all.

When I think about it, I probably have spent, in my life, over $30,000 on my teeth. This all started before I had even left school and certainly accelerated during this year.

# CHAPTER 4

## *CRIES FOR HELP*

There was one thing, however, that wanted to tie in with my bulimia and that was another addiction I had. I had become a kleptomaniac. This was another habit I really couldn't control, up until I was caught stealing in a Ballarat supermarket. I was hopelessly addicted to stealing. I had stolen money from my mother to buy food to binge on and also to buy cigarettes. I was stealing from Shez's father. He had a money jar in their walk-in robe and I had my hands in there quite regularly at weekends. Some of the money I would take to Ballarat, again for food to binge on or cigarettes.

I also had an absolute obsession with stealing soft toys. Shez ended up with a cupboard full of them. They were useless but so easy to steal. Stealing became addictive because of the thrill I would get. It sounds sick, but I was sick. I definitely had no control over it for a while. I don't know whether it was because we never had money to spend for the things we wanted.

Everyone who attended Geelong Grammar School in my time, nearly all had extremely wealthy parents. The girls all seemed to have the latest fashion clothing, makeup and whatever they wanted. They had enormous allowances. I remember one girl had an allowance of $300 a month. And this was back in the eighties. My parents couldn't afford to give us large sums of pocket money. They were educating us at an extremely expensive school and had little left over after they paid our school fees.

My parents were also children born in England. My father, prior to the Second World War and my mother during the war. This meant they were always extremely careful with money and very careful about what it was spent on. They went through the depression in England and were also on food rations at times. Life for them as younger people would have been extremely hard. My mother, to this day, still saves ice cream containers, wipes out butter containers with bread and certainly never wastes food.

I guess I didn't really understand that side of things. So, therefore, I had nothing in comparison to my friends, so I stole it.

Because I was so skinny, I used to be able to go into Kmart or a supermarket and sit a carton of cigarettes under each arm, resting on my hip. The clothes that I wore were always big and easy to conceal stolen items.

One day in Ballarat, when I was at teacher's college, I wasn't feeling particularly well. This was a fairly common occurrence during my bulimic years as already mentioned. I needed to go shopping and I was low on cigarettes.

I walked to the local supermarket, near to where I was living, and tried to steal a carton of cigarettes and a packet of chewing gum. I decided to dump the cigarettes in the store because I wasn't feeling confident about my attempt to steal them. I then proceeded to the checkout and purchased something small, but not the gum.

I was arrested at the front door by a security officer and marched down to the manager's office. I was really frightened about what was going to happen whilst I was waiting for the police to arrive. Fortunately, because it was a first offence, I was let off with a warning. It frightened me so much, I have never stolen anything, ever again.

In reflection, my bulimia was similar to drug addiction. I stole to exist. I needed to fuel the drug, and the drug was food.

My mother never saw my bulimia as a reach out for help. To her, I was just wasting food. Most of the time, wasting food she had spent hours making or purchasing, only for me to fill to myself to the brim and purge at least four or five times a day.

Fortunately, in this day and age, there is more awareness about eating disorders and the damage it will do to a body. There is also exceptional medical help. Pity it was not around in my time.

Until recently, I never really knew how dangerous being a bulimic was. I could have even had a heart attack. Let alone the damaged to teeth, gums, body fluid balances, suppressed pituitary gland and the list goes on. I also read if you vomit more than 14 times a week, you were a chronic bulimic. I was eating and purging, at my worst, 12-15 times every three days.

I had no idea why I was doing this to my body and I also had no idea what I was doing to my body.

At the end of my school years, my sister, Lisa, had a friend whose mother was a child psychiatrist. This amazing woman, Elizabeth Scott, was interested in how I had been getting on. She knew about my bulimia because Lisa had told her. In order to cover up my purging, I used to take Lisa with me to the school toilets as an alibi, so no one would know what I was doing.

I was cross at Lisa for dobbing on me to Elizabeth, to start with. Elizabeth rang and asked if she could have a meeting with me. That first meeting I was supposed to have with Elizabeth, I simply chickened out. I just could not deal with the confrontation. I did not know what I was battling at the time, but it was scary to take any first step. This is not an unusual situation when seeing a psychiatrist or psychologist for help for the first time. I needed to be ready and I needed to take the first big step. The same goes with reporting abuse to the police.

We eventually had a second meeting that I attended with both my parents. We started off the session with a brandy and dry, more than likely to settle the nerves. Then Elizabeth started asking me a few questions.

I am unable to recall much of the discussion we had but I do remember saying to her at some stage, I thought she was looking through me. Her answer was that it was me. She said I was looking into myself and I really did not like what I saw.

My parents and I decided not to have another session with her. This was because she knew my parents fairly well and to find out the more personal side of our family dynamics be a good thing. And she really want to jeopardise Lisa and her daughter Kirsten's relationship. It actually wasn't disappointing because I understood her reasons and she probably knew too much about me anyway.

Another thing to consider, at the time I didn't think there was too much wrong with me and I did not need help anyway. And another thing was, a bulimic needs to want to break the cycle and there is a certain time when this happens. I also needed to want to face my demons and addictions. I was not ready for that yet.

# CHAPTER 5

## *RJ AND THE GOLD COAST*

Shez and I still met up at weekends, even when I was at Ballarat college. We spent the summer and into the autumn of 1984, heading down to Anglesea on Saturday mornings with her father, Ken. Sometimes we would go down with another friend, Lucy. The Anglesea Hotel became a weekend ritual. We would do a bit of work helping in the kitchen and then party and play pool after that. Of course, we would meet guys at the pub and then go on to parties after the pub had closed.

I met a guy whose name was RJ in about April 1984. He was very popular with most people in Anglesea. He lived at a place nearby called Point Roadknight. He was still living with his parents down near the beach. His other siblings were all older and had left home and had careers. RJ was a motor mechanic in West Geelong and drove in from Point Roadnight to work each day.

He was a mad surfer and he and some of his friends would go out surfing even in the middle of winter. It matter what the temperature was, if the swell was up, they went out and surfed. On the winter days, the boys would come out of the water completely blue from being so cold. They all rode planks, which are longer surfboards. It was just a fun time, and I was away from the prison school and my parents. At the time, that is all that really mattered to me.

Because I was still in Ballarat at college when we first met, RJ would come up to Ballarat some weekends and stay. I didn't get my driver's licence until I was 21, so on other weekends, he would drive to and pick me up from Ballarat and we would go down to Anglesea.

I left Ballarat college not long after the second semester began. I had been called to the head of the college's office and was asked to explain why my attendance levels had been so low. I told him I had an eating disorder, and my ill health and low immunity made me very susceptible to any cold or influenza that was going around. I was offered the chance to continue my course, but I really confident in what I was doing, so I decided to leave college and find a job.

When I left Ballarat, I ended up staying at RJ's parents in Point Roadknight quite a lot. I really did not want to be at Geelong Grammar School if I did not have to. I detested the place. If I was staying at my parents, I was out spending time looking for work. Or at my normal very worst, bingeing in the kitchen.

After a month or so, I ended up getting a job in a cafe in Geelong. Also at this time, I had been incredibly itchy in a certain area, and it had happened after a weekend that we had slept in the back of RJ's car, when another friend of his had crashed one night. Consequently, when we talked about this certain discomfort, he said his friend had had the crabs, i.e. pubic lice, leaving some in our bed in the back of the car.

We would often sleep in the car or go parking out the back of Anglesea. We were not sleeping together at RJ's place and had separate rooms to begin with. So, if we were fooling around, it was always in the back of the car.

Back to the lice thing. Before leaving the house in Ballarat, I had also caught up with an old boyfriend, Chris, from Point Lonsdale. Chris came from Ballarat and when I visited him, we mucked around sexually.

I was never sure whether it was him or RJ's friend who gave us lice. But we certainly had a problem. It is an extremely uncomfortable and itchy infestation.

Because of our affliction, RJ made an appointment at a medical clinic in Newtown. The clinic just happened to be the same clinic that Dr Mackey had set up whilst he was still practicing at Geelong Grammar School. It was called appropriately, or more disgustingly, The Young People's Clinic. And who, of all people, did RJ see? You guessed it, Doctor David Mackey. RJ said it was at the clinic he had found out he had pubic lice. He was told the name of a lice treatment and told him that both of us should use it. That would fix the problem.

There was also another comment I remember RJ making about his appointment with Mackey. And that was, he found Dr Mackey very creepy in his manner. Sexually creepy.

When he informed me, we had pubic lice and what we needed to do about it, I remember feeling thoughts of disgust and felt extremely dirty after finding out about our issue. Along with that, feelings of dirtiness because of the doctor who examined him. Other horrible feelings because of his thoughts and descriptions about the doctor too.

I still had no clear recollection of my experience I'd had with Mackey at this stage. I certainly didn't feel comfortable hearing his name or being reminded about his sexually creepy manner.

After we had dealt with the crabs, I became a lot more comfortable. Not long after that, we headed down to the Point Roadknight boat ramp one evening to go parking. Because I was never one to lie and, out of guilt, I told him about mucking around with an old boyfriend. And also, that he may have given me the pubic lice. RJ was extremely cross at me. We had started a little petting by the time I had told him. Then he took his anger out on me physically. The sex was so angry that he really hurt me. I felt like I was being sexually punished. I was in tears.

This was an example of just how shallow our relationship was, even from the start. Because of my erratic behaviour, I would just fly by the seat of my pants sometimes and do things on the spur of the moment. Including doing things with old boyfriends, just for old time's sake. I was extremely insecure and always looking for love and attention.

I enjoyed staying in Anglesea and would try to avoid going to my parents' house if I could. I remember on another occasion, being dropped at home at Corio. The Dawsons, who were great friends of our family, had called in on their way to Mount Buller. Because I did not want to be at home, I just packed a bag and went with them. Penny had a job at a restaurant called the Abom at Mount Buller for the season and I thought I might like to get some work as well. It was also a way to run away, yet again and not be stuck at Geelong Grammar School, Corio. I just could not be there. I would binge and purge the entire time I was there. Every time I set foot in the front door, I was drawn directly to the pantry and so it would begin. One of the reasons why I never liked going back to Corio.

RJ found out I had gone to Mt Buller. He and some of his mates turned up there after driving all the way from Anglesea. He was not happy about me being there. He had heard about the social life at party places like Mount Buller. He was worried he wouldn't see me again if I had stayed up there. We returned to Anglesea the following day.

My next thing to do was try and find a job. I didn't want to be in Geelong or at the school, so I eventually found work later in the year at a local cafe and take away place in Anglesea.

My psoriasis was also particularly bad at this stage, and my arms and legs were always covered in scaly patches. I had had psoriasis since I was about seven but it seemed to become a lot worse when I had started drinking alcohol. And worse again combined with my body being rundown from having bulimia.

During my early relationship with RJ, the world was introduced to HIV/AIDS. As an awareness, there was a great deal of advertising about it. The grim reaper was all over the television at this time advertising and warning against the dreaded AIDS. From memory, when someone contracted AIDS, they could have a rash on their body, which could be red and blotchy. I remember people seeing the rashes on my skin from psoriasis and moving away from me on the bus. I must have looked diseased.

I continued to avoid Geelong Grammar School, Corio as much as possible and stayed very regularly at Point Roadknight. My bulimia was still at a peak and any spare money I had would go on food at the milk bar across the road. RJ's parents lived on the left-hand side of Eighth Avenue and the milk bar/take away shop was directly opposite. I would buy heaps of food for a binge and then go and vomit at the toilets in the car park on Point Roadnight beach. Other times I would binge at his parents' house and throw up in the shower, pushing the contents of my stomach down the plug hole. It was a horrible time. Typically, day in day out, in the lifestyle of a bulimic.

Later on that year, we had a brief holiday on the Gold Coast in Queensland. RJ's sister had been working at a school on the Gold Coast and was moving back to Victoria. We were to travel on the bus from Melbourne to the Gold Coast and then were going to drive home in his sister's car back to Victoria.

RJ's sister was very bitchy at times to me. Even from the very start. In hindsight, I think she was a little bit jealous of me and my relationship with her younger brother. I was also a lot nicer looking than her and had a fantastic figure. She was very plain and a little bit chubby. One of the first nasty comments she ever made to me was about my psoriasis. Because RJ's sister was ignorant, she actually asked me if they were warts on my knees. She was one of those people who would put others down, just to make themselves feel good. Just like a mean girl. She was a very cruel person. I'm sure it had a lot to do with the green-eyed monster.

The drive back from Queensland was done over a couple of days and the only thing that really went wrong was our windscreen smashed as we passed a truck. In those days, you had an emergency windscreen you could use temporarily, until a new one was fitted. There were a few breezy moments on the way home but we arrived back at Point Roadknight as planned.

In 1985, RJ and I decided, with a few other friends, that it would be great to move up to the Gold Coast. At the time, I did not have anything in my life to keep me in Geelong, so I went with him. We drove up there over a couple of days and moved into a two-bedroom duplex unit in Palm Beach. Bunking in with a friend from Anglesea, called CJ. CJ was fondly known as Jacko, after Mark Jackson, the VFL footballer. He was a butcher and lived almost entirely on McDonald's cheeseburgers. Overall, he was a great guy, lots of fun and we all coexisted very happily together.

Because RJ had worked all the way through his apprenticeship and a year or so afterwards, he decided he would like to just go on the dole for a while. Do a bit of surfing, fishing and have a gap year, having some fun. I wanted to spend some time on the beach but wanted to work as well. Because I really only wanted to work part-time, I got a job selling timeshare for a company in Surfers Paradise. It was a commission job and I did only just okay at it. I'm sure it was because of my lack of confidence at the time. Selling timeshare was not a very rewarding job and it felt like I was grovelling at times, to get people through to the consultants.

How it worked was, we would stand on the streets of Surfers Paradise and try and entice people, who were holidaymakers, to have a look at timesharing apartments and the time share aspect. The first resort that I worked for was the Golden Orchid.

We would walk the holidaymakers to a consultant in our resort, who would then explain the concept and hopefully sell them a timeshare. We were paid on the amount of walks we would get in, and the pay rate went up after the first 10 walks. We would have a retainer commission for those first 10 and then the rate would climb at an extra dollar per walk. It was disappointing to have only the minimum walks each day. I really was not suited to this type of job. It was most definitely not an ideal job for a young and insecure person.

Unbelievably, I was asked at one stage, "How much?" In the end, I felt like I was a prostitute with a uniform and folder. Not really healthy talk either for a victim of sexual abuse.

RJ's and my relationship was always up and down. This was because my moods were always all over the place and I was extremely needy.

Another problem I now had was I had become addicted to the weight loss tablets called Medislims. I was introduced to them by an old school friend, who I met up with holidaying on the Gold Coast. Medislims were amazing because they stopped me from bingeing and suppressed my appetite. They were not illegal and you could easily purchase them over the counter at the chemist. The drug in the tablets was pseudoephedrine. I the tablets did not make me feel hungry, so I didn't eat.

Another thing the Medislims did was make me angry and moody. Especially when they were wearing off. They were still a bulimic's dream because I lost a lot of weight when I started taking them. It was also a great dream for me because, from the time I left Ballarat and spent a few months in Anglesea and Corio, I had put on about 10 extra kilos.

Medislims had great effects on my energy levels too. I remember going for a run one night after I had taken one. My boss from work saw me out exercising. He pulled me over to see if I was okay and safe because I was moving very quickly.

Because our flat was just across the road from Palm Beach, I regularly went there for a swim and always a run. It was about five minutes' walk to the sand.

One morning a middle-aged man approached me, as I came up the beach from a swim. He introduced himself as a professional photographer and he asked me if I would be interested in getting a modelling portfolio together. He also said my photo would appear on the front page of the Gold Coast Bulletin. I had always dreamt of the idea of modelling and certainly was in amazing physical shape. Unfortunately, I felt an emotion that was not unusual and that was, I felt threatened sexually. He gave me his business card, and I never said anything to anyone about it. I didn't ever call him.

After time share selling for a second time with another company, I decided it didn't really work out for me. I looked for other jobs for a little while and applied for work at a local supermarket. I started work at a place called Jack the Slashers in Palm Beach. I worked there as a checkout chick. I really liked the job and there was also a chance to go up through the ranks. Jack the Slashers was owned by Woolworths at the time. They were a great company to work for.

RJ had bought a small caravan whilst we had been living on the Gold Coast. We had moved out of the flat in Palm beach and lived out at the Tallebudgera Caravan Park. It was on the outskirts of Palm Beach and a nice quiet place. I could also ride my bike to work and back each day.

My job at the supermarket continued for a few months until we decided to travel and explore more of the coast in Queensland. We left the Gold Coast late in 1985 and headed slowly up towards the Far North of Queensland. Our first stop was on the Sunshine Coast, to Noosa Heads, of course.

Hastings Street in Noosa at the time was still a dirt road. Pretty amazing when you compare it to today. There was a caravan park at the end of the street and that's probably where we stayed when we were there. Noosa Heads was untouched. Unlike the Gold Coast where we had been living. The Gold Coast has been littered with skyscrapers on the beach front for a long time now.

We gradually made our way up the coast checking out places as we went. Most of the Queensland towns in the eighties were just developing and were not very busy. Some were very industrial and dirty.

The Bruce Highway was the main thoroughfare in Queensland and at that time the traffic was not busy. As the highway traversed through many small towns, we had no choice but to stop and have a look around. The difference being today is that the highway bypasses most of the larger towns.

The further north we travelled, the more cane fields and banana plantations lined the highway. There were also food stalls with an honesty system and delicious fruit for sale. And the fruit was unbelievably cheap.

Another strange thing we found were some of the signs. For example: "Beware of falling coconuts" and signs about jellies and stingers. Some of the comments were, "Don't worry, most people who are stung do survive". They were really quite comical.

Some of our travelling was done in extreme heat. We quite often had problems with the Ford XR overheating. Because RJ was a mechanic, he just used to turn the heater up full bore and that would keep the car motor a lot cooler. Obviously, that was more important than our own body temperature. We just drove along with the windows down.

We eventually ended up in Cairns and had seen a lot of nice places along the way. Unfortunately, in Far North Queensland there is absolutely no surf once you get to the Coral Sea. RJ was so passionate about his surfing and because there were no waves, we decided to head back down the coast.

Another catalyst for us leaving Cairns was that Cyclone Winifred was due to hit the far North Queensland coast between Cairns and Townsville.

Heading south from Cairns, we came to a small town called Fishery Falls. The water from the watercourse nearby was over the road but was slowly receding. We weren't too sure about crossing it. We decided to park the car on the north-side and place a cigarette packet on the road. To pass a little time we headed into the pub for a couple of beers. When we returned to the car, the cigarette packet was further away from the water. So, we decided to drive through the water. We managed to get through but ended up with soggy feet in the car. They soon dried out.

I also remember my first impressions of the unbelievably beautiful Mission Beach. They were dampened by pre-cyclonic storms and rain. We stayed a night there and moved south as quickly as possible. Cyclone Winifred hit Mission Beach in early February 1986.

When we were closer to the Gold Coast again, RJ had contacted an old friend, RR. He was from the earlier Anglesea days. RR used to come down to Anglesea most weekends and we would all pile into cars and head down the coast to go surfing. Shez and I would always tag along with the boys, and, at the end of the day, we would end up playing pool somewhere for pots, yet another part of my misspent youth.

RR had said he was going to go fishing down in Ulladulla, NSW. RR's brother, Steve, had been working on the long line tuna boats with a guy who used to live in Anglesea. Russell was a professional fishermen and was looking for a couple of deck hands.

With RJ's love of fishing, he was happy to move down to the south coast of NSW and chase the fish up and down the coast. Deck hands, at the time, were paid 10% of the catch in the eighties. The tuna weighed mostly more than 100 kilos and was cashed on the Japanese markets at 100 plus dollars per kilo. The money was good for a hard-working deck hand. The tuna would be bought from Australia and used for sashimi and sushi in Japanese restaurants. It was a very lucrative business.

I remember hearing about the first fishing shot the boys did and RJ had apparently said to Russell, when they had pulled a big tuna in, "That's not a fish, that's a crocodile." The fish were massive.

Doing a shot on a long line boat could take a couple of days. The boats would steam out to the edge of the continental shelf. The continental shelf out from Ulladulla is about 35km. A shot would then entail baiting a long line, fitted with floats and letting it out behind the fishing boat. Once the line was out, the boat would go up and down it, checking for fish. Normally, if there was a fish on the line, the float would be submerged in the water. Then the fish would be pulled in, gaffed as soon as possible, bled, and gutted. The tuna would then be put into a dry ice box for the reminder of the trip.

There were occasions when a shark would get there before the fishermen. On these occasions all that would be left of a potentially lucrative catch, would be the skeleton or frame. Literally what you used to see in the old Tom and Jerry cartoon's but the frames were a lot larger. It was devastating for both the skipper and the crew.

The boys would be out for two to three days at a time normally, but sometimes longer, weeks, when they headed off to Sydney or as far up the coast as Coffs Harbour.

We stayed at Steve's place for a while, RR in the house and we slept out in the caravan but it was not ideal. So, we all moved into a house overlooking the Mollymook golf course at 22 Buchan street. It was a great spot, and we could walk down to a semi-private beach at the end of the road.

The Mollymook golf club had live bands and we could walk home across the golf course. There were stacks of poker machines there as well. RJ was one of the tinniest guys I have ever met and always pulled a few extra dollars out of the machine every time he played.

Surfing in the area was also fantastic, and we could always find a sheltered beach and great waves. The boys loved surfing there.

With the boys fishing and being away, it became an opportunity to visit more pubs. The boat would pull into local ports along the east coast delivering fish and refuelling as needed. This also meant a few beers at the local pubs and possibly a meal.

When the boats were in Sydney, the boys also visited King's Cross. The Cross in Sydney was a hot spot for all kinds of entertainment and nightclubs.

Even when the boys were back in Ulladulla, they would spend a fair bit of time in the Marlin Hotel. It was getting a little lonely for me at times. Our relationship was also suffering because of this.

I found plenty of work whilst we were there and, apart from looking after two young men, I worked at three different food outlets. You could say I became the take-away queen of Ulladulla.

One particular takeaway was called Tigers. We did homemade pies, sausage rolls, hamburgers etc. I did a bit of cooking at home and would sell my meaty pies in the shop for extra money. I'm not sure how long I worked there before another fisherman called Phil, came on the scene. He would call in and get food on a regular basis at Tigers Take-away. He was working with his father and brother. Then, unfortunately, his father had to return home because he had throat cancer.

Phil and his brother were initially from Port Lincoln in South Australia and had come to Ulladulla to chase the Bigeye tuna up and down the coast. Hoping to make some good money. Phil was gorgeous. He was a gentleman. He and I started spending a great deal of time together. Some days after I had finished work, he would pick me up and we would go exploring. Something that RJ and I had stopped doing or never really did while we were living in Ulladulla. RJ's mates, fishing and surfing were far more important than me. Phil was such a lovely guy, and he certainly paid a lot of attention to me. Far more, than I was getting at home.

Phil did, however, like to smoke pot and had already dabbled in it quite a bit. I had tried it after school and dabbled a bit in Anglesea but RJ didn't really like it, so we didn't get high very much. We just stuck to alcohol.

Phil and I would roll up a number, get stoned and go for a drive somewhere different. We did a lot of laughing. In the end, I had a relationship with him for a while. He was paying a lot of attention to me and RJ was treating me like a doormat. I remember one night the boys had come home from the pub and said to me, "You're the chief cook and bottle washer around here, what's for dinner?".

It started becoming quite confusing to me – what was going on with Phil and being in a relationship with RJ. As usual, I was enjoying being with Phil because of all of the attention and fun but I had been with RJ for quite a while, and I guess it was just a habit.

I remember that Phil was returning to Port Lincoln and he asked me if I wanted to go with him. I should have but I didn't. I felt guilty about what had happened between us and it was a case of; stay with the devil you know. Too scary to just uproot and break up with a guy after two and a half years. Insecure!

In the next few weeks, just before my 21st birthday, I decided to leave Ulladulla. Because of the confusion and how I felt about both guys that I was seeing, I simply did what I always did and that was just run away. I rang my sister Lisa in Geelong and she and her boyfriend came to Ulladulla and picked me up. The boys were out on the boat at the time, and I just could not live with how I had behaved. Running away was always an easy alternative.

There is one important thing I will never forget about Phil. We were out one day and probably stoned, as usual. The discussion came up about other drugs. I had only ever tried marijuana and, apart from being addicted to Medislims, I had not touched anything else. I was frightened of LSD or any hallucinogenic drugs like mushrooms, only because, with an extremely high temperature when I was ill once, I had hallucinated about rats running down the hallway. Incidentally, this was when I was still living in Ballarat. When the topic of heroin came up, Phil had said to me, "Please do not ever try heroin, Jo. Because you will never get off it." He knew about my addictive personality and warned me of it accordingly. Thankfully, I never did.

When I had arrived back to Geelong, RJ was quick to return to Victoria. He had heard about what happened and I guess he wanted to try to sort things out and make it work again. I said to him that he had treated me like shit for six months and what else did he expect. We went out to a quiet spot near Anglesea, talked about things, cooled a few stubbies down with the gas tank on the caravan and, of course, we made up. The only way I ever knew how.

Our relationship was still very unstable for the next two years. We always fought. I was moody and still throwing up and still taking pills. At that time too, I had suicidal thoughts and deep depression.

On one occasion, we had returned from the Anglesea Hotel and had a lot to drink. His parents were not home and we had a big argument. I remember trying to smash my wrists against the ford emblem in the front of the car bonnet. It was quite sharp but I didn't manage to break any blood vessels. I had all intentions of slashing my wrists. Life was still very out of control.

During this time, I made another attempt to get over my bulimia. I decided to get back in contact with Elizabeth Scott for professional help. She was able to refer me to a well-known eating disorder psychiatrist. His name was Dr John Cone and his rooms were at 21 Erin Street, Richmond. His rooms were not too far out of the Melbourne CBD and it was right across the road from the Epworth hospital.

By this time, I was really ready for some therapy. I wanted to find out why I was doing these things to my body. I really wanted to try and stop this horrible self-destructive behaviour.

Our first session was all about my history and my relationships with my family. Then the next few sessions expanded into triggers and interactions in my family. Questions of how I got on with family, on a week-to-week basis. When I felt the urge or had been triggered to binge. Most of the conversation revolved around my mother.

On one of my final sessions, we had been talking about my relationship with my mother, presumably about her thoughts on my wasting copious amounts of food. We were really going over a lot of familiar ground each week. He then turned to me and asked me one question. The question that would be my best life detour yet. He asked me, "Is there anything else that you want to talk to me about?"

Then, I experienced an almost surreal feeling. And everything that started to come out, was relevant.

I replied that I had been having horrible dreams, about the same thing for years. My dreams were that I was always naked and being grabbed and I just could not get away. I was trapped. Then I would eventually wake up.

Then his next question was, "Has anything like that ever happened to you?"

That is when my memory and subconscious completely opened like a book. My selective amnesia dissipated from the experience of my first sexual assault.

It was Geoff Hines. He was the large man in my dreams touching and groping me and I just could not get away from him. After 10 years of having my innocence taken away, I was now able to remember what had happened in Howlong. Dr Cone had helped me find, through dreaming, the memory of my first sexual trauma.

Walking away from his clinic that day was the start of a completely new chapter for me. It meant I slowly started to understand a few things about me.

I caught the train back from my appointment in Melbourne to Corio station. The station was just up the road from Geelong Grammar School. I had all intentions of telling my parents about the discussion at my appointment and I had plucked up the courage of sharing what had transpired.

The evening did not start very well. Mum was not home and had gone to Melbourne to the opera or the ballet with a friend. In the usual Jojo way, I had also upset one of my sisters. This, of course, made my father very cross once again. In his rage, my father walked off to his bedroom and closed the door.

So far, no good.

I stood outside the door and knocked. I began telling him that I really, really needed to talk to him. His answer to my plea was, "If you really have to."

I opened the door and then sat on the edge of their bed. I began telling him about my appointment that day. He listened to me as I explained how and what I had recollected at the psychiatrist's office earlier on in the day. I began to cry and as I sobbed, he put his arms around me and held me. The feelings from his hug were incredible. This was the first time in 10 years, that I did not feel vulnerable or under any physical threat in my father's arms.

As previously mentioned, the sexual assault had always made me frightened of large men, and that, unfortunately, had included my father. And for the record, my father has never touched me in a sexually abusive way.

For most of my life, all of boyfriends, and even my ex-husband, were not big men. I could not feel comfortable around any man that was fat or tall. My father was not fat or tall, but he was very athletic and solid.

From this time onwards, my eating habits did improve, but I remained a chronic bulimic. And I still had many years of living with it.

I have also learned, a lot later in life, that Dr John Cone was a famous psychiatrist for his work with young women or teenagers, who had eating disorders. I had been so lucky to have been able to see him. Thank goodness for my sister, Lisa, and Elizabeth Scott for enabling my psychiatric sessions with him.

This was the beginning of trying to come to terms with my first abuse. It was around a decade since it happened. A decade of blocking out the memory and living with a demon inside my head. A decade of self-hate and unrealised guilt. I really do not have much recollection of my behaviour in those lost 10 years. The memories of those times in my life were blurry.

I had a couple of jobs in Melbourne at insurance companies for a while and a few flings with guys in Melbourne, behind my boyfriend's back. There was always that addiction, to being cared for and loved. I thought that anything that had to do with love always revolved around sex. There was always the attention thing too. A guy who showed genuine interest in Jo, not sex with Jo, was also given a chance.

When I had been working for a while in Melbourne, I moved in with a couple of girlfriends in Brunswick Street, North Fitzroy. This meant I could stay in Melbourne, instead of getting the train to and from Corio each day. It was great fun, and we would go out to fantastic restaurants just down the road and my social life improved. I was still seeing RJ but only at the weekends. I guess, I was really starting to look at where I was heading in life, finally. RJ and I were not really suited. We came from completely diverse backgrounds. There was also an enormous difference in our intelligence. We were both there only to have a fun time really and he, sort of, looked after me. Not very much substance existed in our relationship.

Just before I turned 22, still trying to figure out what I wanted to do as a career. A family friend suggested that I went to see a consultant company in Kew, a suburb of Melbourne called Chandler and McLeod. The friend was very involved with Target Australia and recommended Chandler and McLeod because they could assess me and suggest the best potential life career. Target Australia also preferred their younger management had this type of assessment, before they would interview them for a position.

Chandler and McLeod were psychological consultants and tested IQs in all processes. They also do what is called an environmental evaluation and a temperament test. The results then give subjects an idea of what type of career they are mentally and intellectually geared up for.

I remember the day I was tested. It was quite expensive, and I was in the building for about four hours. It was very mentally tiring to say the least.

To my surprise, the results from my testing and assessments were extremely commendable. I was absolutely staggered to see how intelligent I really was. There was a strong tendency for me to move towards medicine, and I was placed in the 90% of female population in the intelligence tests.

It was quite a shock to me at first. I was in my early twenties and still waffling about trying to find my vocation. There was also a tendency I could become an engineer. But I was keen to try and get into retail management. Because of the results of my assessment, I was interviewed at Target regional office in Melbourne. And not long after that, I was offered a job at the Target Southland store starting a career as a retail sales trainee.

I commenced with Target Australia when I was 22. The first thing I needed to do was find accommodation nearby. I moved into a house with an old friend of my family, Phillip Galloway. He was living in Caulfield with his girlfriend and another person. There just happened to be a spare bedroom in their house, so I filled the spot. I lived there for a while but the commute to work was over an hour and a half and I did not have a car at the time. When I did finally buy a car, the houses lease was up and I had to find alternative accommodation. In order to be closer to the store, I moved to some friends of the family's house, the Sandstroms, in the Melbourne beachside suburb of Beaumaris.

My family had known the Sandstroms since we were all incredibly young. Roy and Sue had spent many holidays with us at Aireys Inlet. Their three kids got on well with my sisters and me. We also visited them in Melbourne at their Beaumaris house in some of our school holidays as children. I have fond memories of watching The Super Flying Fun Show and Hey Hey It's Saturday, which used to be aired on Saturday mornings. We also spent endless hours going bowling and trampolining in their back yard.

When most of my sisters were in their teens, my parents got the awful news that Sue was dying of cancer and did not have long to live. Unfortunately, her cancer spread very quickly to her brain and she did not last long after that.

About six months after Sue had died, Roy met a beautiful lady called Trish. Roy's son, Scott, was seeing a young girl whose mother was Trish. They liked each other from the start and started seeing each other. Eventually, Trish moved in with Roy into the Beaumaris family house.

Trish and Roy were amazing to me and were fantastic to stay with. I was wined and dined every night and felt very welcomed. I had always gotten on well with Roy as a younger person and I really liked Trish. He had made a lovely choice for his final partner.

Trish and I talked a great deal, and we certainly had a lot in common.

She was also a victim of child sexual abuse. And, in her case as well as mine, it was never discussed or dealt with appropriately or at all. We also had a lot of discussion about my relationship with my boyfriend RJ. She knew he was not right for me. He really wasn't, but it was a habit. And a habit that was extremely hard to break, probably due to me being in such an insecure state. Trish and I talked a great deal about things in the months that I was boarding there. She was so beautiful to me and we sorted out quite a few things relating to my abuse.

I stayed at Southland Target for a few months and was then promoted to an Area Sales Manager at the Colac store. Colac is a small country town 80 kilometres west of Geelong.

I wasn't really interested in living in Colac because it is a bit rough and ready, meaning a low socioeconomic area and boganish. Colac was also too far to commute from my parents' house or from Anglesea, so RJ and I rented a farmhouse at Winchelsea.

I remember the place well, because it was an old farmhouse situated on a poultry farm. I couldn't believe how quickly a chicken would grow into a chook in only a matter of weeks. It was also convenient because we were both travelling the same distance to work. We would then head down to his parents at Point Roadknight at the weekends.

I was at the Colac store for about six months and then was promoted again and moved to the Geelong Target store. We moved out of the house at the poultry farm and into a caravan park in Geelong until we found a house in Newtown, a suburb nearby. This lasted only about six months because RJ wanted to move into a house in Anglesea with a friend. So, I moved back at my parents' house for a while.

This was really the beginning of the end of our relationship. RJ was moving out with the boys and was not interested in making a future with me. He had also bought a block of land with one of his siblings and I was never part of the equation. In hindsight, I was thankful.

We had a couple of visits to Ulladulla together, since we had left.

One of the visits was to attend the wedding of RR to a Canberra girl called Odette. The wedding was a disaster for me because I always managed to right myself off, drinking too much alcohol at weddings. I think at the time I may have thought a marriage would have fixed up my life.

We visited one other time to see friends together and it also happened to be the 1989 VFL grand final. We had the most fantastic time watching an incredible game at the Marlin Hotel. Even if the Geelong Cats didn't win. It was one of my best memories of Ulladulla.

At this stage, Russell had a new girlfriend, Sally, because he had split with his partner a few years before. Sally and I hit it off straight away and we stayed connected for a while after that visit to Ulladulla

My relationship with RJ had really been over for a long time but when one of his friends raped me in Anglesea, it just could not go on anymore. He wasn't there to support me and definitely wouldn't let me report his friend to the police on the night it happened. If I had not been stopped from going to the police, I would have been able to have a rape kit done and his friend would have been in a hell of a spot. Where he deserved to be.

Another occasion probably hit the nail on the head and that was when my boyfriend's nasty sister said, in front of me at a family gathering, "When are you going to fuck her off?" I was extremely upset with this comment. She was such a nasty, jealous, bitch of a thing.

After five and a half years together, I broke it off. It wasn't healthy anymore. I don't really know how healthy it ever was. We were from two completely different worlds and I was extremely fucked up. I also remember my mother commenting about him after we had split up. Her words, of course, were pertinent to his social status. He was referred to, as a bogan.

The evening, I told him it was all over, I drove up to the Anglesea lookout in my car, and I played the song by Roxette, *It Must Have Been Love*. I returned to his house and told him it was over and we would not be just having a break. Our relationship was finished completely.

I always had a few boyfriends on the side, during my relationship with RJ. Some were sexual and some plutonic. One particular guy, who was just adorable, was Damien. Damien and I met at Australian Eagle Insurance, before I started at Target. He was such a gentleman. The only problem I had with Damien, was his size. He was tall, well built, and for me, because of my past, he was a scary sized man. I was very fond of him and he of me. We kissed one night but I got so freaked out, I told him that I couldn't. He wanted so much more and I just couldn't have any more than a beautiful, plutonic friendship. We would spend time together at work, go out for beautiful meals in Chinatown in Melbourne. We always had lots of laughs. We were very well suited to each other. But always in the back of my mind, there was this hellish fear of big men.

One of the last times I saw Damien was at his engagement party to a girl he had met at work. She was just so wrong for him. And I suppose I was a little jealous too. I said to him at his own engagement party, to please wait for me and don't marry her. He didn't wait for me, nor did I expect him to, but fortunately, he didn't marry her either.

Then the very last time I saw Damien was at the Hunt Club Hotel in Merrijig and he was happily married to a genuinely nice lady. Funny how things work out sometimes.

# CHAPTER 6

## *NOVEMBER 1989 ONWARDS*

After the rape in Anglesea and the breakup with RJ, I engaged in some very needed counselling. I attended CASA in Geelong. CASA stands for Centre Against Sexual Assault. This is a free counselling service offered to people who have suffered sexual abuse. The sessions brought up a lot of underlying issues that I had from my first assault by Geoff Hines. The counselling helped me to understand a little more about the rape at Anglesea.

The organisation was useful but what I really needed was a clinical psychologist or psychiatrist to help me with what I was dealing with at the time. I didn't find one. I just started to increase my self-medication. I started using more marijuana and drank more alcohol at weekends. Using drugs and alcohol was a useful method of blocking my memory and emotions.

I had started seeing a guy called Craig, who happened to be an old boss of RJ's. Our relationship was really based around smoking dope and partying. We did have great fun but I was attracting the wrong sort of guy for me, once again. He wasn't intellectually stimulating to me. I tended to get bored very easily with him.

I called it off after a couple of months because he was getting serious about everything to do with us. Scary serious and I was on the rebound anyway. I actually think he was going to pop the question on the night I told him it was all over. He wasn't going to be a good choice, and I managed to work that one out fortunately.

I was still working at the Geelong Target store and about six months earlier, we had a new store manager replace the old one. This happened regularly at Target and management was moved from store to store, normally with a promotion.

The new manager's name was BP. After a few months in Geelong, my store manager and I had developed an attraction to each other. He was definitely not in the picture for any sort of relationship because he was married with two young kids. However, it didn't stop the flirting between the two of us.

One of my newer friends that I had met during my days with my ex-boyfriend was Sally. She was the girl that I had met in Ulladulla. We would catch up at weekends and hang out in Melbourne when I wasn't working. She was studying nursing and lived in a suburb of Melbourne, called Brighton.

I had two weeks holiday in September 1990. The first week was spent in Melbourne. I did a day's work at a girlfriend's Target store to help present her linen department in a more attractive way. Then the rest of the week had been a cocktail of drinking bourbon, going out, smoking marijuana and partying until the early hours of the morning, nearly every day. We were waking up at midday and then starting all over again. We were on an absolute party wreckage mission. Most nights we didn't remember how we got home or if we drove home or not.

By the end of the week, we decided we needed to have a much quieter week and headed up to my parents' house in Merrijig. Their house on 10 or so acres was called Noonameena, and was situated in Davies Road, Merrijig.

Sally was absolutely hell-bent on going horse riding in the high country. Another thing Sally wanted and to do, as she put it, was she just wanted to be bonked by a mountain man. All I really wanted to do was go to Mount Buller and go snow skiing.

On the first evening we were in Merrijig, we headed down to the Hunt Club Hotel, to see if she could find just the man. We spoke to a few locals and Sally organised to go horse riding for the day. At the time, Lisa was working at Mount Buller. So, I went to Mount Buller and met with the brother of my sister's boyfriend and we went skiing. I had loved skiing since prior to attending Timbertop.

When I returned from the day on the hill, as we referred to Mount Buller, I met Sally and her riding entourage at the Hunt Club Hotel. She had experienced a fabulous day and a great ride. And, noticeably, was already getting very friendly with Beau. He was the guy who ran the horse rides and his business was known as Mt View Safaris. He did two-hour rides twice a day and two-day weekend rides up into the high country. He had also been a cowboy and was known to be fairly friendly with women.

We returned to mum and dad's place after a few drinks, not before we had organised to go riding the following day.

We turned up at the yards and Beau said to Sally, "I hope that Jo can ride."

Beau was going to put me on a little moody grey mare that had a reputation for tossing most people off. We went on two rides that day, morning, and afternoon. And then, after every piece of tack and every horse was put away for the day, we returned to the Hunt Club Hotel.

Incidentally, I rode that little mare for the next couple of years and she never once threw me off.

The following day, we had organised to go riding again. Some of the horses had somehow gotten out of their paddock and were on the Buller Road. We needed to move them up to the fence line, back towards the horse yards. I had been in the car with Beau and Sally, who were really getting on well, and was asked to hop out and walk the horses up the main road along the fence. I was picked up by a guy who I had briefly met the night before and he was driving a lime green WB Holden Ute. There wasn't much conversation at all whilst we headed back to the yards. I just thought he was quiet. He was seeing another girl from Merrijig, so I never really took much notice of him. He was extremely shy and only really showed any form of communication when he had a few drinks under his belt.

He actually intrigued me and I thought there was more to this guy than meets the eye. There seemed to be a little bit of mystery about him.

Sally and I spent the rest of the week doing rides and, in the end, you could say we were more like the unpaid hired help. We adjusted stirrups, gave people hints on how to rise to the trot etc. Then we would be shouted beers and bourbons at the pub at the end of the day.

This became a weekend ritual. I would finish work at Target Geelong, hop in the car, pick up Sally and off we would go to Merrijig. We mostly stayed at my parents' house. After a while, Sally started seeing Beau a little bit more seriously. When they first hit it off, Beau was still living with his wife and three girls at home. When Sally finished her nursing certificate, she decided to move up to Merrijig and they moved out together. I stayed less at my parents' place and stayed more with Beau and Sally.

As it turned out, I eventually started to see the guy in the lime green ute. He had split from his girlfriend, and we got to know each other a bit better. We enjoyed each other's company at the weekends and used to have a lot of fun. Our weekends were spent horse riding and then hanging out at the pub.

Not really the basis for a relationship. You would have thought that I would have learned that by now. Anyway, it was fun. He seemed like a nice guy, and I had that sense of security because he liked me. Sounds familiar with male friend choices for an insecure girl like me.

Whilst I was still at the Geelong store, I continued with my flirty relationship with the store manager. Even though I had started seeing the guy in the green ute. It was very early in that relationship and at the time, Target and my career were always my top priority.

Incidentally, nothing ever happened with my store manager except for the night I left the Geelong store. I had been promoted and transferred to another Target store in Melbourne. Usually, when someone was promoted and left the store, we would go out for drinks. I was staying at a girlfriend's house in Geelong and asked him if he could give me a lift to her place instead of catching a cab. When he dropped me off and I asked him if I could kiss him, he said, "Yes," and it was very nice indeed.

I was told in later years, BP had kept me at the Geelong store as a manager for a lot longer than usual. Possibly because of the way we felt about each other. If I hadn't been moved to another store, who knows what may have happened. I have seen him only once since then. He had left Target and was working for another retailer. Now, I believe, he is divorced from his wife and has remarried.

After about six months from when I started seeing the guy in the green ute, I was promoted to area sales manager at Highpoint city Target. I moved to the suburb of Footscray and lived with a couple of friends of another one of my girlfriends. It worked out well because the house was close to the shopping centre, where I was working.

The couple I moved in with certainly liked their fair share of dope, so we used to have a smoke on a regular basis but only after work. I lived there for about six months, up until I was transferred to another store in the country at Bendigo.

In the time when I was living at Footscray, I had also attended my 10-year reunion for 1982 Geelong Grammar School leavers. The reunion was to held at the Rialto building in Collins Street, in Melbourne's CBD. I was extremely nervous prior to the reunion. In order to have enough courage, even just to turn up, I had asked my housemate to roll me a large joint to smoke. He then gave me another one to put in my packet of cigarettes for later in the evening.

I arrived at the door absolutely dry and the first thing I said was, "Boy, I need a drink." Marijuana made me very dry in the mouth, so I was extremely thirsty.

There was always a moment of anxiety going anywhere near my year group or anything to do at all with Geelong Grammar School. Too many bad memories and flashbacks would happen when anything about the school was mentioned. So, to make it was easier, I would have a few drinks and/or have a joint. This meant I could block it all out and forget the bad times. You could say that it took the edge off and gave you a little Dutch courage.

I did have the second joint in the girls' bathroom, and the evening wasn't really that uncomfortable. I caught a cab home on my own. I was asked if I wanted to continue partying that night, but I declined going out with everyone afterwards, I guess, I was afraid of being left out of the crowd. At that time, I always thought my year group had never really included me. In my eyes, anyway. It was back to that useless insecurity thing. I didn't have or believe in my self-worth at all.

# CHAPTER 7

## *THE GUY IN THE GREEN UTE*

Early in my relationship with the guy in the green ute, I had asked him about family and parents. He had two elderly parents and two older brothers. When I asked how long since he had seen his parents, he couldn't tell me. So, I decided t I wanted to meet them and we should go and see them.

His parents lived on Mitchell's Island near Taree which is located on the Mid-North Coast of New South Wales. We visited his parents a couple of times, and it was always me that ended up funding the road trips. The guy in the green ute never had any spare money because he told me he was paying off a tax bill.

His parents were extremely basic people and the conversation was quite boring and never went outside the square. It was all about family, the weather, and the vegetable garden. Even when we would go on these trips, I still could not see the enormous difference in us. In hindsight, we were from completely different worlds.

We were together for a couple of years before we were at his parents for a holiday and he asked me to marry him. I said, "Yes" of course and thought my life would really change for the best now. Marriage would just fix everything!

I was still a chronic bulimic but hoped and thought by getting married, my bulimia and my life would get better. Maybe having a few kids would help. Another hair-brained idea that it would possibly and eventually fix me. Fix all my problems.

He was aware I had an eating disorder, and, prior to that, he had helped me beat my addiction to the dieting drug found in Medislims. I had become totally dependent on them in my twenties and was still using them when I went to Merrijig. He said he would try to help me, to even overcome my bulimia. Possibly, going to be my life saviour.

We went to my parents at Christmas time that year. As we were leaving the family get together, he asked my father if he could marry me. I am sure he would have been quite nervous asking my father's permission and, obviously, after a few drinks for Dutch courage, he said, "I would like to make an honest woman of your daughter."

I remember thinking, *What the fuck did that make me look like? A slut, a loose woman, a whore?* My father was lost for words at this stage too. Yet another Freudian slip that really made a girl feel good. Just what I needed when I thought I was happy at last. However, it didn't change my mind. All I wanted to do was get married and live happily ever after with all my problems solved. I had convinced myself this would finally make my life work.

From that time on, plans were made for us to get married. We were second in line to Lisa's wedding, so it needed to be later in the year. We planned to get married at Timbertop in the chapel and have the wedding reception in the old school dining room. Another thing that affected the date for my future husband was the Aussie Rules football finals. I was told that we could not get married until the football finals had finished. Our date was set for the first weekend in October.

The priest who was going to marry us was Father Robin. The Robins had lived next door to us at Corio. Father Robin was the Anglican priest when we lived at Geelong Grammar School. We went down to Geelong and attended a meeting with Father Robin in Point Lonsdale to discuss what it all meant to be married. From a priest's point of view, it was about loyalty and dedication. I wish he had said it was more about being suited to each other. Cleary, in most people's eyes, we were not suited. I was blinded by everything and could not see the ridiculousness at how different we were.

I was also living this ridiculous dream that everything would be great from now on. That my life would change for the better if I were married. Even if I wasn't really sure about the person I was going to marry. Or if it would really work either. Yet another unfortunate and unnecessary chapter to live in Jojo's life.

# CHAPTER 8

## *MY MARRIAGE*

On 3rd October 1993, I was sitting in the front of my parent's car beside my father, heading to the Timbertop Chapel on my way to my wedding. We had spent the morning getting our hair and makeup done and all the usual aesthetic preparations for getting married.

I was nervous about it but had enjoyed a small joint and a glass of champagne. This was just to take the edge off. Whilst my father was driving out of Davies Road, towards the Timbertop turn off, he said to me, "You know, it's not too late to turn around now and go back home."

Wow, what a line dad! What a thing to say on the day. I'm getting married and now you're saying that! All I could think of at the time was, *everyone has turned up to be at our wedding and how would they feel if I didn't turn up?*

Both my parents obviously did not think I had made a desirable choice for a future husband. My father was now giving me, the better-late-than-never opportunity to change my mind. He knew full well, this was going to be yet another Jojo disaster. He never once said to me, "I don't want you to marry this man." He never once said that we weren't suited. I sometimes wished that he had. In hindsight, we were not suited at all. The only thing we had in common was we both liked riding horses.

That really sums it up. Our marriage was based on our love of riding horses.

I really did think my husband was a solid person for me at the time and I knew he loved me. That is all I really wanted. I just wanted to be loved. I also wanted someone to keep me in control and in check. I thought he could be this person. Probably not the things you look for in a husband, but I was incredibly insecure and extremely messed up. I really thought he was just the right man for me.

I just wanted to be married and live happily ever after.

I had wanted to get married at the Timbertop chapel, because it was the only place I really ever liked religion. My parents were religious, and I wanted to please them as well.

The view from the chapel was of the surrounding mountains and hills. It was beautiful. An aspect you get in a lot of places around Mansfield district. The chapel window and altar faced out towards the Buttercup Valley which was another place so beautiful at Timbertop. It was also the freedom feelings I got from being in the mountains. Just an incredibly beautiful spot in the High Country.

In hindsight, my father was right in having the car conversation on the way to the Timbertop chapel. Our wedding video showed every bit of doubt in my mind about getting married. The look on my face whilst I was walked down the aisle, showed I was screwed up with total confusion. One twisted smile emanating from one confused, young bride-to-be.

We went ahead with the ceremony as expected. After our photos, we headed down to the Timbertop dining room for our wedding reception. Our reception was great fun and, for once, I chose not to drink very much at all. In the usual fashion my father had warned me to be careful about how much I had to drink. From experience, whenever I was stressed or uncomfortable, I would grab a drink. Just so I could deal with things.

For once, I did as he asked.

Everyone had a great evening, and the speeches went off well.

Something that really sticks out in my mind was I remember when my father was speaking. He had mentioned something my grandmother, who was still alive, had said. Her words were, "Please don't ever let Jojo get bored."

After all the other official speeches were finished, my husband stood up and said, "On behalf of me wife and I…" This brought cheers from the congregation. I felt like cringing up into a little imp, because it was very obvious, I was now planning to spend my life with someone who was from a completely different tribe. I suppose it would have been a great deal worse if he had referred to me as the Missus. One term I will never tolerate being referred to.

For our reception we had a band playing called, The World's Worst Band. They were a local Merrijig band and were nothing like their name. Everyone said they thoroughly enjoyed the reception.

The only other thing that stuck out as being really awful at the wedding, was something one of my close girlfriend's boyfriends had said to me. We were saying our goodbyes to people all in a row and I came to this particular guy. He gave me a hug and then told me he had always wanted to fuck me. Not really the kind of thing you would normally say to a new bride. Wow. Why do people always say things like that to me?

For our wedding night we stayed at Pinnacle Valley Hotel, which was close to where we had our wedding and reception, and my new husband fell asleep in the bath. Too much to drink, as usual. Not an ideal way to start a married life.

Our honeymoon was also a nothing. His parents came and stayed with us in our flat for a week and we did not leave Merrijig. Besides all of that and, because we didn't have any money, we couldn't afford to have a honeymoon anyway.

My husband and I came from two completely different upbringings. We were two different people from light years away. I am an incredibly intelligent woman, and my husband had a basic work background. His parents were simple people. My parents had careers in teaching and were well associated with people from a different tribe. My family talked about politics and had discussions about remarkably interesting topics.

We went on through our marriage drearily and slowly drifting apart for too many years. And for the obvious reasons, we could never really connect or have any form of intelligent conversation. Every time we went away on holidays, I hoped it would get better. I thought it would get better. It did for the time we were in a different environment but then it went back to the same old, same old. The stupid thing was, I just didn't know or have the self-confidence to just leave and start again.

Another marriage wrecker for me was my husband could never hold down a decent job. I simply lost respect for him. Not to mention, I became, almost from the day we married, the major breadwinner. I had resigned from my fantastic, well-paid Target job, because I couldn't get a transfer to the Shepparton store. This store was the closest to Mansfield at the time. About an hour and a half away.

Before I was married, I was working in the Bendigo store and about to receive a generous remuneration and go into senior management. My husband refused to move away from Merrijig. As a result of this stubbornness, I gave up my $35,000 per year in 1993, with benefits. Instead, I took an enormous salary drop of $13,000, with no benefits and started work for Coles supermarket in Benalla. This was so we could stay near Mansfield at Merrijig.

On another note, my husband, within days of getting married, had just told the guy he was working for, to stick his job where it fit. Whenever he had any difficulty with people he worked for, or alongside, he would just crack it at them and leave.

My husband was a daily drinker and always insisted on going to the Hunt Club Hotel. He told me, this is where he would pick up a lot of his work. I rarely ever drank during the week, so I insisted he spent less time in the pub and drank at home. We were newly married and needed to start putting a house deposit together. He had also lost his job. Money spent on beer was money not going into our savings. Incidentally, my husband rarely picked up enough work at the pub to even cover the cost of his drinks.

I stayed at Coles supermarket for only six months as a manager. I was driving an hour each way, every day, from home to Benalla and back. I never really liked my job at Coles. It was a hugely different management style to Target. I had also hurt my back at work whilst there. It was an injury that had happened previously, and I had worsened it one day at work. The driving back and forth was also making my back worse. Another reason for leaving. So, I decided to find myself some work in Mansfield and locally in Merrijig.

I became a waitress at the Merrijig Motor Inn and also cleaned the motel rooms there on busy weekends. I had three other jobs in Mansfield, one at the Roundabout Cafe in the kitchen and behind the counter. Another job helping with inventory at the local Mitre 10 and I also worked at the Mansfield veterinary clinic as a vet nurse. I just loved working. I also needed to work so we could pay the rent and eat. At that time, I was the only one working. Money also covered my husband's and my habits, smoking, and drinking. He flittered in between jobs, sometimes working and mostly, sometimes not.

I loved my numerous jobs but especially enjoyed working at the veterinary clinic. Everyone there was smart and we had fantastic conversations. Another bonus was being able to watch certain veterinary procedures. In my spare time I sometimes enjoyed going out on call with a vet. For example, if there was a difficult calving to attend to. Or watching pregnancy testing in cattle. It was a fantastic experience. I was also spending time with intelligent people. It was very stimulating. I certainly did not have the same mental stimulation at home.

Within a short space of time, I soon became very friendly with one of the vets. He had an amazing bedside manner with pet owners, and the bedside manner went a lot further than that. Again, I had found someone who made me feel like I was as smart as he was. The relationship went on for quite some time, but the vet always had other women on the leash as well. So, once again, it not a good thing to do for my fried brain. The result of sexual abuse confusion. He was a total womaniser, and I was totally sucked in by him.

Fortunately, he left Mansfield veterinary clinic and headed off to work at his own practice in Melbourne. I also left not long after that, because I was offered a few private apartments at Mount Buller to look after and clean. The money was also exceptionally good. I left my job at the vets after about 18 months.

Whilst I lived in Merrijig and from the very first weeks of my marriage, I had a fantastic neighbour who, even to this day is one of my most special friends. She was the spark that helped me deal with and really helped me endure my marriage. I had to endure it, because at that time, it was what I thought I needed. Robbie stood by me, through all of the rough times and we also had a lot of good times together. We had a love for life. Toast with Promite and tomato for breakfast, champagne, and we also both loved a smoke and a bit of hooch here and there. Laughter was always our choice of beverage, as well as others. I don't think I had laughed so much, up until I met Robbie. Well not in Merrijig, anyway. I still had my fabulous Geelong girlfriends.

When everything was doom and gloom and boring at home, this wonderful person, in those years, helped me laugh again. Robbie worked at the Almrausch, a ski instructors' accommodation at the time and was head of the kitchen.

In the first couple of years of being married, my husband and I were living quite close to the Timbertop campus. I hadn't really thought too much about Geelong Grammar School during this time. However, somehow, I heard about the campus having trouble with some of the girls with eating disorders.

So, I decided, because I still had an eating disorder, that I would offer to speak to the female students at Timbertop. I was extremely passionate about helping girls early before there was a chance they could end up in the hideous world I was still living in. At this stage I was into my 13th year of the living hell of bulimia.

Not only was the age of girls in this year at school, a crucial time for sexual development, but interestingly, it is also an age when eating disorders start and progress. I am not a particularly good public speaker, but I decided I would try and get a message across at this tender age. Hopefully, to help prevent eating disorders. I began with talking about my anorexia and then my bulimia nervosa. I also spoke about some of the causes of my own eating disorder.

I told the girls about my dentist bills and how many fillings I had at the time. After I had spoken, I asked the girls to ask me as many questions about eating disorders as they wanted and I happily answered everything I could honestly.

It was just one of those simple things I could do to help. It was little snippets in life like this that have helped me to try and help others. It also gave me the slightest bit of therapy because I was talking openly about my own struggles. It was also some small connection with Geelong Grammar School. I do not understand why but I felt like it was a good thing for me to take part in.

On September 16th, 1995, my husband's brother was going to get married. This was to take place at Mataranka in the Northern Territory. It was also the date of my 30th birthday. Priority here was not, as usual, about me. It was about his family. I was literally just an accessory. A wife, or should I say, a missus?

My husband's brother was a military police officer at Tindall RAAF base, just south of Katherine in the Northern Territory. My husband travelled up for the wedding and then started working up there. He was hoping, if he could stay in some decent work, I would also go and join him.

Working was always an issue. I was almost praying, even though I was not at all religious, that he would finally hold down a job for some time. We would then be in a position to put a deposit on a house.

I stayed in our rented house in Merrijig and got someone to move in with me for a while. When I moved back to my parents' house, I signed the lease over to her. I stayed at my parents' house, until I headed up to Katherine. I had my 30th birthday on the same day that the wedding was held in Katherine. I celebrated with a couple of friends.

Two weeks later was the AFL grand final. For most football games during the season, my husband and I used to go to the Merrijig Hunt Club Hotel to watch the game and have a few drinks. Another excuse to go to the pub.

Because it was the grand final, I made an afternoon of it and there were a lot of people there. After the game, I returned home for a shower then headed back down to the pub. After drinking in the afternoon, I always needed a sleep and would go home, eat, sleep, shower and head back out. It was a ritual I became accustomed to. Alcohol with no food always made me sleepy. I guess that alcohol was something I should have never participated in. But it was now becoming my numbing agent.

I also loved the partying, if there was a band on. This particular night, there wasn't but I was invited to a party in Mansfield. I do not remember how I got there but I ended up at the party.

That was my next mistake.

I had fallen for a man I had known since kindergarten in Mansfield. He was well known for his womanising, was fun and extremely good looking. He was also full of charm and becoming highly successful as a farmer. All the appealing things I had been missing out on in my marriage.

We ended up getting together that evening and I went back to his farmhouse for the night. We met on a couple occasions, but he said he never wanted a relationship. He also knew I was married and there were no promises. Once again, I was a sucker for it. Sex was happiness and I was confused with being loved. And he was another one of those sucker men. You got sucked in and they just loved visiting the black hole. The black hole of a woman. The only thing that was on their mind. *And you sweetheart, of course, were the greatest vulnerable target.*

My husband had found himself quite a decent job in Katherine and started talking about saving money for a house. *There was a bit of hope, I thought.* Because things were on the improve with his work, I decided to go to the Northern Territory. In October, I drove to Katherine with one of my sisters. We stayed with a few friends along the way on the east coast of Australia.

We stayed a couple of nights with my husband's best man and wife at South Ballina. My husband and I had stayed there before, so it was a good place to spend a night or two.

I had a conversation with Gail about my marriage and my uncertainty and she posed a few questions to me about it all. She knew it would eventually fall apart but I still could not see it. Yet another warning not heeded.

My sister and I then visited my girlfriend, Robbie, who was looking after her parents' house in Burleigh Heads on the Gold Coast. We had a wonderful time and really could have stayed. I really didn't want to go but it was another give- the-marriage-a-go trip. Another holiday that I had said to myself, things will get better.

On our way, we visited Barcaldine in Queensland and went through the Australian Stockman's Hall of Fame in Longreach. It was a bit of an adventure for us, and we were also towing my husband's tool trailer with us to the Northern Territory. We stayed at Mount Isa and then headed up to Katherine. We lasted about two weeks in Katherine, much to my sister's disappointment.

The entire time spent at RAAF base in Katherine was ruined by the constant drinking of my husband and his family. It was always about how we got pissed when we are going to get pissed etc. I was also, at the time, starting to drink a lot more. But it was only to mask my existence.

The last night we were there, we had gone to a rugby match, and I had experienced yet another silent panic attack. This was because of a comment made to me. It was about a man I was introduced to at the rugby match. After the introduction, I was then told, in the not too distant future when he saw me again, he would be playing with my bottom. I felt instantly sick. I told my husband that my sister and I were going back to Mansfield. I told him I really needed to sort my head out. Finally, and hopefully.

My sister and I returned to Merrijig. We drove for three solid days. I cried nearly all the way home to my parents' house. It was here I started, once again, to try and heal my childhood sexual abuse wounds. I read books and spoke to our beautiful neighbour, Kate Eggers. I cleaned for Kate and started doing other local houses in Merrijig. This was just to keep me fed. Kate gave me a couple of books about healing and we could talk very easily because she had experienced quite a similar and difficult upbringing. She had also suffered from sexual abuse as a child. She was incredibly endearing and empathetic.

At this time too, because I was doing anything in my power to try to heal myself, I finally plucked up the courage, after 19 years, to go to the police. I made a statement regarding my assault by Geoff Hines and I was interviewed by a policewoman in Wangaratta, Victoria. After my statement was taken and a few days later, I was contacted by a detective who wanted to find out more information about Geoff Hines. This concern was probably due to me saying in my statement that he had offended other little girls. He fit the child sexual predator model. Nearing the end of our conversation, he asked me if I wanted to press charges. My confidence was lacking. So predictably, I declined. I did reiterate that I was reporting him because I was trying to protect others in the future.

Another reason was, I was afraid of going to court and did not want to see this horrible man ever again. It was also truly clear it would be his word against mine. Maybe I had watched too many movies where these situations were just thrown out because proving beyond reasonable doubt was a gruelling process.

There was also always the thought I would have been doing something wrong in my parents' eyes. Dobbing in a friend, a friend that had been a friend of theirs and also the association that came, of course, with Geelong Grammar School.

This was probably because of the reaction I had received from my mother. I asked her once in one of my healing times, why my parents had never done anything about my abuse by Geoff Hines. She told me they didn't ever do anything about it, because they didn't want to hurt his family.

What the fuck? What about my hurt? What about how I had sent turmoil and hurt through my entire family? Was she taking the blame for him? Or was it because of the guilt, shame and embarrassment associated with one of their friends? So, did I just have to forget it and get on with life as if it had never happened? Apparently so. Just get over it!!!

There was the first glimpse, after I realised what he had done to me in the psychiatrist's office. Now there was a glimpse of the road to finality after reporting him. After all, it had only taken me 19 years to make the assault known to the police.

Life did start to improve in some ways. There were feelings of relief that I could prevent someone else from being hurt. It did make me feel a little like the old Jojo again.

Whatever that means.

I'm not sure whether it was November or December but in that same year I had an accident which was definitely a wakeup call. Another life changing moment. I had gone to the pub to meet with friends for a drink around lunchtime. I had then gone back to my parents' place to have a sleep, something to eat and a shower before returning to the pub. I was also hoping I might catch up with the farmer I mentioned before.

I drove my car down to the river and parked on the same side of the bridge that our house was on. It was an easy way to crawl up the road in the car when you had had a few drinks and hopefully avoid the police. I crossed over the river and wandered up to the pub. I spent a couple of hours in the bar and decided I wasn't really in the mood to party that night. So, I decided to have an early night. I had a friend who was always at the pub with his two boys. I asked one of the boys, Orion, to walk me over the bridge to my car. Earlier on, when I had got to the river, I noticed there were some young guys camped on my parents' house side of the river. And because I was always wary of being vulnerable and sexually assaulted, I decided I needed a chaperone to walk me back to my car.

Orion came down to the bridge with me quite happily. Incidentally, the bridge was the old one we used to play under when my mother had picked me up from kindergarten in Mansfield. It had long been decommissioned and a new one built. It was made from large pieces of timber laying side by side with a narrow gap in between so the water would drain off the bridge. Either side of it was a rail all the way along. Hopefully, if a person was to walk over it and lose their balance, the rail was there to stop them falling off.

As I said, the bridge was decommissioned and closed only to vehicles. Orion headed over the bridge in front of me and, as I came up from ducking under the 'road closed' sign, my two-inch high, RM Williams heel went down a gap in the bridge floor. It tipped me completely off the bridge and I was left hanging there, trying to grip the bottom safety rail. The top rail was long gone. Orion heard my cry for help, but I couldn't hang on. I fell and knocked myself unconscious. I do not remember falling or calling out to Orion, which I found quite strange. The power of the protective brain. Also, possibly that selective amnesia thing again.

I woke from my unconscious state to find myself in the Mansfield hospital. Beside me was a local doctor tending to my broken ulna. When I had fallen, because I am left-handed, I had put my left hand down to break my fall. I then punched myself in the left eye and, knocked myself clean out.

When I asked what had happened, I was told I had fallen off the old Merrijig bridge. Because it had been on the way home from the pub, I was stirred a little about it later. Everyone was sure I had been drunk.

The next day, Lisa picked me up from the hospital. Robbie then called in to Lisa's house to collect me, and we attended a Merrijig fun run or some sort of new fundraising event. I had a plastered arm and a great shiner on my left eye. The first thing I wanted to know, was where I had fallen. We walked to the spot on the bridge where the rail was missing. To my amazement and relief, I had missed the rocky concrete support of the bridge, missed the river, and missed being impaled on a steel post that was sticking out of the ground. I had landed beautifully on a patch of green grass.

Orion had raced back to the pub and raised the alert because he couldn't see me. One of the older guys had scooped me up off the ground and taken me up to the road, so I could be placed in the ambulance.

I could have died. What A wake up call.

My recovery time was six weeks in plaster. Because I couldn't get work in Mansfield, I stayed with my older sister in Hawthorn, a suburb in Melbourne, and went to work at the Melbourne city Target store. I worked in the fitting rooms for a few weeks. During this time, I was approached about becoming a Target manager again. I declined because my confidence was shattered and I still thought my marriage would save me.

During the time my ulna was healing, I was able to work one-handed. By the time the Christmas break and the New Year events had come around, I was working as a waitress and a cleaner at Pension Grimus, Mount Buller. The idea was to save enough money to go back and try with my marriage again.

I was never, ever going back to Katherine after leaving previously. The white people were smutty and a bunch of drunks. Unfortunately, with life in the armed forces, people are hugely different. A lot of their social life is alcohol and if my husband wanted me back, it definitely wasn't going to be there.

After a little bit of enquiring, my husband got a carpentry job over at Mission Beach in far North Queensland. As soon as I could drive and had enough money, I took our Hilux, armed with some dope, my dog, named Molly, and some Guarana tablets to keep me awake.

The first couple of nights, I stayed with a girlfriend, Sally, and her father and stepmother on the Central Coast, just north of Sydney. We had a great couple of days together, going to the beach and just hanging out. I still wasn't sure I was doing the right thing but I thought perhaps things would change. Didn't I always think that?

The next couple of nights, I stayed with husband's best man and his wife. We had been there before together and I also had been with my sister in October but this time I was on my own. Gail and I did a lot more talking about our marriage and I guess she also wondered why I was still going to have yet another go. After all, she had already told me they thought our marriage was doomed from the start.

After a couple more days and driving over 1300kms from the day I left South Ballina, I arrived in Mission Beach. I had called my husband from Townsville to let him know where I was and find out where he was working. When I arrived at Mission Beach, I went straight to his work, hoping for an enormous welcome. Instead, I just got a simple hello. No hug and no kiss. Another big letdown.

When I first arrived, I thought the place was an absolute paradise. There were palm trees, beautiful beaches, and islands just off the coast. We walked our dogs along the beach and chatted away to each other. It was what I had expected our honeymoon to be like. Maybe it could have worked if it had stayed like this. We stayed in a caravan park for a few weeks and then rented a house for $150 per week. We had absolutely nothing. We slept on the floor, our fridge was an esky and we only ever had enough money to buy a few things to eat. Money was also spent as a priority on cigarettes and, of course, he always had to have his beer.

Everything in Mission Beach was extremely expensive. It was a transient little tourist place with just one supermarket at the time, who would charge you to the moon and back. I found work easily and my husband, as usual, seemed to lose work easily. I started cleaning and slowly built up my working gear and then began my cleaning business, Merrijig Cleaning Services. I had worked for a few real estate agents in the town and ended up with about 20 occasional rental apartments to clean.

The former apartment cleaner, Lyn, had set up a quoted cleaning system. She had wanted to further her career in the real estate business and became the property manager. The cleaning job was easy money because I was quick and had an eye for detail. Lyn also gave me a method to follow with quoting rental places, and it worked a treat. I was earning good money. Another little benefit of this job was that people would leave perishables and sometimes the odd bottle of wine or beer. A nice treat sometimes and always. This also included everyday foods, such as butter and bread. It actually helped us to eat sometimes.

My husband still could not get work or any work that was ongoing, so he mentioned about going down to Noosa Heads. In his early twenties, he had worked for a guy who was a registered builder and highly successful. Successful also meant that my husband might eventually be busy and stay employed.

So, just as I was setting up another small business, I was moving again. Changing locations and uprooting again, so that my husband could get a job. And hopefully hold down one for a considerable amount of time.

Because I had set up the business and couldn't leave straight away, my husband drove down to Noosa to set up ahead of me. I then gave a month's notice to the real estate. This was so they could find a suitable replacement. For that month, I stayed with a lady I had done some cleaning with at a local resort. She was married and had five children. I helped them out with a little rent money.

After a month, my husband flew to Cairns and we drove down to Noosa together. He had rented a house in Doonan which is about 20 minutes out of Noosa Heads in the Sunshine Coast hinterland. It was quiet and just like a little country town with no hustle and bustle. Suited us just fine.

I managed to get work easily at two local resorts cleaning. He managed to stay in his job for a while. By the time I had been there for three months, I picked up a contact in Sunshine beach looking after 20 apartments. The properties I looked after were all occasional rentals and the real estate agent also had some other work with bond cleaning. Bond cleaning was when a lessee had vacated the rental and I would bring the house or unit back up to scratch. I had employed a few staff and was now running a great business, once again.

In early August, of 1996, I woke in the night with extremely bad stomach cramps, and I was bleeding very heavily. I assumed I had miscarried. I had never had period pain. Probably because I had amenorrhea, where I didn't get my period for most of my child-bearing life. This was caused by being run down from my bulimia nervosa.

I had wanted to have children since we were in Mission Beach, thinking that would change everything in my married life. I would be able to raise them in paradise. This is what dreams were made of. Happily, ever after fairy tales.

Around September 1996, I started getting nausea, especially in the afternoon. And because I had been wanting to get pregnant, I waited for my missed period. In my case, probably because of my eating disorder, my periods varied all the time and they could be anything from 35-50 days apart. Well, it didn't come, so I went to the doctor, to get a test.

The test returned positive and, according to the ultrasound a week later, I was around six weeks pregnant. It was amazing. I was finally pregnant.

Being pregnant was the brand-new start to looking after a new life and also the beginning of looking after my body finally. My eating disorder didn't just stop but I was a little more careful about what and how I was putting food and nutrients into my body. I also wasn't throwing up anymore. You could say my first pregnancy was the one that started me saving my life. My bulimia nervosa was not going to beat me finally. Apart from having a little bit of morning sickness, especially in the afternoon, being pregnant was no different to being normal. I still worked and kept doing everything I had always done. I was eating a better diet and felt great.

I had built up yet another small business in Noosa. I had quite a few girls employed and was doing similar work to what I was doing in Mission Beach. I was enjoying the work and my little business was growing slowly.

To my disappointment, we only lasted around six months living in Doonan. After Christmas that year, my husband decided he wanted to go back to Mansfield. This was because he missed the lifestyle and was very homesick for Merrijig. Probably the beer and a few blokes at the Hunt Club Hotel more to the point.

However, I was glad to be going back to Mansfield because my parents and Lisa were there. Lisa was also pregnant with her second child, Tom.

We left Doonan for Mansfield in March of 1997. We drove both cars down and, apart from the many pee stops due to my pregnancy, it took us three days.

As usual, I went straight back to work. I cleaned for a few local private people and also at the Merrijig Lodge. I had to work again because my husband was only getting a few days here and there. He had a few days of cattle work and the odd fix it job on a local farm.

We were also able to stay at my parents' house in Merrijig, so we could have free accommodation and hopefully save up to buy our own house. Saving money just never happened. My income had always fed us and provided for us.

I worked up to and including my pregnancy due date at the Merrijig Lodge and I picked up a few local houses to clean as well.

My oldest child, a boy, was born 8.40 am on 6th July 1997. After being in utero for 42 weeks, he had very long fingernails, flaking skin and weighed eight pounds two ounces. He was healthy and my labour was only eight hours.

During the course of my pregnancy, I had put on 25 kilograms and weighed a healthy 85 kilograms. I was absolutely enormous, but I hadn't vomited intentionally for over nine months. Finally, my bulimia nervosa was ending its days.

Within the first two weeks, I had lost over 14 kilos, including a baby and a placenta. I was so determined to lose all my baby weight and quickly. It was like an obsession again. I just could not stand being fat. But I still managed to refrain from bingeing and purging.

There was another incidence, about my husband that comes to mind. When my son was born, his father decided it was most important to wet the baby's head. This ritual seemed to go on for quite a few days, if not weeks. I had stayed in hospital for about five days to get a handle on being a brand-new mother. This was certainly different to carrying a child. My husband came to visit us every day, but the head wetting continued in the evenings. Any excuse to have a lot of beer.

One of my husband's groomsmen had come to Mansfield for the weekend and they were to catch up at the Hunt Club Hotel. And yes, this was going to be yet another night of wetting the baby's head.

Being a new mother and not at all experienced, I had a few problems with my son as a little baby. He was quite colicky at times. These bouts of colic and irritability would normally occur in the early evening. He would scream after feeding and was always very windy and very difficult to burp.

I was having an enormous problem on this particular night. The baby had fed well but then just screamed in pain for well over an hour. I didn't really know what to do in this situation and was becoming terribly upset. I tried putting him down, bathing him; I tried everything. Then I rang the pub to speak to his father. The first response was, "Oh, just one more drink."

After half an hour had passed, with more gut wrenching screaming from our baby, I rang him again. I asked him to please come home. I was answered with the same excuse that I was given earlier - just one more drink. This happened a couple more times. By this time, I was ready to throw the baby at the brick wall. Obviously, I didn't but I was so upset and so cross and I was now crying.

Not long after, my husband walked through the door. The first thing I did was give him the baby. The next thing I said was, "You are a c&%$!"

He said, "No, I'm not."

I said, "Yes, you are a c&%$."

The baby head wetting stopped after that and, fortunately, I learned how to deal with the baby's colic. Just another example of the lack of any support from my husband.

By the way, he never apologised for this behaviour. I can assume that from my husband's upbringing, a woman's and mother's place is in the home. That is their job entirely. Pity he just didn't know how to work or support his family as the breadwinning father.

My father was due to retire from Geelong Grammar School at the end of 1997 and my parents were going to move from the school to their house, Noonameena, in Merrijig. We had been living there rent free for about six months. Remembering that they had offered us their house so we could save for a deposit for a house. One weekend before they had retired, they had come up to stay, bringing with them, my youngest sister. My husband and I had been arguing. More than likely over money and work, or lack of his work. We were sitting outside on the verandah both having a drink and a cigarette.

There was one thing my husband always found extremely difficult to understand and that was the way my parents had dealt with, or not dealt with, my child sexual abuse. My moods, obviously, would go from normal to fractured in an instant. I was erratic and this was due to my not dealing with or not even knowing that I suffered with Post Traumatic Stress Disorder.

He would sometimes say things to me like," You're fucked in the head, Jo!" or he would threaten me.

I remember him saying once, when our first baby wasn't even born, that if anything was wrong with him, it would be all my fault. He bullied me, at times, because of my weak emotional state. I guess it was because he wanted to be in control of me. Sometimes he wouldn't get this control because I was always doing exactly what I wanted to do. I also remember another thing I was told as a newlywed and that was, I was his wife and I would do as I was told. Or course, I retorted by saying, "I am Joanna Herbert, and I will do what I want."

It was the same mentality I had unfortunately witnessed a couple of times with his own parents. If something was wrong with his father, it was never his father's fault. It was his mother's fault or someone else's. His father was always waited on by her. She was owned by him.

My husband tried the same tactics on me. It had been, instilled in him through his parents. But I was never going to be owned. Maybe looked after by a man, but never, ever was I going to be a man's possession.

I went inside from the front verandah to say hello to my parents when they arrived from Geelong. Then, completely out of the blue, my husband came storming into the room and called my father a fucking, gutless bastard. My parents were aghast with these comments, and I was extremely embarrassed. My parents, of course, said nothing to him in reply.

Then he stormed off to our bedroom. I followed him, and in a state of shock I told him to pack his stuff and leave. My husband always got a little Dutch courage up when he had been drinking and this time was absolutely no exception. He packed a few things and then he left. We were all quite astounded and, as usual in my family, it wasn't discussed any further.

The following morning, I was talking to my mother at the washing line and trying to work out what I was going to do. The baby was only a few months old, and I certainly did not know what the next step was. I remember clearly her saying one thing to me and that was, "There is the chance if you have more children, one of them may turn out like their father."

Typically, because of my hopeless insecurities, I thought I would once again try and patch this mess up with my husband. Knowing my parents were going to move up to Merrijig in the not-too-distant future, we had already organised that we would move up to our friend, Paul's house. This would be until we could find a place to rent. I packed up the baby's and my things and drove up to our friend's farm. On arriving, I put all of our things in place. Because there wasn't anybody around, I decided to put the baby back in the car and try to find my husband. Hopefully, we could sort out what had happened the previous night at my parents' house.

I drove back down to a friend of my husband, Robert's place, which was down the hill, and pulled into his driveway. To my absolute disgust, there was my husband and he was staggering around. He was absolutely intoxicated. I don't know whether he had kept drinking since he left my parents' house or had started early that day but he was totally inebriated.

After I had got over the initial shock of what I was seeing, he then asked me, to drive down to the Hunt Club Hotel and get some more beer. Out of complete stupidity, I proceeded to do just that.

What was I thinking? I was so confused, about what to do. I had just packed all our stuff up, moved out of my parents' house, put everything away at Paul's place with a small baby and then found my husband extremely drunk and wanting more grog. I was torn between the devil and the deep blue sea. Of course, I made the wrong decision again. I went to the pub, got some beer, dropped it off and went back to Paul's with the baby.

There was never any apology and never any mention of anything that had happened at my parents' house. It was as if it never happened. This was a recurring reaction from my husband to these sorts of situations throughout my marriage. I just had to simply put up with it.

We found a place nearby to live in Buttercup Rd, Merrijig within a few weeks. Paul's house wasn't really suitable for a small baby because it was quite often an alcohol-fuelled party house. I was not interested at all in drinking, because I was caring for a baby and he was still being breast fed.

The house in Buttercup Road was quite spacious and close to Lisa's place. I would drop my son there for her to look after him, whilst I went to work cleaning somewhere. She had two small children at home and didn't need to work because her husband was a good provider for his family. Totally unlike mine.

There were also times when Lisa would go to Mansfield with her elder son, Josh, and leave her younger son, Tom, behind with me. It was a family barter system with other advantages too. Lisa and I both, at some stage, had fed each other's baby when they were hungry. If the other mother was away, there was always breast milk on tap. Lisa has told me in recent years that Tom more than likely got his love for hot spicy food from being breastfed by me.

Before Christmas, in that same year my son was born, my older sister organised for my son and me to fly to Port Macquarie. This generous gesture was to enable my new son's grandparents to meet him. We didn't have enough money to visit them with him and they were also too old to travel to Victoria. The trip was lovely, but I remember feeling the way I had previously, that we were from different types of upbringings. And my husband's parents were hugely different people to my parents.

I continued to breast feed for about five months until my psoriasis started becoming too painful. My son also got his first tooth at this time and tried it out on me. Ouch! My psoriasis was always manageable when I was pregnant but played havoc when my oestrogen dropped, in periods of breastfeeding or just prior to childbirth.

I also had to go back to work quickly after I had him and, as you know, the old income was not there, if I didn't work.

When my son was about 10 months old, I drove to Melbourne for the day to meet with a prospective employer at Snow Bookings Only. I had heard that a local Mansfield person at Mount Buller had lost the contract and I had enquired about taking it on.

Snow Bookings Only were a Melbourne-based booking service for the Mount Buller ski resort. They had a free call number and around 25 private apartments. They also took bookings for some of the other accommodation establishments on the mountain.

Because of my earlier experience with private apartment cleaning at Mission Beach and Noosa, I was extremely interested in their private apartments. Therefore, it made a lot sense to apply for the job. The interview was successful, and I got the job. I did the necessary quotes on the individual apartments and expanded my small business, once again.

Before the first season, I was to inspect and bring the apartments up to a respectable level of presentation. I spent long hours in the apartments cleaning. Unfortunately, the earlier cleaning contractor had really let things go. And because of my experience, in order to make money on quoted apartments, they needed to be at a certain level of cleanliness to begin with.

I was paid for some of the spring cleaning that I did, but I did an awful lot it for love. This was so I could make good money a lot easier, during the ski season. I had also learned from experience, that when people go into a clean apartment, they generally tend to leave it clean. My first season went very well. I put this down to all the extra effort I had put in prior to the opening weekend. I employed local staff, which was not always easy. But I managed and along with my management skills acquired from Target Australia, we all seemed to go in leaps and bounds.

I also had a great deal of help employing people for my business, through my girlfriend Robbie. She was now employed at a place called Work Trainers. This was a government job agency set up to help people find work and a help for the long term unemployed. Meaning, they could get off the unemployment benefit and have a job.

This also meant I was employing a truly diverse range of people. Some girls were bright and energetic, and some were hardly employable. They all seemed to have come from the school of hard knocks. They all knew of each other and sometimes did not get on particularly well. It was an enormous gamble some days, working girls together.

I once had a near punch up between two girls at the top of a building at Mount Buller. I learnt very quickly that these two girls could never work together ever again. Apart from the expletives and the embarrassment to my business, there were no injuries. Just a little bruised pride.

After my first year at Buller, I was approached by another holiday letting lady, Julie, who also had a need for a contract cleaner. This was mainly for doing body corporate work on the mountain. In addition to that, Julie had more private apartment work than she could not manage on her own, so I gained a few more apartments with her. In addition to that, there were other owners at Buller who would call you and ask you to help them out. Other jobs were also obtained by people seeing you go from building to building with cleaning gear. They would just walk up and ask you if you could fit them in.

Sixteen weeks of flat-out work was more money to me than I had seen at any other job over a 12-month period in my entire working life.

I also had other jobs in Mansfield and Merrijig and employed more staff to cover these jobs. I also started to pick up work with builders, now and then. Some of the builders were in Mansfield and some built in the summer months at Mount Buller.

In around early December 1998, whilst we were away visiting my husband's parents, I discovered I was pregnant again. My due date was going to be during the ski season, but pregnancies did not change my work ethic, and I had managed to clean well late into my first pregnancy. So, what was going to be any different with this one?

I also still managed to mow the lawns at 40 weeks pregnant. There was only ever one hiccup with being pregnant and that was, I sometimes needed to take a detour to get around a tight gap. Because of the increase in my size, I could not squeeze through narrow gaps anymore.

I had set up such a great business at Mount Buller now that I definitely wasn't going to let a pregnancy get in my way. I had built up a good team of girls to do my regular work and employed extra casuals on my changeover days. We had a good season. Ski seasons are sometimes dependant on the amount of snow and/or rain. Seasons could finish as early as mid-August and some went until early October.

My second son was due in early September, so the season had been easy whilst I was pregnant as it was one of those years, fortunately, that did not go on forever. It had finished around mid-September.

I did, however, have a few, no brain, pregnant head muck ups. One particular day had been a big changeover day, and we all came off the mountain exhausted and well after dark. I made it a habit to do my books every night. Reconciling and invoicing, as well as making sure all jobs were done.

This particular evening in late July, I did my recap of the day, and, to my disbelief, we had missed an apartment. I could not contact the guest or get a message through to them. So, I got back into my Toyota Hilux and proceeded to travel on my own, for the 40-minute drive back up to the mountain. It was very dark and I waddled down to the apartment with cleaning gear in hand. The door was answered by a lovely couple who were a little puzzled as to why I was standing at their door. Firstly, because the apartment was clean and also, why would I be cleaning it in my apparent, very pregnant state?

I explained the problem, and they said the apartment was satisfactory when they arrived and there was no need to clean. I said I would get someone into service it, free of charge, the following day and they were incredibly happy with that.

The day I was due with my second son, I remember standing in a bathroom and yes, I was still cleaning. I did, however, find a few difficulties getting through trifold shower doors at nine months pregnant.

The following day, I stopped working. The girls that were working for me, were quite capable of doing a couple of cleans and doing a fantastic job at that. They just simply took my vehicle with all the gear and a list of what they needed to do. I would always pay one of the girls more than their normal hourly rate to be in charge and there were never any complaints.

On the 11th of September 1999, late in the afternoon, I sat down on the back verandah to have a beer with my husband. Then, suddenly, I had this warm, wet feeling between my legs. It was then I realised, my waters had broken. My husband and I were expecting this at some stage because I was now a week overdue.

We bundled our son into the car, with his toddler bits and pieces, and took him to my parents' house at Noonameena. We then headed into the Mansfield hospital. I had not started any real contractions by this time and when we saw a midwife, she wasn't really too fussed with my state of labour. She gave me an enormous hospital bed pad to put between my legs and told us to go out and have a light meal. We decided to go to the local tavern to have dinner.

When I was in labour with my first child, we had gone through the entire night before he came into the world. My husband definitely did not want to go through another laborious night without a meal. Especially another eight-hour labour. By the way, I was the one doing all the arduous work. After all, I was the one having the baby.

We met a girlfriend at the meals counter when we were ordering. Sarah asked me what we were doing there? I just told her we were having a meal because I was in labour. Sarah made sure our meal was quick because she was worried, I might have the baby in the tavern.

Around 8pm, we had finished eating and I went to the loo. Apart from my water loss, I had noticed there was some meconium on my hospital provided pad. Meconium is the sticky faecal matter in a baby's bowel whilst they are in utero. This also meant my baby had passed a stool and it was now in my water. I knew it could be dangerous for the baby. If he had inhaled some meconium, it could cause huge problems. It was definitely time to go back to the hospital.

I had started more frequent contractions before the meconium appeared. With each contraction, I would resoak the pad. It was like one of those uncomfortable feelings, when you are at school and your jumper goes around your waist because you think you may have soaked menstrual blood through to your dress. I kept asking my husband to see if I had a wet patch.

We arrived at the hospital to be greeted by the midwife, and I went into the room I had been allocated. Beside me was another lady who had just had her first baby. She was pretty wrecked from the whole ordeal. All I could really worry about at the time was what t-shirt I was going to wear into the labour ward. I wasn't really in any great pain at all.

I thought at this stage, I would be in for a couple of hours of labour at least. At about 8.25pm, I went into the labour room and the midwife gave me the usual internal examination. I was seven centimetres dilated. Normally, before you start pushing you need to be 10 centimetres dilated. Not long after the internal, I started asking where my doctor, Rosemary Thompson, was. She was down the hall, doing an X-ray on someone with a fractured bone.

At 8.30pm, my doctor came into the labour room, clothed in a brand-new pink shirt. The first thing I said to her was, "Can I push?"

"Yes," was her answer, and then, "Oh my goodness, there's a head."

I covered my doctor and her brand-new pink shirt, with help from my new baby, in blood. My second son was born at 8.40 pm. Labour was noted at only 10 minutes in duration. It was a bit of a shock for me and the baby, and we were a little shaky, to say the least, but both well. My husband was, of course, happy. This was only because he did not have to be up all night again.

In the following days, my new baby boy was an absolute breeze and so perfect. A couple of days after the birth, I thought it was about time to tell Snow Bookings Only about my news. I rang from the hospital and asked for the lady in charge whose name was Maria. We talked quite regularly, and it wasn't unusual to discuss something, at least once or twice a week. I was given a lot of free reigns with my contract on Mt Buller. I was also the on-mountain person who could deal directly with the owners of an apartment or with a paying guest.

On answering the phone, I asked her if she was sitting down, and if not, I thought that she had better. After she made sure, she was seated, I told her my news. I simply said I had just given birth to a baby boy.

She was absolutely amazed. She wondered, how I had done it. There had been no inkling of my pregnancy during the ski season, and I hadn't handled anything differently with my contract. Things just seemed to work well.

Her response was lovely. I was delivered to the hospital a beautiful bunch of flowers, some chocolates, and mountains of well wishes from her staff. Just one of life's nice memories.

I continued to work for Maria for a couple more years, until she offered her business to a woman who lived on the mountain and who also had a few apartments of her own to manage. I kept my job and went on to subcontract to her, also adding a few of her apartments to my list.

When my new baby was only two weeks old, you guessed it, I had to go back to work again. I would bundle my older son off to daycare in Mansfield, put the tiny baby in the car and drive to Mount Buller. As an extra in my vehicle, I had to include the entire accessory kit. There were nappies, bibs, vomit cloths, extra clothing for baby bum blowouts and a pusher so he could have something to sleep in. And on top of that, was all my equipment that I needed for work. This was also probably not the best scenario, for a woman who has only recently had a baby. Unfortunately, it was the only way around my husband's very usual lack of work and not much income.

It was an enormous task trying to work whilst feeding a young baby. At least an hour's interruption for every feed. Plus, with the loss of blood after having a baby, I was putting myself at risk of haemorrhaging.

Other scenarios of doing it tough, were when we moved houses. It was me who did most of the organising and the packing up of everything. He did, however, move the heavier furniture on a few moves.

When our second baby was incredibly young, we had to move house because our lease was expiring. My husband had a farmer friend whose mother was moving into Mansfield and was renting out her small cottage, which was also on the farm. The rent was going to be considerably cheaper than our previous rental. This also meant it was a way of not paying out so much of the money I was earning. And possibly, we could finally get a deposit together for our own house.

In the first few days of living there, I remember sitting in the run-down cottage, breastfeeding my baby, and all I could do was laugh. How were we still living in a dump, now with two young children? We could have been living in our own place, if only my husband had any sort of work ethic. Or at least a regular job. This was one of the worst places I had ever had to live in. The small cottage was a run down, two-bedroom shack that desperately needed re-stumping.

The water to the house came from a dam. Having a shower was just like washing in water that reeked of duck shit. I would dry reach in the shower quite often, especially when the water level in the dam was low. We had a drinking water tank, and I would use water from it to bathe the children. I could not bear for them to be bathed in that smelly duck water. Nor did I think it was very hygienic. Most of our washing was taken by me to Mount Buller when I worked there. For the other times, I did do some washing down the road at the Merrijig Lodge. Fortunately, because I worked there, I was permitted to wash there from time to time.

The cottage, to say the least, was very airy. There were gaps at the top and the bottom of the louvre windows, and I would stuff clothes in them in the winter to stay warm. The house was freezing in winter and stifling in the summer. We did have a fire but that meant getting wood. And, of course, that was always another issue, because my husband did not have or could not afford a chainsaw.

We stayed there for about two years. We were still living there when the Twin Towers were bombed in America, two years after he was born.

Later on, that year, we were told we had to move out of the cottage. It was going to be fully renovated, and a member of the family was moving back in. We were given only two weeks' notice. We moved after six weeks because of my knowledge of real estate law; I knew that was the legal notice that you needed.

Thank goodness I was still working for the booking agent at Mount Buller that took over Snow Bookings Only. Her name was Deb. Deb had an unfinished house in Sawmill Settlement which was closer to Mount Buller. It was on town water, had three bedrooms and a washing machine and a bath. I was absolutely wrapped with the water situation, especially after the duck pond experience in that dive in Merrijig.

The day of moving, my husband was on one of his latest hopeless adventures. He had a government-funded contract for installing long drop toilets out in the high country. He would be gone for days in a row. It was never an easy time for me with the two young boys on my own. And, of course, having to go to work as well.

As you can well imagine, I had to move house on my own. Fortunately, that great girlfriend of mine, Robbie, and a few people from her work helped me out with the move. My husband came home from the bush dunny job and the first thing he said when he walked in the door, was, "Fuck!"

This was his first response to moving into the house at Sawmill Settlement. We really had no other options. I reminded him again, that we really needed to buy a house and he needed to keep in work. Because of our lack of money and his lack of work ethic and motivation, my husband often used to say, "I wish we could just win the lotto."

Well, that was not ever going to happen.

We didn't stay in that house for very long, thank goodness. I never let anyone visit us there either. Apart from Robbie and a couple of girls that lived nearby. I was just so embarrassed about the house and the condition it was in, that I didn't invite my parents there even once. It was an unfinished, no ceiling house, that would be frequented very often by possums. The possums would eat our food off the bench and make a great deal of noise at night.

The major coping mechanism at this time was, of course, alcohol. I would drink every day now and it helped me to sleep and to also put up with the frustrations of my husband. We finally started talking about my husband getting enough work, so we had enough to put down as a deposit. He had his builder's licence now and had got that whilst we were living in Merrijig. The problem was, he could never really land a decent house to build.

I continued to run my business, on and off the mountain and still had a good enough income to pay for daycare for two children, rent, food and alcohol. My husband earned money and just kept spending it on carpenters' tools and trying to improve his business. Which never really ended up being a success at all.

My income was ours and his income was his. Any holidays we went on were always funded by me. Most of them were to see his elderly parents in Taree in New South Wales. And like every other time that we had been away, I was hopeful this time things might improve in our marriage.

On other occasions, I did manage a few holidays on my own. I would fly up to Noosa with the boys and stay in an apartment. This happened most years at the end of the ski season. I really needed a break because I had put in seven days a week, for 16 plus weeks. And because I had hardly any time with my little boys, it was a fantastic way to relax and enjoy. I am sure they did not miss their daycare either.

On another occasion, in order to have a break, I had asked a friend of the family if I could go down to their Anglesea house and stay there for a week. I was willing to spring clean the house and do some gardening in exchange for my rent. This exchange was accepted and I packed the boys into the car and headed for the coast.

One of my other intentions was to go down to Point Roadknight and walk along the beach with the boys. It was a beautiful spot, and I have enjoyed it since we were kids and had our holidays at Aireys Inlet. We would sometimes go and swim there with family friends.

I had also spent a great deal of time there when I lived with my boyfriend RJ and his parents. We had vehicle roof surfed on the boat ramp, gone fishing and swam etc there for the five and a half years we were together. There were a lot of fun memories, even though there were plenty of awful ones too.

I took the two boys down to the beach and we parked in the car park near the boat ramp. Just as we were getting out of the car, across the car park came my old boyfriend's mother. Her name was Gloria. Gloria loved the beach and always, as far as I can remember, would go out most days for a walk.

My time with my boyfriend's parents and family had really taken its toll. During those five horrible years, they all had to live with me at some time. I was a noxious, nasty, temperamental, suicidal bulimic. I had behaved so badly that when I asked Gloria at this chance meeting if I could see my ex- boyfriend's father, she told me he never wanted to see me again.

Gloria also told me, that RJ's and my relationship had only been about sex. I guess it was to an extent, because I needed sex for love. And sex was love. I didn't know any better, so that was the way it was. After we had got over the analogies, I sincerely apologised to her for how badly I had behaved. She forgave me, which was a great comfort to me. But I knew her husband never would. I had to let that one go through to the keeper.

During our meeting, Gloria updated me on how the entire family was and the grandchildren she had. She adopted my children like she would her own. She kept referring to herself as nanny to my children. It was a beautiful time, and we spent quite a bit of time together. I was so pleased to have been able to say sorry. Gloria was always so good to me. I had a lovely time with the boys for about a week in Anglesea, after that.

Life with my husband in Mansfield was very dull and when I returned from these little trips, I was back to work, and nothing really changed in our lives. We never really did anything or see anything in the Mansfield district. This was because he always said we couldn't afford it. Not even a drive somewhere nice on a Sunday. We just stayed at home and went on drinking binges with friends at the weekend in Merrijig. No wonder, we were never getting anywhere buying a house. My husband also wanted to buy in the rural area, but we never had a deposit more than 10 percent. In Mansfield, at the time banks would not look at you unless you had at least a 20 percent deposit, in order to buy a rural property.

We finally managed to engage a finance broker who came through with a loan for a house in Mansfield. That was it, we looked at a couple of properties and eventually bought a house in Highton Lane. It was three bedroom and two bathroom and in a fairly nice area. There were neighbours each side of us but there were no neighbours at the back of the house because it was a paddock.

It was great to finally be in our own place. Highton Lane needed a few renovations done which my husband should have been able to do in his spare time. Considering he always had quite a bit of spare time.

I was also extremely excited about the garden. There was hardly any garden when we arrived, so I personalised it and it really felt like mine. I built garden beds, a vegetable patch and did quite a bit of planting. It was my first taste of gardening that I was passionate about. Probably because it was at my first ever house.

Long before my marriage was really over and even before my daughter was conceived, there was a guy who worked with Robbie, who had taken interest in me. He was a nice-looking guy, and he was smart as well. The only problem was that he was married too. Anyway, he was one of those guys that had plenty of extramarital relationships or flings with women behind his wife's back. He was another real charmer or should I say womaniser? Similarly, just like the vet, his bed side manner was quite flattering. He was one of those guys who could tame any girl. Of course, I became totally sucked in from the start. He would flirt and have his eyes on me every time I went into Robbie's work. It was flattering and nice to be noticed. Much nicer than the way I was being treated, like a doormat at home.

I was wanting to have another baby, so I tried to forget about the married man for a while and focus a little on my own marriage but mainly my business. I found out I was pregnant with my daughter in February 2003. We had been at a friend's 50th birthday and I woke in the middle of the night throwing up. I had a couple of drinks at the party, not knowing I was pregnant. Obviously, the throwing up was a telltale sign. This had also happened when I was first pregnant with one of the boys.

I desperately wanted to have another baby now that we had a house. I had actually tried for over two years but drugs and alcohol use had dictated that my body was not capable or well enough to have another baby at that time. Thank goodness our bodies protect us. I know the same situation would have occurred with my chronic bulimia for all those years.

I was so excited when I had an ultrasound and found out this one was going to be a girl. A friend had told me, if you know when you are ovulating, then wait until the next day and it will most likely be a girl. For the first time, I had felt myself ovulate, I knew it was right. And that is how my daughter was made. I was rapt to be having another baby and maybe this was the one that would fix it up my marriage.

By this time, my business at Mount Buller had grown to 80 private apartments. And I employed 15 girls to cover my contracted work. It was hard at times matching teams of girls that would get on. A lot of the staff were young girls with no qualifications; some were completely brainless.

Most people think they can clean but not how I wanted it done. I had to sift through a lot of girls over a couple of seasons and eventually finished with a fantastic team.

I also employed a couple of girls I would pay at above the award. This was to cover them for having greater responsibilities and meant they could be in charge when I wasn't around. I also paid some of the girls more when they were training staff for me.

Because of it being my third pregnancy, I got more tired during the day. I took a few days during the week to be off the mountain to do paperwork etc. I needed to have an afternoon rest as well sometimes. This was probably because I was 38 years old and a little older than my other two pregnancies. The days I was working on the mountain, I would have a little rest at one of my business colleague's flats. Or sometimes a lie down in one of my apartment owner's flats.

Along with a small office at our house in Highton Lane, I had also set myself up with a little commercial laundry. This was handy for the linen from apartments coming off the mountain. I had been paying enormous fees at the local commercial laundry in previous years and wanted to work on my business, as well as saving some money. I employed Lisa to wash for me. She had a young son, and it was easy for her to work and care for him at our house. I also did some days of laundry when I was at home.

From some of my earnings, we made a few improvements on the house. I put a spa bath in our bathroom and a new shower glass unit. I had worked for a lady at Mount Buller who was always forgetting to pay me. She happened to have a spa company in Melbourne and one season she paid me with a lovely spa bath. It was well and truly above what she owed me for her personal cleaning.

We also put in a new kitchen to replace the orange taps and tiled benches etc. These were the good old relics from the eighties.

Things had also cooled down for a while, with the married man whilst I was pregnant, but he would make comments to me sometimes, like, 'We will just have to wait for a while'. Or just tell me that I was currently on hold. Really, it was very cocky - excuse the expression - of him to feel that one day I was going to be at his liberty. For me to be very unhappy in a marriage and also very vulnerable. It seemed this was all this guy needed.

Yes, there are men out there that just walk over vulnerable woman and use for them for sex. Sometimes I have thought, *Do I have an "I'm easy" sign written on my forehead? Or is there a breed of men out there, that think that they have some God-given right to have a relationship with any woman they choose? Married or not?*

During the course of the season that I was pregnant with my daughter, I decided to sell the Mount Buller part of my business. A girl named Kim, who had been working as a supervisor for me, decided she would like to buy my business. This also included my Toyota Hilux. She knew how to drive the car and was familiar with all of the apartments and she had the support of the staff.

I sold her my business in September 2003, with the car for the sum of $40,000. One of the considerations of selling my business to Kim was also to do as much washing from the mountain at my house. This set me up with a nice income and I could keep nursing my baby. My earnings were over $1,000 per week. I had always intended to feed my daughter for 12 months and this worked beautifully for all concerned. It also saved Kim a lot of money. Not to mention the confusion that was often tied in with the apartment linen. To make things easier for the staff, I made sure the linen was always put back in the correct quantity for the apartment.

Kim had bought a thriving business. I always invited her to seek help from me if she needed it. She could ask me anything, from structuring staff and changeovers etc, to managing her accounts. I was always there if she needed me to help with the running of her newly bought business.

Her first season in 2004 was very sketchy and she fell in a big heap not long after that. At one stage, she even offered to give me the business back. I totally declined.

Because of the ongoing doubts about my marriage, I started going out on my own with friends on a regular basis. I also tried to get away from time to time. And this time, I was really looking for an excuse to get away and be with the married guy.

I had made an appointment in Melbourne to meet with a linen manufacturer. I had bought linen from her company for my commercial use and for my private apartment owners. This was prior to selling my business. We had become friends through my dealings at Mount Buller and she invited me to stay at her converted factory house in Collingwood. We went out for dinner and had a great catch up with each other. On the following day, I organised to see another contractor about material used for protecting windows on building jobs. This was another hair brain idea of my husband's. And, of course, I was going to get stuck doing all the work.

Because I had intended to stay another night in Melbourne, I made an excuse not to return home. My idea was to finally spend a night with the cocky married one.

After my meeting with Protecta Window, the cocky guy and I met in Canterbury Road at a lovely hotel. He had arrived with a nice bottle of champagne. Probably to settle the nerves. We chatted and then things started to happen.

I am sure he had done this all before. We had a great night, and, in the morning, I had told him I was over my marriage. I also told him I liked him a great deal. His response to me was, he was very tied up financially with his wife. He also told me that a breakup of his marriage would cost him too much to dissipate it.

I really liked this guy a lot and was obviously totally sucked in by him. Unfortunately, or maybe fortunately, he was not going to change a thing for me, so I was used up again and had made yet another wrong decision.

In late 2003, my husband finally managed to get his first ever building job as a registered builder. This job continued into 2004. By the end of the financial year, he had been paid for all his work but not yet paid his subcontractors. As you can imagine, his taxable income was huge.

Well, it was huge compared to what it had been in the previous 11 years. When he had his tax done and could produce his taxable income, he told me what it was. The next question he asked was, "Where has all the money gone, Jo?"

He had the nerve to blame me for spending all his earnings. My answer was, I was not dripping in diamonds and fur coats, so I did not know where the money was.

I actually did know where it was. He had not earned that money at all. He just could not manage his business or his books. Hills and valleys need to be put in the same financial year. He had been paid for the job in a financial year but not paid his contractors until the following financial year. Pretty simple stuff really when running a business.

By this time, my respect had really dwindled, and I was thinking about how I could get out of my marriage and still support my three children. I started drawing at straws. I even entertained the idea of having my fortune read. The following is how this transpired.

In 2004, I had an older lady working for me, off the mountain and her name was Margaret and she was a very spiritual sort of person. She also did a bit of eyebrow and leg waxing etc. on the side. She was great to visit and, quite regularly, I would go around to her house, have my eyebrows and eyelashes tinted. Then we would have a chat over a Bombay Sapphire gin and tonic.

We would chat about a variety of subjects. She had experienced a marriage breakdown and a few relationship muck ups and was good to talk to, because of her own experience. She knew I was going through my marriage breakdown at the time and she had told me, when she had some difficult times, she had her cards read by a psychic. I was intrigued. She also told me things had worked out roughly the way this psychic had predicted.

As I was confused as to what, how, when of any sort of future without my husband, I decided to get her telephone number and get a reading done. The psychic's name was Adele.

It was a little unnerving to start with and really, would I believe everything that was said on a telephone call with a woman who was a complete stranger? How much would she really know and how was she going to know how things would turn out for me?

During my reading, the psychic knew a lot about my past, including my abuse. She knew other things about my childhood too. This included being jaundiced at birth. I was quite amazed at some of her knowledge. I must admit, I was sceptical on some things. But she was saying things that I really wanted to hear and also, really wanted to believe. She was fairly spot on with some things about me and about my husband. It was quite an unusual experience to have had a reading done by a psychic.

I discussed my experience with a few other girlfriends, and some were interested in having a reading done. So, I organised to have a psychic reading party for those that were interested. There were others who were also having difficulties in their marriages. We were all at about the same stage and trying to find a way out.

One of the girls, in particular, had lost her husband to melanoma a few years prior. She had a reading with Adele and, much to her amazement, she spoke to her dead husband. Another dear friend had lost a child from a brain tumour, and she heard his voice. No, we had not all had a big joint and we had not had a few fried magic mushrooms either. It turned out to be an extremely successful party.

I liked Adele and we chatted throughout my dissolving marriage and even afterwards. If anything, she bestowed strength on my decisions. She was also fantastic therapeutically with my healing from child sexual abuse.

After speaking to Adele one day, she gave me some homework to do in the evening. I sat outside alone on the back verandah. The assignment Adele set for me, was to write a letter to every person who had ever sexually abused me. The purpose of the letter was to acknowledge what had happened to me and to forgive them. Following the writing of the letter, I was instructed to burn it in the fire drum outside. You could call it, setting my forgiveness free. This little assignment was to enable me to release the trauma and, I guess, feel pity for them. It also helped me to believe the abuse was not in my control and it was not my fault what had happened to me.

To my horror, there were so many people who had abused me throughout my life. I just kept writing letters, remembering the next one and the next one. In total, there was a ridiculous number of them I had identified as my sexual abusers. Some had been boyfriends; one had been the brother of a girlfriend. Every one of them had been people known to me. There were a few, where I didn't realise what had happened to me at the time but it was actually sexual abuse. The worst thing too, was I only, just at that time, realised it was sexual abuse. I had been sexually abused from the age of 11 years for over 30 years.

I had either blocked it out with selective amnesia, or I thought that this may have been normal behaviour sexually. I had let this happen to me. But it wasn't normal behaviour and that is what is so confusing. I was so confused about how I had let it happen in the first place. Why didn't I stop it? Was I frightened?

The most amazing thing that came out of all this strange but therapeutic homework was, one particular sexually abusive person was finally identified. It was Dr David Mackey. The doctor at Geelong Grammar School, Corio.

During my letter writing to him, I had flashed back to that day in the medical centre. The vision of the high window behind him, the blinds, and the sick look on his face with that disgusting paedophilic grin. I am sure I had dreamt about it but, up until then, I had never identified the traumatic incident. That selective amnesia habit again, I guess. I also never realised he had digitally raped me in the surgery that day.

It was a great piece of homework. One of the best ways to realise what had happened to me over all those years. I do believe there is some spiritual energy in this world. Good and bad. It was just another experience in life that helped a little and then helped a lot.

Respect for my husband had dwindled increasingly. We had started doing some marriage counselling in late 2004. My husband had refused to see anyone in Mansfield. I think he was worried about people knowing that our marriage was finally over. So, we found a marriage counsellor in Benalla. Even our sessions in Benalla were extremely frustrating. This was because, the only thing he could ever talk about was money and his building business. He could never admit there was something terribly wrong with our marriage. Maybe he did not think there was anything wrong at all. He was looking at everything outside our relationship. He was not looking into what a healthy relationship between two married people is supposed to have.

During the counselling stage, he also decided to do some reading into mental health and depression. Another desperate measure to see if this could save our marriage. His entire family had a history of depression. He came to me and told me he thought he was depressed and had been to see the doctor about it. He was prescribed antidepressant medication and, for a brief time, I think they may have helped. But at this stage, there was not much that could really change the downward course where our marriage was heading. Or the feelings I no longer had for him.

I just really could not respect him anymore. I really could not stand him being near or touching me. I told him I wanted him to sleep on the couch and if he was near me, I did not want him to touch me.

We fought a lot, and our arguments were often fuelled by alcohol. I also smoked a lot of dope to cope with what was happening. To cope with how boring and mundane my life had become and to take the edge off living with such a frustrating man. There is one thing to mention that came out of these alcohol-filled arguments and that is,

I am ashamed of what my children would or may have heard during these outbursts.

## CHRISTMAS 2004

Everyone in Mansfield has Christmas breakups and the crew at Robbie's work were no exception. I went for drinks at the Mansfield Hotel on the Friday night before Christmas and we celebrated. Robbie and Mark left to go to their respective homes, which left two of us at the bar. The married cocky one and myself. We left the pub together and made our way down to his office. After some conversation, things started to happen. I ended up getting home extremely late and snuck into my bed. My husband, at this stage, was sleeping on the couch.

We still made an attempt at our marriage, with further marriage counselling in January and early February 2005. He was still sleeping on the couch and, in my opinion now, there was no way he was ever going to sleep in the same bed as me again. Obviously, it was really very unfixable by this stage. I had also been involved with someone else, even though that had turned into another one of my disasters. I was also spending more time on my own going out with friends and working a few after hours jobs, so I did not have to spend time with him.

At our final counselling session over in Benalla, I had said I would give it another go again. I guess that was because I felt really sorry for him.

The next day, I was due to go to a Mansfield house to clean for the lady I had worked with at Mount Buller. We had had a lot of conversations over the last few years about respect in a relationship and other issues. She previously had a marriage breakdown, divorced, and remarried.

I walked into her house feeling so numb. I had not slept well and was regretting what I had said to my husband about giving it another go. I just could not give it a go. I could not do it anymore. It was always wrong and nothing, not even holiday time, or island living, or our having children or any friend, could ever make our marriage work.

The following night, we had a great friend and her new boyfriend around for dinner. After they had finished dinner and left, I told him he had to leave. Our marriage, for me, was definitely over and it could never work again.

It took a week or so for him to find a place to go. He moved into a shed in Merrijig at a friend's property. I helped organise some furniture from Mount Buller for him and some beds for the children to sleep on when they were staying out there. That was it. After all that time, it was finally over. It had taken me years to pluck up the courage to do it, and I had finally done it.

Between my ex-husband and I, we decided he could have access to our children every second weekend from Friday to Sunday. We had discussed a sum of money to help me with food, clothing and school fees. An amount of $50 a week per child was agreed on by both of us.

The day he left was really awful. When he left the house, he was sobbing and bawling his eyes out. It was also, unfortunately, in front of our children. My older son remembered it well. I am not sure about the effects it may have had on my second son, but my daughter was only 15 months old, so I don't think that she knew any better.

Marriage breakdown is an awful thing at any time. I know I made a lot of wrong decisions, which led me into marrying a person I was not suited to. I have made the wrong decisions with most relationships I have had. And even though I thought he could be a rock for me and because I knew he loved me, it just never ever worked. And it could never ever work. We were so different. It was not his fault, it was mine. I should have listened to my father on my wedding day.

Unfortunately, this was always the pattern from my younger days when looking for love. I gravitated to someone who I thought would be strong for me, not to someone that was suited to me. I believe now my sexual assaults have played an enormous part in my bad decision-making. This has especially been when it was about relationships. I have always chosen partners for all the wrong reasons.

A few weeks later, after we had split up, he came to the front door to get the children for the weekend. On leaving, he said to me that he could have given me the world. My reply to him, came without any thought at all. It was, "Well, when were you going to start?"

On reflection, sadly giving me the world would not have worked either. That was not what I was looking for anyway.

My marriage, however, introduced me to many who were amazing people in my life. People who became friends, found in so many places in Australia. People I would not have met if I hadn't met my husband. Life is like that. We find different connections in our lives, that sometimes later, turn into disconnections.

On another thought, our marriage has given us three beautiful children. They are grown up now and independent, strong, intelligent young people. I am glad I had my husband's children, and I could never ask any more of such great young human beings. And yes, my mother was right. I do have a son that is emotionally and mentally very much like his father.

On one of my first child free weekends, I added another bit of finality to my life. It happened in March 2005 and with the cocky married man. We had tried to find some time to get together after I split from my husband. He texted me to say he was going to be down in the Yarra Valley on a Friday night and invited me to join him there for a catch up.

He flew hot air balloons as an extra job. These balloon flights would take place in Mansfield, as well as in the Yarra Valley. Because he was staying at the ballon flight owner's house, he asked me to book a room at a hotel in town. I picked out a really nice hotel in Yarra Glen and it was not cheap either. He arrived with the usual bottle of bubbles early in the afternoon. He stayed a few hours and we enjoyed each other's company.

On leaving, he told me he would return later that evening. He apparently had a bit of organising to do with flying balloons the next morning. I totally understood that. A few hours later, I doubted he was going to return.

Then, he simply didn't show up. He never called to say he was not going to come back. He dropped me like a hot potato. I went straight down to the bar, bought a bottle of champagne and drank myself to sleep. I was devastated. What an arsehole, womanising bastard!

I woke up the next morning and had a shower, then returned to Mansfield. I felt totally numb. I felt like I'd been used up, spat out and had dirt thrown in my eyes. I felt like a hooker who was not paid. He even had the audacity to leave me with the bill for the hotel room.

On returning to Mansfield, I packed my overnight bag for the weekend and headed out to the Cattlemen's Get Together. This year it was being held out in the King Valley at a property on the Rose River.

The Cattlemen's Get Together is an annual event held in the Victorian high country. It varies each year and the location changes. It is all about racing in the bush, competing in other cattlemen's events and normally has great entertainment at night. It is a great party weekend.

The King Valley is a beautiful spot in the high country and there are rustic wineries, scenic farms, and it is another entrance into Victoria's high country. It is a magic spot.

I was going to camp with Robbie that weekend. During the drive out there, I still kept thinking about what had just happened. I felt awful. I felt totally abused. I felt like absolute shit.

I arrived out there at about 11am. I was still in that delirious state, trying to work out what had just been ripped out of my inner self. We chatted for a while and obviously Robbie had sensed something was really wrong. She then said, "What the flip is wrong with you?"

My answer was, I had been used up and dumped by a guy, who only thought about the use of his penis. Without any trouble, she worked out who it was. She had seen us in action when flirting, and she had also seen his behaviour with other women. And yes, there were a few of them. Of course there were!

As a result of his behaviour, I have never spoken to him again, in person. However, some of my girlfriends sent him some pretty awful texts about wombats. Meaning that just like a wombat, he eats, roots and leaves.

Something that happened later was even more depraved. He found the audacity to text me after six months and wanted to have a catch up. I did not think so. Another using arsehole who hurt me and took advantage of my vulnerability. And that is the ultimate question, why do we let these men woo us and then use us as their little sex toys?

# CHAPTER 9

## *RAPES AND MY EXPERIENCES*

This is a piece that I have thought about a lot and it is also educational. I still do not believe we were taught any of this as young people and I hope now it is taught in schools and also at home. I have always done my best to encourage my children to speak up if anything ever happens to them. I have also reiterated that people do not need to be strangers to do such horrible acts. And yes, they can be highly regarded people too. There are a lot of priests, doctors and politicians that have sexually empowered themselves. Empowered themselves enough to abuse children and rape women.

The reaction to a sexual abuse also needs to be recognised by the victim. The abused person is the victim here. And it is abuse. It is no persons right to be the perpetrator.

Quite often, people around an abused victim can perceive that their manner is different and something sinister may have happened. This also needs to be acted upon.

Rape is sexual penetration, whether it is with a digit, such as a finger and/or a penis, that penetrates an intimate area of a female or male without consent. Areas that are within a certain distance from and include intimate areas. Below the belt, to be exact, and above the thighs.

Sexual consent was something that I ever taught by my parents or during my school years. Sexual consent is a free and informed agreement between people to participate in a sexual act. This agreement is only present when there are mutual and genuine feelings about wanting to engage in a sexual act, making actively sure the partner does too.

Geoff Hines digitally raped me when I was an 11-year-old though, at the time, I didn't know that it was digital rape. I did not consent, apart from letting him kiss me good night. And even though he never asked me, I did not want him to kiss me or touch me in the way he did or the places he did. My reaction was with an involuntary response. This inbuilt ability to freeze and go into survival mode.

The two boys at school who were my boyfriend's friends never asked me; they just did what they did. I immediately zoned out and went into survival mode. I did not touch them whilst they were playing around with me. I did not know what to do at the time. I was in a numbed state. I concentrated on a spot on the wall that I knew about and just pretended I wasn't there. It just wasn't me. It was like my skin grew over my eyes for a while and I did not see anything, until it was all finished with. I became safely and comfortably numb.

These boys were also popular at school and this may have been wrong at the time but maybe I let it happen because it was an act of acceptance. Maybe I wanted to be part of the group. Being part of 'the group' was very real at Geelong Grammar School. I was insecure and thought what they were doing was wrong, but I didn't want to displease them.

I never told anyone about it until now. They, however, told my boyfriend. I did not consent; I simply did not know what to do.

Freezing was the best survival mode. I would look at something and pretend it was not my body. *It's not my body; it's not my body.* I got out of my body to learn how to make it stop. It makes sense when someone talks about an out of body experience. That is survival mode.

After one of these experiences, there were feelings of guilt and shame. On the occasion mentioned above with two close friends of my boyfriend, one of the boys left. Then I proceeded to give the other guy some satisfaction in return. I do not know why I did this, to this day. Was it to be accepted? Accepted for what or as what? I was just so confused about what love was all about. Or was I confused about what was sexually expected of me as a female?

These are some of the confusing emotions that happened when I had been sexually abused. And these confusing emotions turned into confused behaviour. Behaviour that wasn't justified. Behaviour that didn't ameliorate a thing.

Being initially assaulted as a child made it harder to stop these things happening. Who do you trust to love you? Is sex love? All these questions are so confusing and become more confusing in the mind of a sexually assaulted young person.

I do not need to tell the Dr Mackey story again, so I won't but another time when I had lived down at the beach for about five years up, until I was about 24 years old, I was still a suffering bulimic and incredibly moody. I was also very much an insecure, young woman.

We had just done our mid-year stocktake at Target and I had an enormous week at work and was very tired. I was staying with my boyfriend RJ at his house in Anglesea. As usual, we had gone to the pub and there was a party back at the party place. There was a heap of friends there and we were spread from the living area to the verandah outside. Our bedroom was off the living area and he had a double bed pushed up against the wall, on the outer side of the house.

My boyfriend was having an in-depth conversation with one of my friends outside. I was extremely exhausted from my 60-hour week at work and was tired after being at the pub. I had one or two drinks at the party and then headed off to the bedroom and climbed into bed.

I have no idea what time it was when I was woken. For all my life, I have been an extremely deep sleeper and extremely hard to wake. I woke up on this night, with a man on top and inside me. I put my hand on his back thinking it might have been my boyfriend. It was fat and hairy. My boyfriend had a surfer's body, and he was not a hairy guy.

I said firstly, "Is that you RJ?" because I wasn't fully awake.

And the guy said, "No, it's Stan."

I screamed out at him, "Get off me! Get off me!"

I quickly put some clothes on and went out into the living area and into manic mode about what had just happened.

I remember a good friend, Steve, just holding me and making sure I was okay. I wanted to go to the police about it, there and then, but it was so late. I was also talked out of it by Steve, because Stan was, supposedly, a friend of most of the Anglesea boys.

The next day, I stood in the shower for hours. I was dirty; I was so dirty, and I just couldn't get clean. I did not give him any consent; he just helped himself.

He was not my boyfriend, and I really did not like him anyway. There was no way in this world, that I would ever let a man like that near me. He was fat like Geoff Hines and hairy too. *Fat fucking, fat fucking awful, hairy, fucking fat. Disgusting.*

I spent the entire day on that Sunday in the shower, but I just could not get clean. I just could not get this man out of, or off my body. I felt so filthy.

The following day, the numbness and horror lingered. I went to work on the Monday at Target, because we had a 15% off sale storewide and they were always big retail days. One of my female bosses took one look at me and asked me if I was okay and I burst into tears. I told her what had happened and then she sent me home. I went back to Anglesea and resumed my obsessive cleansing in the shower. I still could not get him off my body.

This was the first time I had had to deal with rape as an adult. But it was a very familiar feeling I experienced. That of sheer panic and uncontrollable anxiety. I could not breathe properly. I could not think. It was like a bad nightmare but it had happened in real life.

That same day, I went to the police station and made a statement. I didn't do the statement to go for a conviction but I wanted to make the police aware of what sort of guy Stan was. They said I should have had swabs done and done a rape kit within hours of the offence. Unfortunately, because I was talked out of it by Steve, I could not prove that Stan's fucking fat and disgusting semen was inside me.

I believe that after I had reported it, they interviewed him and gave him a warning. I also had to partake in an AIDS test, which added to my emotional trauma. I had two tests a month apart. Fortunately, my results were the same. They were negative.

There is one more instance I need to include in this chapter. And stress that, unfortunately, when completely inebriated and blacked out during an alcoholic episode, I did not have the ability to say 'no' or even know what was happening. I was not in any state to consent to sex.

When my marriage was over, I told my husband he was not allowed to touch me anymore. This was around early December 2004. A few days before Christmas, we had taken our three children to an end of year party at Bells Earthmoving, whose offices I'd cleaned. The Christmas party was at the Mansfield football club rooms and it was always a generous party with plenty of food and, of course, alcohol. As usual, I drank too much. Well, that was always a common occurrence for me at that time. Because of the caved in state of our relationship and marriage, I was drinking to oblivion most nights. On this evening, there was no exception.

I do not remember but my husband had driven our children and myself home. I had blacked out, as usual, and had no recollection of how the evening, after we arrived home, had transpired.

I woke the next morning and, to my horror, worked out I had been sexually abused. I said something to my husband about it. He then told me he had said to me in my inebriated state, "You know what you need Jo? And that is a good fuck."

He tried to tell me I had said, "Just do it." I had a blackout. I was in an unconscious stupor, and I do not remember a thing after we left the party.

After he told me what had happened, I was mortified, disgusted and proceeded to have the usual panic attack that always comes with these situations. What followed after that was the 'I can't get clean in the shower' mode. I locked the door into the bathroom and stayed in the shower for ages.

I felt nauseated the entire day. The same feelings appeared like they had done after the rape in Anglesea. And that is why it was Rape. There was no lucid consent.

Other woman and rape

I have been incredibly lucky to never conceive, as a result of non-consensual sex - Rape. However I have come across other beautiful woman, who have had children as a result of being raped by their husband or partner. Yes, this does happen. One particular example has come to mind recently, as we are still in contact.

She was, when I first met her, a single mum. I employed her for many years and she was a lovely person, hardworking and had really done it hard. She had two sons, the younger became very good friends with my second son, and an older son.

Amazingly enough, her younger was an absolutely brilliant young boy. He was sent to a special school to study because of his amazing talent. His mother decided he wasn't going to waste his ability and he has excelled ever since.

This brilliant child was the result of nasty abuse, followed by a rape. His conception was unplanned and indecent. It was bastardisation. I can only imagine the guilt and resentment that would have gone through this beautiful woman's mind when she discovered she was going to have a child. A child that was created as a result of rape. I applaud her strength in keeping the child.

I also have another beautiful friend who had to endure the same act from her husband and fell pregnant.

Someone very close to me was raped by her husband when she was semi-conscious. She had a fall and, because of her state, he thought he would just help himself. He did it because he thought it was his God-given right.

What gives a man the opinion that he is entitled to rape a woman? Even if she his wife or his partner?

This is an important reason for teaching our children at home what is consent and what it means. I would encourage schools to do the same when teaching sex education. Consent is not well understood and needs to be taught with clear definition.

# CHAPTER 10

## *DAVID*

When I first moved to the Mansfield district in 1993, I wanted to earn the same amount of money that I previously earned whilst I was employed at Target. When the Coles job fell through, I found many jobs in and around the Mansfield area. One of my jobs was working at a milk bar in Mansfield. The milk bar was the Roundabout Cafe.

One particular morning, I remember this guy with a mullet came in to the milk bar. He was larger than life. His voice and laugh could be heard throughout the room. Even spilling out into the back of the shop. To me he seemed to be a very happy person.

I believe, at the time, he was seeing a slightly older woman than me, who also was working at the milk bar. He had an enormous presence. It was David.

I didn't really think too much of him or the moment but there was an impression. He had a mullet and I wasn't particularly fond of the hair style and thought they were a little boganish. A mullet is an Australian hair do, short on the sides and top but long at the back.

Incidentally, I also had a friend who was renting a house to him, or her mother was. This friend was actually one of my bridesmaids. It is funny how people emerge in our lives without being invited. Is there a magnet effect that draws human beings towards each other? Or is it that you put likeable people in a bank, so they can be withdrawn out later, when the time is right?

Another brief meeting I had with David was when I was in full sail and pregnant with my first son. We had returned from Queensland and my husband had a few farm jobs. This job was at a local farmers' yards in Merrijig. I had taken my husband something to eat for lunch and a cool drink. They were drafting out cows and calves and then marking the male calves. This means cutting out their testicles. David's job, at the time, was as a stock agent and he used to help out with some of the farming jobs. This helped with keeping clients and was more of a loyalty task. Also to keep good public relations, some stock agents did extra unpaid work.

He probably didn't take any notice of me anyway because he had his head down with a sharp knife in his hands. I think I was introduced but it was not a notable event. Not for either of us.

Through my next pregnancy and for a long time afterwards, David didn't appear in my life. I was still trying to work out what my marriage was about and thinking it was going to get better. I remember coming across him again at a friend's barbecue. He was seeing Robbie's sister, Kim, and we ate out on a deck looking at a beautiful vista in Booroolite. Booroolite was a little community close to Merrijig. David was also there with his noticeably young daughter.

After that, I didn't really see him at all.

In the final year of my marriage, I made a few changes to work and to childcare arrangements. I had been trying to work things through, always providing for the kids and paying for their childcare.

In order to get away from my husband, in the afternoon and early evening, I chose to do a few after hours jobs. One was at the garden supplies in Mansfield and another was at Bells Earthmoving. I wanted to go to work and then just get home at night with kids sorted, have a drink and go to bed.

That was the way it was by then. I loved my kids but did not want to spend very much time at all with my husband. When I told my husband he needed to move out, I continued enjoying my evening jobs and would get friends to look after the kids.

I did, however, structure my after-hours jobs, so I worked at the weekend and on a Saturday morning. This was so that finding childcare was easier. The kids went out to their father's every second weekend, so Friday and Saturday were always easy, when they went out to Merrijig on a Friday afternoon.

I was always trying to find things to do, with a little extra at both my weekend jobs. This was because I was not getting much help financially and needed money to feed us. There was also the continual upkeep of my house in Highton Lane. Gravel for my driveway and wood for the fireplace were the main needs. I would do a barter system for wood and gravel with Vicki at the garden supplies for work done during the week. That was sometimes the only way we could afford to be warm.

My husband, on one occasion, did do a wood run with me and the kids. I had the feeling he thought it was going to make our marriage work. It wasn't happy families at all anymore, in my eyes. It was just getting some wood. And the marriage was irreparable.

One Saturday morning, I was busy doing some windows at Bells Earthmoving and needed to lift a window out to clean the outside pane. I was struggling with it and this gentleman strolled in and asked if I needed a hand.

"That would be lovely," I said.

Then he took the window out so I could clean it and placed it back in the frame for me, after it was cleaned. We started talking a little about cleaning and he asked me if I was interested in cleaning his house. His wife was soon to be returning from America, and he needed a hand to clean a few things, to be ready for her return.

A job was a job, so I said, "Yes," and we arranged to catch up and have a look at the house.

I visited David's house at Paps Lane with my daughter for the first time before Christmas 2005. I was a little nervous at going to his house to start with. This was only because David was a big man and I was now, a vulnerable single mother.

I turned up at his house, and we sat outside on a leather lounge. I had never been there before but had been told the view was lovely. I found myself looking at one of the best views I had ever seen in the Mansfield district. We talked about the job at hand etc. and I got the job. We had a couple of beers whilst I was there and then I needed to go home. My excuse was to go home and feed and bath the children.

I was still extremely cautious of David for a while, because of his height. Remembering that all tall, big men frightened me, and I did not really feel comfortable around them. In the end, I figured he was married, and it really didn't matter because I was only going to see him when he was paying me for cleaning.

I started working for him for a month or so. And after this time, his wife had decided to stay in America for good. Their marriage was over.

He was incredibly happy with the job I was doing at his house, so he became a regular customer. We started this ritual where the girls and I would go once a fortnight and clean. Once I had let him know how much he owed me, he would call in to my house to pay me on his way home from work. David was working at a quarry up the road, and my house was on the way home.

Payment for my fortnightly clean soon turned from a stop and chat, into a longer stop for a beer. Then more chat and another beer. Then the phone calls started, discussing when I was cleaning next. Work related phone calls were then followed by extra phone calls. Then phone calls that went on into the late hours. Then more calling in on the way home without any reason. Then he would pick me up to go wood collecting. Then extra call ins when cleaning hadn't been done. We were really starting to see a lot of each other.

David also had some friends down the road who wanted their house cleaned on a regular basis too. He invited me down one Friday night and I went with him to meet these friends, in hope that I would pick up another cleaning job. I drove to his house, and he drove us both down to the house at the end of the road. We stayed for a while and I got the job.

When we returned to his house, he offered for me to stay on the couch. I declined because I had a few scrambled fears and feelings. Fears because of his size and feelings, because I was really starting to like David a lot.

Another night, he asked me out on a date to one of the local restaurants. During the evening, I found myself holding his hand. He dropped me home afterwards and gave me a peck on the cheek and said goodbye.

There was one other occasion that really blew me out of the water. I was working at Bells on a Saturday morning and in walked David as neat and tidy as usual. We chatted for a while, sorting out the next cleaning date and, when he said goodbye, he gave me a peck on the cheek in the boss's office. These funny little meetings were becoming very frequent.

I remember a phone call with him one night and, after talking for about four hours, I piped up and said, I thought that something was going on here between us.

David was also starting to help me around my house; with the jobs I couldn't do. He fixed things, he built me a woodshed and mowed my lawn. All the jobs my husband did not do. I always mowed the lawns anyway, even if I was 42 weeks pregnant. My husband would sit outside and watch me mow, whilst he was drinking his beer.

On one occasion, David and I went to get wood together. The children were at their fathers for the weekend, and I had organised for the kids to be dropped off at 4.00pm. Knowing that, we decided we would get back and all the wood would be stacked in the wood shed, long before the kids arrived home.

We had loaded up the back of David's Toyota with wood and were back at my house unloading at about 3.40pm. At the same time, the kids and their father turned up. The kids' father thought the worst, of course. He dropped them off with a foul look on his face. I hadn't even kissed David at this stage, but my ex-husband had already heard we were seeing a bit of each other and assumed he was taking a lot of interest in me.

The next morning, I had a phone call and a message left on the answering service. He rang to say he wanted a divorce. That question was simply answered. I rang him and said, "Yes, no problem," and told him the papers for divorce were organised and already in the mail.

Long before I even started working for David, I had decided to be myself again. Just after my husband and separated, I had organised my divorce and property settlement. I engaged a local family lawyer to draw up the formalities. And, in order to save some money, I learnt what I was required to do for the property settlement myself. I also changed my name back to Joanna Herbert. I just wanted to be me again. Well, as best as I could be, with my history.

I also had great intentions to keep men out of my life for quite a while. My track record had been too hurtful. I had married the wrong man, and I did not want to go through another agonising relationship I wasn't happy in. No more emotional pain for a while. I also had not had any serious intentions for another relationship, since I had made the big mistake with that cocky married man in Yarra Glen. I was definitely made out to be the fool there.

David's and my relationship slowly began to flourish. He courted me for at least six months before he even asked me if he could kiss me. This sort of courtship had never happened to me before.

On the night that he finally kissed me, we had gone to a great friend's party at a local Mansfield pub. The night was fun and we flirted with each other all night. We had decided to walk home to my house from the pub, so no one was driving a car.

On the way home, we laughed and chatted. On the corner of Ailsa and Collopy Streets in Mansfield, he stopped and asked me if he could kiss me. No one had ever asked me that before. They had just done it and hoped it was okay with me. It was a very nice kiss and I am not sure whether one of my feet was in the air, but it was lovely. After the kiss, he escorted me home and there was a bit more kissing in my lounge room. David did not stay the night, and he left to go and stay at his son's house around the corner. David picked me up the next morning and he took me out for breakfast.

After that weekend, David asked me if I would like to go and stay at his house the following Friday evening. We had spoken every night during the week, and he visited my house for the usual beer on his way home from work, more than once. We had conversations to all hours of the night on the phone. I am sure that he was getting a little tired by the end of that week.

It was very nerve racking to be going to David's house, but I knew this guy was really special and he treated me so beautifully. Fears were always there, because of too many abusive people I had allowed to come into my life. But with this man, I was willing to try it. And hopefully it would be vastly different from all my earlier relationships. There was only one other issue I had and that was the age difference. David is 16 years older than me.

Because it was the kids' father's weekend, my children were packed up and out at their father's house straight after school. It was Friday afternoon, and I was to catch up with Robbie for our usual champagne at 4.30pm. I was incredibly nervous about staying with David at his house. I told Robbie of my intentions and her reply was, "Oh, another old man."

That comment did hurt me a little, because there was absolutely no comparison to the old man who I was married to for years. A dreary, depressing, and boring old man. David was simply different in so many ways. You could say we were both from the same side of the street.

Robbie and I finished our champagne and then another girlfriend, Rosie, turned up. I was really starting to get more nervous now and could not seem to get into the car. People kept visiting. David must have thought I had changed my mind about staying.

Rosie was in a related situation in her life to me, with her marriage nearly over, and we caught up regularly. We had a close network of girlfriends. You could call it the sisterhood. We were all there for each other. Just what women need.

Finally, I found myself on my own and managed to get in the car and drive up to the Paps. Yes, I stayed the night. It was lovely.

Our relationship blossomed. David took me out for dinner regularly and always treated me so beautifully. During my marriage, I always had to pay when my husband and I went for dinner. I was never really taken out and treated, because I was always the one having to pay and mostly from money I had earned.

I have been treated the same way, only a couple of other times. Or let myself be treated this way.

Probably because being paid for on other occasions, may have given some men the right of ownership, I was always scared I was going to be violated again. Or I thought, I would have to end up being the one giving my body up for love.

When David and I first started seeing each other, there were warnings and rumours from other people. One of my brothers-in-law had said to me to be incredibly careful of this man, because he had a bad reputation with women in the past. This particular brother in law needed to have a good look at his own reputation. Not the perfect dedicated partner after all, it seemed.

Another female friend had told me I needed to be warned about David because when someone moved in with him, he turned into a monster. I think that might have come from one of his ex-partners. I have come to believe that she was the monster in their relationship, as it turned out.

On another occasion, I had gone down to Melbourne to stay with David whilst he was working at Dromana. There were rumours going around about him having a female visitor. Guess what? That was me. Too funny. People tried to make our relationship rocky as much as they could but with no success.

My ex-husband was also trying to cause a bit of havoc. Expectedly. I was being called a slut all over Merrijig. He was also telling people that David started seeing me even before my marriage had finished. And it was most likely the reason our marriage ended. All made up stories.

For the record, I started seeing David 16 months after my marriage was completely over. I had a property settlement, and I was also divorced from my husband. My life and identity was totally changed back to being Joanna Herbert again.

David came with his own past life and baggage as well. He had two sons from his first marriage. And another child, his daughter Nichola, from another relationship.

Because of the children he already had, David was definite about not having any more children. I also assured him; I was happy with my three children and definitely didn't want any more either. I was nearly 41 years old when we started seeing each other and I had definitely gone past the pregnancy and baby era. Let me give you the tip.

We talked about this extensively and I told him I could not do the contraceptive pill, because it did my head in with premenstrual tension. I had also had yo-yo periods for all my fertile life, because of my eating disorder and the only solution was for him to have a vasectomy. So that was it. He got it done.

The next thing was David was keen for my children and me to move to his house at the Paps. At the time, I told him we needed to give our children time, and I also did not want to rush into moving in with him for a while. It was new and maybe another chapter but definitely an undetermined one. I had divorced my husband, been on my own for only

16 months and really, I needed some more time to come to terms with my new life.

When you have had a time where you may have evolved a little, you need to take time to change. Moving in with him with my young children, wasn't an option for me or them just yet. I wanted to reestablish myself as a woman who could look after three kids and have a job that gave us everything we needed. I didn't want to depend on a man who was very new in my life and didn't want to feel obliged to anyone. I wanted to be completely independent.

By this time, my ex-husband had gone down the usual track where he had no income. So, he stopped paying the child support we had agreed on. I guess that was because I was in a relationship as well and he was still extremely hurt. It could also have been a way to try and get back at me.

I put up with the no money for quite a while and just kept a running sheet of what he owed me. I was hoping he would one day get some work and then pay me back. He still continued to have the children every second weekend and if I needed him to have them, when I went away.

## BROOME SEPTEMBER 2006

David had an absolute bug for travelling when I first met him. He would go on variety bashes, raising money for disadvantaged children, trips to the bush with the boys and long trips with other guys his age. These trips would take him all over the country for weeks on end.

In 2006, the first year we started seeing each other, he did the Canning Stock Route in WA. The day he left, the local florist turned up with a beautiful bunch of red roses for me. It was such a lovely surprise, and I had never been treated like that before.

When David was away, it was an incredibly long eight weeks and communication was limited to a satellite phone. Not a great telecommunication but that is all he had. When he finally arrived home, he gave me a beautiful gold bracelet from Kalgoorlie and lots of hugs.

I mentioned it would be great to go on a holiday together. I had been to Broome, WA with Shez the year before and loved it so much, that I wanted to go back. We started saving a sum of money each week and, by early September, we were cashed up and going to Broome.

Another thing I need to mention about David was, he detested the use of any illicit drugs. When I first started seeing him, I was still smoking marijuana. It was very early in our relationship that I felt I really didn't need to smoke dope anymore. I also wanted to remember what we discussed and also things we did. Marijuana always played havoc with my short-term memory.

It was on our way to the airport to go to Broome that I decided to stop using marijuana. So, I threw my dope smoking one hitter out, in a bin at a roadside stop on the way. When I got back into the car, I announced to David what I had done. Then I told him the reason I threw it out, was because I didn't need it anymore, now I was with him. It was a great way to start our holiday in Broome.

Our days were spent lying on the sand reading and listening to music and swimming at Cable Beach. We went out for meals and just had a wow of a time together. My first real holiday with a man. Totally spoilt and treated like I had never been treated before. It was also great to be back on a beach as well.

There is one occasion I do recall and David quite often reminds me of it. I used to wear a g-string in those days and most of the time, I was topless. Only because I could still get away with it. I had strolled down to the sea in just my g string and was splashing about on my own in the waves. The next thing, a buggy started to drive towards me. There was someone yelling at me to get out of the water. Because I hardly had a stitch on, I was a bit sceptical about leaving my coverage. It wasn't until he told me the shark plane had spotted a shark in the patrolled area on the beach. I walked out of the water and up the beach trying to cover up a bit. David was roaring with laughter by the time I got to my towel, watching me fiddle about trying to cover my tits and bits.

He turned to me and simply said, "Thank goodness, I didn't have to explain to your parents that you'd been taken by a shark on our first holiday."

I moved into David's house on 1st July 2007 with my three children, a cat named Willie and a dog named Tessa Bear. I had had the cat for a long time and he was one of those cats, that would settle anywhere. Tessa Bear was a Belgium shepherd and about two years old. I had bought her for security at my house in Highton Lane. Being a single mother with three children, I was a little paranoid. So, I decided to get a dog that could really woof. My father had German shepherds when we were young and I always thought they would be good security dogs.

My children were still going out to their father's place every second weekend from our house at the Paps. On the other weekends we were at home with the children, David's daughter, Nichola, would sometimes come and stay.

After we all moved up to David's, my ex-husband stopped paying me totally. He had run down all his work and had absolutely no money. Because I knew I wasn't going to get any help from the kids' father, I stopped them from going out there. I never really liked the environment they were in anyway. They were spending most of the weekends surrounded by serious drinkers or at the Hunt Club Hotel. As a result of me stopping his access, he started doing a few things to try and change the situation.

I was contacted by a group called Relationships Australia. They explained to me, rather than getting involved with the Federal Magistrates Court, we would schedule a mediation on the phone. This mediation would sort out child access for their father and child support payments for me. Remembering that child support was for the upbringing of the children and not for the ex-wife's personal expenses. Not, as thought by most men who have to pay it. Many think we women are having the time of our lives with it.

The mediation worked out super well for the kids' father. He got to have them every second weekend and week on week off in the school holidays. I got the rotten end of the deal. Because he was not earning any money through the books, he ended up paying one dollar per day for three children. I clothed them, fed them, and paid for school fees, football memberships and to say that was fair, was completely wrong. At the time, to add to costs, one of my children was in pull-ups because of his bed wetting at night. They cost a dollar each day. Thanks for that being covered by my ex-husband. What an extremely mighty contribution you have had to your children's upbringing, as always.

My children and Nichola got on very well. My second son was a little younger than her, my eldest son a bit older and my daughter was still only four years old. Nichola looked after my daughter a lot and they both used to play horses and jumps on the front lawn. They could just be normal kids, which was fantastic.

In later years, the kids would be down in the paddock or on the motorbikes riding around the farm. Farm life is a great life for kids. And also, for big kids, like me.

We also did a few camping trips over the years. This was one of the first opportunities my children had at camping. David always had an amazing set up and we would take both his vehicle and my car out to the bush somewhere quite regularly.

I remember, one of the first weekends David and I had together on our own, he was down at the shearing shed doing something. I decided to walk down to the shed, to take him some water. I remembered back to how wonderful it had been all those years ago living next to Marcus

Oldham's farm, as a child. And now, I was living on a farm again. It was incredibly special to have felt this way. I quite often, on the way home from work or town, thought about how lucky I was to have met such an amazing man. I would literally have to pinch myself.

I was so in love and, I was absolutely sure, it was for the first time in my life.

When I first moved up to David's, he was still working for Bells Earthmoving. They were doing crushing to make product for the roads wherever it was needed. He started working at a place called Dromana near Melbourne and then even did a stint down in Geelong. They then worked on bypasses on the Hume Highway, north of Albury and also other overpasses further up the Hume. He was working away most of the time during the week. As the work increased, so did the distance from home.

The next lot of work was at Lake Cargelligo in New South Wales. This was about six and a half hours drive from Mansfield. David was leaving on Sunday afternoon for work early on Monday and then coming home very late on Friday nights. He was exhausted most of the time at the weekends. Hardly surprising!

By the time he was up at Lake Cargelligo, we were running about 600 sheep at home. Further down the road, we had another 600 sheep on agistment. The humidity was particularly bad this summer and that was always a sign for a green fly season.

The green fly, Lucilia Cuprina, normally strikes sheep on moist or soiled wool. Areas affected can be urine or faeces-stained wool and skin wounds. Sheep become poor and struggle with the parasites feeding on them. Green flies are typically more abundant in humid conditions.

Because our sheep were getting struck, I needed to check on them more regularly. I was rounding them up at home into the yards every second day. I would put them through the race so I could see if they had been struck. Then treat them if necessary. On the off day, I would often find the odd struck sheep out in the paddock. For me to be able to treat it, I would have to get the dog to catch it first. All I would have to say to old Bo was, "Was get hold of it," and he would gently bring the singled-out sheep down. Holding it there until I could treat it.

The treatment was something else. KFM apparently stands for Kill Flies and Maggots. It is carcinogenic and smelled like it was seriously bad. It did, however, do the trick. No sooner had you put KFM on the struck sight, it would immediately erupt with maggots. David assured me KFM was an abbreviation for kills f——ing maggots. So, from then on, I had a vendetta against maggots.

Another horrible incident that happened when I moved to the farm, was my dog, Tessa Bear, got the taste for sheep. The day it happened, Nichola and my daughter had taken her down into the front paddock for a walk. There were a few merino ewes amongst our mob of wethers that we had managed to join with the neighbour's ram. He had actually jumped the fence and helped himself. Then when the job was done, he just popped back into his own paddock. As a result, we had four fat lambs on the ground.

The children took Tessa too close to the sheep, and she delighted in having her first taste of lamb. She also had the experience of the chase for one. The children told us about it and we were not too concerned at the time. I had also told David I was happy to find Tessa Bear a new home. He told me he liked her and that would not be necessary.

In the previous weeks, we bought a new flock of wethers, and they were up at the back of the property and in the adjacent one. We had a barter system with the next-door neighbour and could use the property as long as we looked after the fences.

David was still working away with his job and I was at home alone with the children. One morning, on my way to work, I noticed a sheep in the front paddock in the neighbour's property. I noticed it had a bit of wool hanging from its neck and hindquarters. It was standing out on its own. This was a sign that there was something wrong with it. When I spoke to David about it, he said he would have a look at the weekend when he was at home.

Tessa was chained up to her kennel during the day as usual and when we were home, she normally hung about on the verandah with David's dog, Bo. On the Saturday morning, Tessa had turned up at her kennel. She was soaking wet, covered in sheep's blood and smelling of wool. David took one look at her and told me to tie her up. Then he went off in the Toyota for a look around the farm.

He returned after about an hour and was very distressed. He had found mauled sheep everywhere. They were in the dam and some of them had drowned. They were also strewn all over the paddocks. He told me to stay at home with the children and said he would be back. I insisted on going with him and we hooked the tandem trailer on, grabbed the .22 and proceeded to drive around the paddocks.

We had to shoot over 30 sheep to put them out of their misery and loaded 40 altogether into the trailer. Some of the dead sheep had even started to go rotten. It was obvious Tessa had been doing this for a while. I cried all the way around the farm with him. It was one of the most devastating things I had ever seen.

We then had to pile all the sheep up under a dead tree and burn all of the carcasses. It was just a horrible and heartbreaking day.

What my dog Tessa had done was the cruellest thing I have ever seen. If had a gun, I would have shot her myself. David did not want to shoot her and insisted I find her a loving home. I did remove her from our property, and she lived a great life back in Mansfield until she died at the ripe old age of 13. Not a bad innings for a shepherd.

I really loved living up at the farm. There were also some extremely trying times we both managed to battle through. The only problem was, we weren't spending enough time together because of David's work. I was also becoming very lonely. So finally, after working in my own business, tending to sheep, and feeding and looking after three children on my own, I told him I was really struggling.

Then it eventually had to come to - could he please stop working away and get a job nearer to home.

It started worrying me that I was using old crutches for support again because I wasn't coping. What this really meant was, I was smoking a lot and drinking way too much. He left Bells Earthmoving soon after that and found work locally with his son at his garden supplies and earthmoving business.

# CHAPTER 11

## *DAVID RELATIONSHIP STRUGGLES AGAIN*

David had always told me his first marriage had not been a happy one. He had married the widow of his best friend. She was a widow because her husband had been killed in a water-skiing accident on Lake Eildon. David and her dead husband, Winston, were best friends. They had been friends for years and worked in shearing sheds together.

Another thing they did in their free time was to water ski on Lake Eildon. They did other projects together, including building a boat for ski racing before he died. On the day Winston lost his life, they had been waterskiing racing near the town of Eildon. They had skied all day on the lake and were on their way home to Bonnie Doon. They were both quite tired. When they went to cross each other on their ropes, Winston had gone headfirst into the bank. He was dead at the scene. Winston's wife and young daughter were also in the boat and saw the accident. Another one of David's friends, Norm, was driving the boat. It was tragic.

Because David was a gentleman, he looked after Winston's wife and daughter, post his death. It was probably out of sympathy, in the end, that he married her. He was only 21 years old and thought he should do the right thing by her and her daughter. Winston's wife was from a different side of the street in all ways. It was chalk and cheese.

David and his first wife had produced two boys. By the time the boys were growing up, it was inevitable the marriage was not going to work. She was extremely unhappy and started drinking more frequently. David would get home most days after a long day at work, to find no food on the table. David was always working hard, shearing in those days and did fence contracting in the off season. The marriage ended after about twenty years.

The reason why I have included this is because of my own on and off drinking problems throughout the years. Whenever I was triggered or upset, I used to drink myself to oblivion. If David were away, I would sit out in the garage, smoke my head off and drink. David was starting to see an unpleasant recurrence happening with me. He started to ask questions like: Do you need to drink to be with me? Or do you need to be drunk to make love to me?

I guess he was also doubting himself because of my drinking habits. He sat me down a few times and we talked about alcohol, and he tried to help me with the problems I had with it. As explained in other chapters, my problem with alcohol stemmed from needing to block things out and, a lot of the time, to get to sleep.

His first wife's behaviour was mentioned because he was having a bit of deja vu, except, this time it was with me.

We talked about a lot of things that had happened in my life, and I told him about my being interfered with, abuse and raped by my parents' friends. And that nothing was ever done about it except leave me with thoughts of abandonment and hopelessness.

I went through especially bad stages as well when I was due for my period. I would always have a drinking bender about that time of the month. Probably because I was more emotional during the oestrogen dump. At these times, things had got so bad I sometimes had suicidal thoughts of driving into a tree on the way home. I, fortunately, managed to turn those thoughts around when I thought about my children and our future together.

Then there were other occasions, including every time we got together with my family, I would be triggered by something and get really drunk. Other things would also trigger me, including David sometimes, and I really hated that.

After battling with this for some time, I decided to make an appointment to see my doctor. I spoke to her about my dreadful pre-menstrual tension, and she said she could prescribe me antidepressants. I told her, I couldn't possibly take them, because I was scared they would make me put weight on. The fears of eating and getting fat had returned. I wasn't going to go back there. Eventually, I managed the pre-period doldrums with a natural medication and things improved for a while.

The suicidal thoughts started coming back again and the trees were looking good and sturdy enough to drive into on my side of the road. I didn't want to go down this path, because finally I did have a lot to live for. My children and David.

The only solution was to get some professional help. I decided to make another appointment with my doctor. The day I walked through her door, I broke down in tears and said, "I am not acting this time, and I really need to get some help."

She talked to me for a while, and we did a mental health plan. She referred me to the female clinical psychologist in Mansfield. I had not told David, at this stage, what I was struggling with. I probably didn't even know myself. I certainly did not want to lose our relationship and I just couldn't do this on my own anymore.

I started seeing Kate, my clinical psychologist. What an amazingly special woman. We both liked each other from the start, which was especially important. Because of this, she said that it would be fine to see each other on a regular basis.

We started with going through everything past, present, the whole kit and caboodle. Kate was specialised in the trauma I had experienced and also in the way I didn't deal with it. She diagnosed me with Post Traumatic Stress Disorder (PTSD).

The PTSD had stemmed from the very first assault but I had definitely found a great deal of extra strength with all the other abusers. I had anxiety from then on and would regularly have panic attacks and run away. I didn't realise this is what I had. It wasn't until 30 years later I found out about it. And I still had absolutely no idea of how to manage it.

The sessions I had with Kate were amazing. She was able to help me work through a great deal of my amassed problems. My relationship with David improved and my alcohol problem was being managed by myself, better than it ever had previously. Finally, after all this time, I was in a relationship I wasn't constantly trying to sabotage.

Another issue, incredibly important in our relationship, was broached about 14 years ago. Because I had been so honest with David about my horrible past and the sexual abuse I had suffered, David found it easy to tell me his deepest, darkest secret in the world. He told me he had been sexually abused by the local priest in Mansfield. This happened over a considerable period of time, and he had only been nine years old.

He had suffered all these years with his own guilt, shame, and horror. He hadn't told anyone about it until me. He was so frightened of being bullied by his peers about it. If he had told his parents at the time, he would have been punished. And to add to that, he probably wouldn't have been believed by anyone either. He sadly, was just like me. He too, had all of the same thoughts and the total confusion with love and sex.

In a sad sort of way and because of our awful pasts, we have both managed to grow closer together. David is the best person in this world for me, and I am the best person for him.

# CHAPTER 12

## *STUDIES AND FIGHTING THE GOOD FIGHT*

When I had attended a few more sessions with Kate, other things also started changing for the better in my life. One of these was the belief I could do more with my life and possibly start doing a few educational courses of interest. And, because I realised I had been such a failure during my further education as a young person, I wanted to start educating myself again. So, I enrolled myself in a diploma course. This was to, firstly, use my brain, as well as maybe give me some sort of reward for learning. Or some reassurance that I was still academically capable.

At the time, my two sons were also getting to their later years of learning and we could discuss subjects, such as physical education or sciences, like biology. It was also proof I could be something. It was always in the back of my mind what my father had always said that I was not a university graduate.

I enrolled in a Diploma of Sports Nutrition online and loved every moment of it. Learning was an amazing feeling, and it had been put on pause for quite some time. I passed with flying colours.

I was working for some great people at the time doing my cleaning and I would often talk to them about the course I was doing. One lady in particular, because she knew how passionate I was about nutrition, mentioned to me about the possibility of a McDonald's outlet coming to Mansfield. The lady was also friendly with someone whose son had a position of higher management with the fast-food giant.

At the same time, a huge battle was going on in Victoria between the Tecoma community and McDonald's. The town in the Dandenong ranges near Melbourne was the site of a long and contentious battle against the construction of a McDonald's outlet. Their plight was because of increased rubbish, traffic, and the impact on local businesses.

That was it. This started off a great sense of urgency and excitement in me, to do something about it. My concerns were: the nutritional health setback on the Mansfield community and, similar to Tecoma, the impact on our local businesses. Mansfield had evolved over the last 20 years as a small town with lots of lovely food places to choose from. It was these food outlets I was very protective of. Those small unique businesses in my town.

The only way to stop the threat was to run a petition. And put it to our council as a community wish. I set up a petition notice and started distributing them throughout the town in as many businesses as I could. I put the petition in the schools, and I set my car up as a protest vehicle with banners and placards on the inside of the windows.

There was a district population in Mansfield of around 8,000 people at the time. This included holiday property owners. My final tally against McDonald's was over 4,000 signatures. This also included school children. I was absolutely thrilled with the result. It was definitely power to the people!

As a result of the petition, I was approached by one of the town's doctors. I was invited to join a committee that would ensure McDonald's never came to the town of Mansfield. We met regularly at another member's house and managed to devise a way to stop the fast-food giant getting into town. Unfortunately, it wasn't for any of the reasons I felt strongly about. Eventually, it was knocked out of any contention by signage rules held by the council. The big yellow M sign would not be allowed in the town.

It was an interesting time for me. Our committee was made up of two doctors, a home economics teacher and a member from the local council who was interested and participating in the health of the Mansfield community. One of the doctors had done a thesis on McDonald's years ago and let us in on little known facts about the food. The buns are so full of sugar they make you crave Coca-Cola. The kids' meals come with a toy so children will eat McDonald's Happy Meals. This also associated the kids' foods with an increased yearning for eating the fast food.

We also learned a great deal about Jamie Oliver's plight to uncover some of the untruths of McDonald's food and its preparation. The ammonia-tainted mince in burgers.

Another concern was certain studies had been done on the topic of obesity and the occurrence of it. This study noted that secondary schools, in the vicinity of one kilometre from a McDonald's, had a higher incidence of obesity. Mansfield, at the time, had a higher low socioeconomic community as well. Studies have shown that people with this income status, make poorer choices with regards to food they buy.

During my childhood, McDonald's was a treat that only happened a few times a year for my family. The same applied to my own children. It is not part of a nutritious diet.

Another interesting reaction I had, was being verbally attacked by a woman at my daughter's ballet concert. The woman had seen the McDonald's objection notices on my car. Her attacking argument was her daughter would get great training and would be employed by McDonald's if they came to town. Interestingly, the woman was grossly overweight and so was her daughter.

# CHAPTER 13

## *DEATH KNOCKS*

It was part of the post McDonald's protests that started people seeing me more as the person I was. Previously, because of my work, I was seen more as a cleaner, than someone who had any intellect. This event was helpful with my confidence too.

Unfortunately, there was a stigma attached to people who cleaned. We were supposedly complete 'nuff nuffs' in most people eyes. I was treated badly by people I worked for from time to time.

Interestingly, this was also something that came up when I was attending Geelong Grammar School. The Madges, as we referred to them, were people who came from Corio. Corio is a very low socioeconomic suburb in Geelong. It was because of this snobbery, I became a victim of it when I became a cleaner.

When I had my first child, I rang an old friend from school and I remember she said, "Oh, you don't actually clean do you?"

On the other hand, I was also treated beautifully by some extremely wealthy and intelligent people, and these were the ones that made my job as a cleaner so worthwhile. I made close friends with some of these people and to this day, we are still close.

Unfortunately, people I have become friendly with through cleaning, have also died too young. One of whom, was a great friend of David's before I started seeing him. His name was Ross Ray. David had known Ross through his work as a stock agent. Incidentally, I had also cleaned for him, when he sold and vacated a house in the Mansfield area. I met Ross and Mara a few times after that. We had gone out to dinner with them in Mansfield.

Because Ross and Mara loved the Mansfield district so much, they had bought and built on a property in Merrijig. On completion of the build, I had offered to do a builder's clean on the house for them, because the clean hadn't been done properly when the house was finished.

On other occasions, David and I would also go to their house for the day, quite often to help plant trees and tend to the garden for them. David also mowed the lawns when Ross didn't have time. We also checked on the cattle David had bought for Ross. We started spending a lot of time with them when they were up for the weekend. Ross and Mara were both in the legal profession and extremely busy people.

One weekend, in May 2016, David and I were attending a bike race meeting at a nearby property. David's grandsons were all competing. At around 11am, David received a distressed phone call from Mara. She explained that Ross had gone out on the quad motor bike to check on a fence where the neighbour's sheep had been getting in. They were due to go to Melbourne for a family function and he still had not returned home. She had tried to call him on numerous occasions but he wasn't answering the phone. David and I drove my car around to the property.

David and Ross had chatted on the phone the night before about the fence and David knew where the sheep were getting in. He intended to fix the fence during the week. When we drove up the driveway, David pointed to the fence line on the hill. What we saw was a four-wheel motor bike lying upside down.

We arrived at the house and Mara rushed over to us. She was extremely distressed. David told her we would go for a drive to have a look at the fence. We got back into the car and drove as far as we could up the hill to where we had seen the bike. We both ran from the car over to the quad bike. David was in such a state of urgency he tore his Achilles tendon running towards him. David was yelling out, "Ross, can you hear me?" as he ran up towards him.

When we reached the bike, Ross's body was ashen grey. He looked like he had been dead for a while. The first thing we needed to do was get the bike off him. We do not know how we ever did it, but we lifted the four-wheel bike uphill and off his body. David checked for a pulse but there was nothing. We returned to the house, called the police and ambulance, and told Mara the tragic news. She was devastated and so were we.

David returned to the bike to wait for the ambulance, and I tried to do as much as I could to support Mara. She was in a state of shock and walked out of the front door and started down the driveway to the road. I followed behind her just in case she needed me. On the way up to the Mount Buller-Mansfield road on Hearns Lane, the ambulance pulled up to talk to me. I knew the guys because one of my jobs was cleaning at the ambulance station. They asked me what had happened and enquired about Mara's mental state. I told them Ross was deceased and Mara is trying to process, as best as she could, what had just happened.

When Mara finally returned to the house, she said she wanted to go to our house at the Paps. She collected a few things and her briefcase. Then she, in a beautiful tribute, sprayed herself with Ross's aftershave. We got into my car, and we drove out the gate for her last time.

Whilst driving into Mansfield, I asked her if she needed money or had enough money. Knowing that Ross's bank accounts would be frozen. She said she had some money. She then started to tell me how Ross had prostate cancer and had also had heart surgery to put a pacemaker in. They had experienced a bad health scare in recent months.

When we arrived at our house, Mara still felt the need to walk, and she headed down the driveway at our place. She just needed to walk herself through things. When she had put her thoughts in place, she returned to the house.

Mara made a few phone calls, one in particular to a close friend who was also a barrister. She was to come to our house for moral support. Then Mara started phoning other people, but then kept giving the phone to me, so I could tell them about the tragic news.

It was an extremely difficult day for all of us. Mara was picked up by her family and driven back to Melbourne later that afternoon. She was incredibly grateful for the support I had given her that day. There were times when I just didn't know what to say or do. All I could do was try and be there for her and give her some space as well as support.

In the following weeks, David and I attended what was the biggest ever funeral I had ever been to. It was held at St Paul's Cathedral in Melbourne. The service was incredible and magnified every beautiful, intelligent, and humorous side to Ross.

We attended the wake near the law courts in William Street. Mara and her family thanked both David and me for the support we had given the family. It was an honour to have known such an incredible human being.

There is another sad but special story I would like to tell. Another thing that goes with my cleaning business in the Mansfield area.

When I was a little girl and living at Timbertop, I remember going to kindergarten in Mansfield. One of the boys in my class, Chris Stoney, was from quite a large farm in Mansfield and my mother became friends with his mother, Helen. I remember going out to the farm and Helen would fuss over us and then Lisa and I would go out and play with her children. The Stoneys were another family my parents had met when we lived in the Mansfield district.

During the time I had my business at Mount Buller, I had cleaned for Helen. When she first moved into Mansfield, I had returned many years later, to the same farmhouse. Helen employed me to clean the house, so a new manager and his wife could move in. Then, she looked me up again a few years later and asked me to come back and clean for her on a regular basis at her new home in town.

We would have a cigarette and a cup of coffee together and a jolly good laugh. I got on with my job, and we would meet again after another fortnight.

In the years David and I were travelling, Helen would simply cope with her house and have me back when I returned. Sometimes, Helen would be away when I wasn't travelling and I did a few extra hours for her, for love. I remember cleaning the entire outside of the house one year. This was to give her a lovely welcome home surprise.

One year, when we had been away, I noticed that Helen's bathroom wasn't how it normally was. Her toileting had changed. I remember mentioning my concerns to her daughter. Her reply to me was, "Don't worry about mum, she is very stoic."

When you clean at people's houses, you pick up certain health signals from time to time. Because of my interest in people's health, I had done some research into common diseases and ailments to fill in some time while we were travelling. These illnesses and disease were always more common in our ageing population.

The following year, I returned from holiday and went to clean for Helen. We sat down together and talked about our travels etc. Then she hit me with some extremely awful news. She told me she had pancreatic cancer. Her next question to me was, would I be prepared to do this journey with her. Wow, that was extremely personal. But, of course, I accepted.

Helen had already had some treatment by the time I had got back from my trip. She was losing her hair slowly. We chatted away as usual and then I did her cleaning.

Progressively, her health became worse. Helen had chemotherapy and other treatments. She was put on steroids for a while to pep her up, but they are more of a mask than a treatment. Each fortnight, she became more jaundiced. She really deteriorated very quickly. This is what happens with the untreatable pancreatic cancer.

The last day I turned up to clean for her, her son, Chris, and his partner at the time, were in the kitchen. Helen was now being cared for by the family 24/7. I walked in through the back door and was greeted by Chris. Helen was calling out, and Chris asked me to go down and see what she wanted. In fact, he told me, I was being summonsed.

Helen was having terrible problems with toileting by now. She greeted me by saying she was having a terrible day and had forgotten I was coming in. She also told me I wouldn't be needed today and sorry that she hadn't let me know. She was also cross because no one had turned up to shower her. She was sitting on the loo and didn't have a stitch on. She was completely yellow from the jaundice. She told me she was going to be admitted to the hospital in the next day. I asked her if I could visit her there. She didn't really give me an answer, so I leaned over, gave her a kiss on the forehead, and said goodbye.

I was quite distraught. I picked up my cleaning gear at the door and headed out to my car. I sobbed uncontrollably for a while then went to see a friend for a big hug.

Sadly, Helen died in hospital a couple of days later.

David and I reserved a place in the church for her funeral. She was a very much-loved person in the Mansfield community and there were people spilling out into the church hall. It was an honour to have known such a fun and loving lady.

# CHAPTER 14

## *THE ROYAL COMMISSION*

On 12th November 2012, the Australian Prime Minister, Julia Gillard MP, announced the establishment of the Royal Commission into Institutional Child Sexual Abuse. This royal commission was established by our Governor General, Dame Quentin Bryce, on 11th January 2013.

The royal commission findings were collected through until late June 2015. On 1st September 2015 the commission held a public hearing in Melbourne to inquire into the experiences of former students of Geelong Grammar School.

Because of the facts that were uncovered by the royal commission about child abuse at the school, a letter of invitation to speak up was sent out to all old Geelong Grammarians.

**I never received this letter.**

In early 2015, I was contacted by Kate Eggers. Previously in my story, I have spoken about Kate and the immense help she was to me in my earlier years, of trying to heal from my abuse.

Kate was my parents' next-door neighbour in Davies Road, Merrijig. Kate had helped with flowers at my wedding and helped me more with a bit of friendly counselling when I needed to talk. She was a great friend of my family and soon became an incredibly special friend of mine.

She had called me to let me know, there was a letter circulating amongst Old Geelong Grammarians and earlier parents of the school. It was about the Royal Commission into Institutional Child Sexual Abuse. As we had previously discussed my experience, she thought I would like to see the letter and have the opportunity to act on it.

Apparently, I was supposed to have received this letter but, somehow, I never did. It has always made me pose the question, why not? I am also sure my parents would have received this letter. But interestingly, it was never mentioned. This letter has since set off the last 10 years of my life, up to and including now.

David and I have had a fairly temporary, nomadic life from about 2014 and we were about to spend a few months on another trip away. Most years, we were on the road from the first weekend in June and returned in the early spring. Our main aim was to escape the cold Victorian weather. As well as staying warm, it has always been a dream for both of us to explore our amazing country.

We left Mansfield in early June 2015 and headed towards the Victorian country town of Cobram. The purpose of going to Cobram was to visit the Tuppal woolshed. The Tuppal woodshed was once a working 72 stand shed. It was also noted as the Rolls Royce shed in Australia in its time. We spent a few hours just looking at the history of shearing and this beautiful old building. You could imagine the noise of the shears and the sheep being yarded and moved about.

Also, at this time, I was in the midst of trying to learn about shearing and shearer's cooking. I would hopefully gather enough information to write a book about it, with lamb recipes attached. Yet another one of my hair-brained ideas.

We also travelled through the town of Hay in New South Wales. Hay has quite a large shearer's museum. Whilst we were at the museum, I researched everything and anything about being a shearer's cook. I had only had a small experience at our own farm in providing for shearers. This was because our shearing only lasted typically for a couple of days each year. This type of cooking was a full-time job. It was a way of life, being a shearer's cook. After a couple more days travel, we arrived in the outback New South Wales town of Broken Hill.

I had been thinking about the letter that Kate Eggers sent me, and it was getting closer to the cut-off date for reporting to the royal commission. After a great deal of thought, I plucked up some courage and nervously rang the number provided. I spoke to a woman, telling her about my unfortunate experience with Dr Mackey. We spoke for about half an hour and, in that time, she also set up another appointment for someone else to call me and talk about it further.

Because we were on the road, and sometimes didn't have mobile service, I needed to make a time that I knew we would be in a certain place, where I could use my phone. We had been held up, in the previous days, because some of the roads had been flooded by heavy rain.

This is a common occurrence in certain outback places in the winter. Especially in the southern states of Australia. Another reason we had been held up was because some of the roads weren't sealed and became very muddy when wet. Also, when the roads were wet, you were not allowed to drive on them. This is because it causes an incredible amount of damage. If you did choose to drive and were caught using a dirt road, it could be very expensive. Penalties and fines at the time, were enforced at $1,000 per tyre, including spares. We were towing a dual axle camper trailer with one spare.

Fortunately, we arrived safely and legally to a town called Tibooburra and I was on time for my phone appointment. I received my phone call from the royal commission on 16th June 2015 and spoke to another person for well over an hour. She had also informed me, if I wanted to, I could go to the police and make a statement. It would then be processed from there. In other words, an investigation would take place conducted by the Victoria police into my allegations against Dr Mackey.

It was a lot to think about. I didn't report anything further at that stage. I don't know whether it was because I was frightened about digging up the past or because I wasn't ready to, or too frightened to start meeting my demons. My demons were always a scary thing. And yes, they were always there. I was always having vivid nightmares and often triggered into live conscious flashbacks.

Post my phone call, there was a lot of discussion with David, and we brought it up a few times during the rest of our holiday. We finished our trip, taking in a part of outback Queensland, including visiting Longreach and a few other historic towns.

There are some fantastic museums in Longreach, including the Qantas museum and the Stockman's Hall of Fame. When we visited these remote places, we tried to learn as much as we could on our Australian history.

Before we started to head slowly home, I ended up meeting up with a girl from school, after 32 years. Her name was Helene. We had played sport together at school and had also finished our schooling in the same year. I had put a post on Facebook about how I was dipping my feet in the sea at Bowen. We went south a little from there and camped next to a railway line for the night. When I checked my Facebook post, Helene had piped up and said her father had some property near Bowen.

We exchanged phone numbers on messenger. I then called her, and we spoke for a while. She told us that we were very welcome to stay at her father's house. The following day, we put the address into our GPS and realised, to our surprise, that it was just over the highway from where we had camped for the night. So amazing after so many years of no contact. And amazing, that we were not far away.

We went to the address and set up our camper at the front of her father's house. The view was sensational, and the beach was at the bottom end of the garden. I was absolutely rapt to be staying in such a beautiful place. We had views of the sea with islands as a backdrop. In appreciation for letting us stay there and, also because the place needed a little maintenance, we busied ourselves with some gardening and other handyman chores.

After staying at their house on the beach for a few days, we were absolutely delighted, because Helene and her family drove up to see us. Not just from down the road. They had driven from the Central Coast, just north of Sydney. Over a 2,300-kilometre drive!

We met her husband and young family and stayed on the beach front property for a few weeks. The house was situated at a place in Queensland called Brisk Bay. A small community just south of Bowen. During this time, Helene took us over to her father's island and showed us around his other blocks on the beach. Helene then teed up some work for David to do the following year if we wanted.

Since leaving Geelong Grammar School and also entertaining my life-changing experiences, I had lost contact with most people from school. This was because, not only did I feel so out of touch with my year group, but I had also lost all my confidence and never really thought anyone from my year group wanted to see or catch up with me. Those years were an exceptionally large, void space for me.

Helene and I did discuss a few things about Geelong Grammar, including our school memories, both good and bad. I told Helene about the Royal Commission into Institutional Sexual Abuse and that I had reported Dr Mackey. I also told her I wasn't sure about contacting the police at the time. The way that I looked at it, it was really more about letting the royal commission know just what sort of man he really was.

In early spring, we returned home to our farm. After returning to Mansfield, David and I decided to invite my parents and David and Jenny Yencken up for a meal one evening. We always have a jolly time with the Yenckens, great conversation and plenty of laughter. Because the royal commission was being highly reported on, the conversation finally got around to what was being said and seen in the media.

David Yencken had once been head of the Geelong Grammar School council. He commented that he knew nothing at all about what had been going on at the school for all those years. My parents had the same inclination and agreed with him.

Because of the current conversation, I piped up and told everyone I had spoken to the royal commission in June and reported to them what Dr Mackey had done to me. I didn't elaborate on what had happened to me, as it wasn't really the time nor the place.

David then told his own story, about how he had been abused by a local Mansfield priest as a child. He then went on to say, he had absolutely no respect at all for the church. The conversation changed pretty much straight away. Probably because of the shock of our confessions. It wasn't really dinner party chat.

After that night, there was never a conversation brought up by either of my parents about what their friend, David Mackey, might have done to me. Never ever, a question asked. And never ever, an apology offered. I felt extremely abandoned and quite confused with their genuine lack of interest in the overall health of one of their daughters.

For the next two years, the royal commission was still on my mind. II was happy at this stage that I had reported Mackey and didn't follow up doing a police statement. Aside from that, I was ignorant of what the court processes were about and how the judicial system worked. In other words, I was happy with my contact with the royal commission to get justice. What I didn't realise at the time, that making a statement would have a great deal more bearing on the criminal case.

# CHAPTER 15

## *DAVID'S HEALTH GOES DOWNHILL*

In February 2017, David and I received some terrible news. David was diagnosed with prostate cancer. After numerous tests and a great deal of anxiety, a tumour measuring 35mm was found on the left side of his prostate gland. David had none of the usual symptoms of an enlarged prostate. The result was initially from routine blood tests.

We proceeded to go through the usual cancer scans, MRIs, Positron Emission Tomography (PET) scans and then biopsies. A very trying time for both of us and very busy time moving around to get tested for everything related. Mansfield isn't set up for cancer treatment, so we were on the road a great deal in order to have appointments. We had appointments in Wangaratta and most of the radiography appointments were done in Albury, New South Wales.

After all the testing was done, we had a phone call from David's urologist. He discussed the results of the biopsy and informed us the tumour was malignant. He then said the only way to deal with this tumour was to remove the prostate. This would have to be done as soon as possible, otherwise he would not be around for too much longer.

On 2nd May 2017, David went into surgery for over six hours, and a radical prostatectomy was performed. The surgery was longer than usual because there was other questionable tissue found in the area of David's perineum. He recovered well in the first few days and was released from hospital after about seven days. He came home with drains and catheters attached and was placed in my care. There was also care provided by the Mansfield hospital community nurses.

David's post-surgery healing was progressing normally and appointments for removing catheters etc. took place and all went well. We had a few complications with the removal of his lymph drain. We eventually had to visit the emergency department at Wangaratta District Hospital. The attempts at the removal of the drain were extremely painful. No one in the nursing department seemed to know how to remove it. David waited for a registrar to do the job. Finally, after some serious pain medication, it was pulled straight out.

I was very curious to have a look at his drain and donned a pair of surgical gloves and picked it up from inside the rubbish bin. I examined the drain closely and, to my shock, found it was a flat drain about six inches long. The drain was attached to the catheter, which resembles a pipe. It was the catheter that could be seen outside of his body. The nurses, in their attempts to remove this drain, had twisted it around and around and then tried to pull it out. I now understood why David was screaming in pain when they had tried to remove it. It was like a thick plastic corkscrew turning inside his newly healing body.

I showed the drain to the nursing staff, and they too were a horrified after I had told them about the earlier attempts to remove it. Because I couldn't help myself, I mentioned the drain issue to a lovely lady that I was cleaning for. Peta was very senior amongst the nurses in Mansfield. Her response was for me to write a letter of advice for a teaching nurse to bring it up in a nurses' meeting, so it could be discussed and addressed.

The drains inside post-surgery are not necessarily what they seem like from the outside. Please find out the shape of a drain beforehand, and prior, to removing it.

Also, post-surgery and during his recovery, David started to act a little differently. Unknown to most people, there is an extreme hormone imbalance after prostate surgery. We weren't really expecting such changes to happen. I totally understand now what it is like to deal with a woman with Pre Menstrual Tension or menopause. After we had realised this phenomenon, we managed to sort that out together. It was the culprit for what was causing all the extra stresses and anxiety. Not to mention the idea that David might even die.

We were told David needed to have another Prostate Specific Antigen blood test three months post-surgery. In a male with no prostate, this result should be zero or less than 0.012.

We went away as usual in mid-June on our yearly trip and returned to Brisk Bay. We caught up with Helene and her family again but this time we stayed on one of the beach blocks her father owned. We kept ourselves busy with tidying up the blocks and fencing them off, in preparation for their sale. It was a lot of fun, and we had a beautiful place to stay in exchange for work we both enjoyed.

David's Prostate cancer was still on both of our minds. He had a PSA blood test whilst we were there, and it was around 2.28. This result was certainly not desirable, as it was an indication the cancer had started growing again. We organised an appointment in Townsville which was the closest large town.

I drove David to Townsville Hospital, which was about two hours away and he had another Prostate Specific Membrane Antigen PET scan. This scan would show up any metastatic prostate cancer which is where it may have spread to other organs in the body or into the lymph glands. Nothing was detected during the scan and David was told to keep getting three-monthly Prostate Specific Antigen testing.

The worst thing about any cancer is the waiting for test results. There is also the idea in your head, you may not have very long to live. And, in my case, my lifetime partner was possibly going to die.

I spent most of this trip walking along the beach every morning in tears. I would ask myself why? On top of everything that had gone wrong in my life, why was I now going to lose the man I adored? He was the right one to come along eventually and then he was going to be taken away from me.

We stayed in Brisk Bay for a few months on this trip. We spent more time with Helene's family and thoroughly enjoyed the warm winter weather. David went fishing and I started walking more and more for my sanity. Exercise at any time, seems to help me greatly process my good and bad feelings about almost everything. It's a great way to let off steam. I certainly did this most days at Brisk Bay.

In August, we started slowly on our way back to Victoria. We travelled towards the west through Lawn Hill National Park, Adele's Grove and through the Diamantina. Being in the outback is definitely one of our favourite places to be. The vastness is mesmerising.

We made our way back to Victoria by early October. All the way home, every moment was special. This might have been our last trip. Who would know?

# CHAPTER 16

## *FEELINGS OF ABANDONMENT*

In early January 2018, I had seen on social media that Mackey had been accused of sexual-related crimes and would be facing charges in the Magistrate's court in Geelong. The Geelong Advertiser news clips were all over the internet. Finally, the Royal Commission into Institutional Sexual Abuse had facilitated and begun proceedings against this horrible predator.

As a result of the headlines on social media, I sent out numerous messages on messenger. I made sure I thought carefully about who to contact. Some of the girls from school were vulnerable types and could possibly be a potential victim. I told them I had reported to the royal commission and I was now definitely going to report it to the police. I also made it clear, if they had had a similar incident with Mackey, to report it as well. One other person did come forward as a result of my message. I was so thrilled I could help at least one other person.

My first response, of course, was to ring my mother. Well!!!!

I began by saying to her, "At last, the horrible man is going to get his justice."

Her response to me was she and my father already knew about the criminal charges held against him.

I asked her, in amazement, "Why didn't you tell me about this?"

To my further shock, my mother simply said, "It was because I just didn't want to tell you."

I was dumbfounded and felt incredibly alone. Abandoned again. At that time, I couldn't think properly to ask her why and just simply hung up from her.

I was extremely confused and upset at her reaction. I also could not understand her not wanting to tell me she knew about this. From my own mother, this was also extremely upsetting. A denial. Why? Because it was one of their friends? Because, as she said at times, sometimes things happen to little girls that we just need to forget. Does that give child sexual abuse some sort of normality? And does it give a male predator a right?

I continued to converse with the group on Facebook for quite some time. Unexpectedly, I had plenty of sorries and mountains of support. It was unexpected because as I stated earlier, I really lost contact with my school year group and always felt like I was unimportant and never included.

The following day, I had organised to visit my godmother, Vanessa, at my parents' house. Vanessa lived in Scotland and had a daughter, Victoria, who lived in Sydney. Vanessa was over here in Australia, to catch up with Victoria and also to see my family. When I went to visit my parents' house, I had a lovely chat with Victoria, who is a doctor and, because of my interest in health and nutrition, I really enjoyed her company. It was also great to talk to Vanessa. We chatted for a while and drank tea.

When it was time for me to go, Vanessa offered to walk me out to the car to say goodbye. I wasn't sure what we may have been going to talk about but she certainly sent me messages she wanted to speak privately. So, in order to have some privacy, I told my parents to stay inside. I had a great excuse, because it was over 40 degrees Celsius outside.

Vanessa and I spoke for a while about the Mackey affair. She told me my mother had kept saying on the previous night, "The poor man, the poor man, the poor man."

Vanessa also told me, my mother had told her and my father, not to mention anything about the royal commission or Dr Mackey to me when I visited that day.

As a result of hearing this, I was absolutely devastated about how my mother had reacted. I was also feeling very betrayed by her, because she had told Vanessa to be non-vocal about it, whilst I had been there. Was my mother in denial that this happened?

Vanessa and I hugged and cried for a while together and we finally said goodbye. She also told me, she couldn't understand my mother's reaction and, in fact, never could understand my mother's reactions to a lot of things.

From there, I went into an extremely, overreactive and manic state of panic. I couldn't go home to the farm. I needed to just run away and be on my own. So that I could cry or do what I needed to do to calm down. I rang David and told him I was safe and would be home later.

Due to my massive panic attack, I drove out to a client's house, which was vacant at the time. This same house had previously belonged to Ross and Mara Ray. I sat on the master bedroom bathroom floor and just sobbed. I stayed there for over an hour. When I was feeling a little grounded, I rang a couple of friends. Every time I told them what had happened, there was another period of sobbing.

My feelings of abandonment continued. I felt especially abandoned by my mother. I could not believe in my wildest nightmares that she had pitied him and not pitied me. And what about all the other children he had abused. How could a mother do that to her own daughter? Why would a mother not protect and console a daughter in a very needy time? Why does my mother always abandon me constantly when it comes to things to do with their friends and Geelong Grammar School?

When I finally returned to the house after a few hours, I told David and my older son what had happened. Both of their reactions were immediately to go around and see my parents and give them a piece of their mind. I said to both of them, it wouldn't be worth it. This is because both my parents just didn't understand. Or maybe just didn't want to. Possibly guilt, because it had to do with their precious Geelong Grammar School and secondly, because this was another one of their close, creepy, sexually-abusive and disgusting friends.

Fortunately, neither David nor my son went around to my parents' house. As soon as I was at home and composed, I wrote my mother a letter. It was about what she had said to Vanessa and what I thought about her, because of these reactions.

# CHAPTER 17
## *LETTER TO MY MUM*

**THE LETTER TO MY MOTHER DATED 23/01/2018:**

*Dear Mum,*

*It is with great sadness and disbelief that I need to write to you. It is without hesitation or regret I would like to tell you, I am so disappointed in our relationship that I find it hard to spend too much time with you.*

*I, fortunately, have a great network of caring people in my life, who will slip into any role that needs to be played. They are, actually, some of your friends. And, as a mother myself, my aim in life is to support, protect and nurture my children, for as long as I am alive. I will keep them out of danger, as much as possible and, if they are to enter into any danger or circumstances they find uncomfortable, I will be there to guide them through. No matter what it takes. This, to me, is what mothering is all about.*

*I would never in my wildest dreams, put a friend ahead of them.*

*I am absolutely devastated and very disappointed about your reaction of what is happening in Geelong.*

*Do you not believe that this friend of yours wouldn't be caught and that he violated me and many others whilst he was in a position of trust?*

*In fact, he has a rape conviction already.*

*What also amazes me is that a good friend of yours, and Emily's godmother, Sue, was kept in denial and put up with this man's behaviour. Not to mention the devastating effect it must be having on his children right now. This animal was giving young students internals for no apparent reason, other than satisfyingly the animal in him. How would you feel, if dad was doing the same? You wouldn't be saying, "Poor him."*

*I am also reminded of your reaction to the Geoff Hinze interference. To say you wanted to protect his family and you didn't know what to do. That sends me an incredible stack of mixed messages.*

*I was also informed how you told Dad, on Friday night, not to mention things to me and then just sat there repeatedly saying, "The poor man".*

*The poor man is the predator, friend or not, who has ruined many girls lives at Geelong Grammar School. And I am sure he has done the same thing, when he opened a "Young people's clinic" in Newtown. Why did he leave the school?*

*How do you feel for his wife Sue? He hid this from her. Put yourself in her shoes and try to say, "Poor man." The 'poor man' has a wicked, mental disease.*

*I am not the only one who has gone to the Royal Commission. I have heard other familiar names, of people close to you, that have reported him. I would never disclose their names but they are very familiar.*

*Maybe, if I hadn't been assaulted by your friend, you would have a little more heart and sympathies for the lifetime of hell he has imposed on other people. There will be always somebody worse off than me. This is not for pity. I have learned to live every day, dealing with this and will, I am sure, until I die. But I will never let it happen to anyone else, if I can help it.*

*All the evidence will unfold and you will, hopefully, see what a disgusting man he is. Your friend, who you entirely support, played with my clitoris and he actually turned me on. I was 15. I can still remember the sickening delight on his face as he knew he was stimulating me. Can you imagine at that age, how confusing that would be?*

*You trusted him to help me with an eating disorder and he abused his every right and to add salt to the wound… it turned me on. I was the same age as my own daughter, innocent and naive.*

*From the first day he saw me, he was saying inappropriate things and was very smutty. You sent me to him to get help and he made it 1000 worse. He knew I was an easy target. I am sure he premeditated the whole thing. He broke your trust too.*

*Why do you think I stopped seeing him?*

*Condoning that sort of behaviour, from a man you call a friend, has riddled me with disgust.*

*I hope that one day, you will realise what "just get over it", means to someone, who has been physically and mentally violated. You just can't.*

*I am disappointed I feel this way and you are so old-fashioned, you can't see or want to believe, the damage this has done. The damage to others is my first concern. Fortunately, I have learned how to deal with this.*

*It is very disappointing to have to email this letter to you but every time I have tried to talk about this in the past, you have just fobbed it off and told me to just get over it.*

*I am making a formal statement at the Mansfield Police Station tomorrow morning at 10.30 am. It's time this man is brought to justice for everyone's sake.*

*Your daughter,*

*Joanna Herbert*

The following day, on 24th January 2018, I made my statement at the Mansfield Police Station, regarding my experience with Mackey. From that day on, legally events really started to heat up.

As a result of the letter to my mother, she contacted me via email and said we needed to talk. My parents, at the time, were visiting people in Geelong, so I had to wait for a few days for their return.

I asked to meet only my mother, because my father had always been so pro Geelong Grammar I thought he would not really hear anything I was talking about.

When I met with my mother, her first words were, "What have you got to say to me?"

I replied, I had already spelled it out in that letter.

"You need to talk to me."

We talked for a while and she said she would support me but that was as far as it ever went. I never really thought she meant it. She had never really supported me before. Why would she want to start now?

# CHAPTER 18

## *SHEZ' WEDDING*

Our annual trip in 2018 was to begin in late February and we were taking my daughter out of school for about four months. She was in Year Nine at Mansfield Secondary School. I had discussed this with the school and there was set work to do, so she would keep up with her learning. There were comments made to me by the school that she would miss quality time in the classroom. I took these with a grain of salt.

In Year Nine, at any school in Victoria or Australia for that matter, classrooms are full of disruptive young boys and some girls. Consequently, not much is learned. I have two older sons and both of them were very distracted in this year.

My daughter, because of her time out of the classroom with us, happened to learn an incredible amount of worldly education, anyway. David and I would set her other work to do. But mostly, the entire experience was incredible.

Our trip started with attending Shez's wedding in Warrnambool where we would stay for about 10 days. We visited museums and my daughter and I had lovely walks at the beach.

After we left Warrnambool, we travelled west through Victoria, visiting the blue lake at Mount Gambier. We drove up through South

Australia and then headed up to Darwin, as quickly as possible. David was very keen to do some fishing and has always wanted to catch some barramundi.

Barramundi is a fish found in salt and freshwater, in the northern states of Australia. During the warmer months of the year, it is more active and catch rates are generally higher. During the build up to and during the wet season, water temperatures can be up to 10 degrees Celsius warmer, than during the dry season.

We made great time heading up to the Northern Territory. We did, however, have to sit in a highway stop, just north of Barrow Creek in the Northern Territory for a few days. This was because we needed to wait for a cyclone in Darwin to hit and move out across the land in a rain depression.

Once we were back on the road, we headed out to Mount Bundey army training camp, to stay with our great friends and hopefully catch some barramundi. David and I had stayed with friends, Pam and Des, in 2014, at Mount Bundey. David had a long-time friendship with Pam, because he had worked for her father years ago at Mount Buller. Then they had rekindled that friendship, when I had come on the scene. I worked for someone who had previously been married to Pam's brother. We had that network connection.

It was while we were at Mount Bundey, I first heard from an amazing detective. This detective was the person in charge of the Mackey case, at SANO taskforce in Melbourne. SANO was a specialised unit within the Victoria police that investigated reports of child sexual abuse. This sexual abuse can be both historical or current.

This female detective had contacted me to discuss my statement. In addition to that, at a later date, she was to inform me of court dates for the committal hearing involving Mackey. The hearing included another 20 other survivors. I was astonished to hear how many people he had sexually abused. I was glad they all had the strength to come forward. Interestingly, his sexual assaults had involved both male and female students.

The committal court hearing was to be carried out over a few weeks, starting in late August and into September, 2018. My court date was set for 5th September.

The detective stayed in contact and telephoned me a couple of times while we were at Mount Bundey. Talking to the detective was quite an emotional time for me. It brought up lots of bad childhood memories and sometimes I would cry.

On other occasions, we would have a great laugh. She was fantastic to deal with, and we were on the same level. We were also about the same age and managed to digress away at times to discuss things we did in the eighties. Including the dyeing of hair and the outrageous fashions, including large shoulder pads, pink Mohawks, and super big fringes.

Her earlier experience as a detective had made her very in tune with the type of offender Mackey was. A couple of times when we spoke, she made mention of him leaving a dirty trail for many, many years. Even decades. She actually once referred to Mackey as a serial sex abuser.

By this time, Geelong Grammar School was trying to do its best for all of us and were getting involved with all the Mackey survivors. We were offered access to a clinical psychologist named Pauline Ryan and one other human resource professional. I made contact with both these women who were recommended. They were extremely helpful to me.

I had further consultations during this trip with Pauline Ryan, in particular, and she was a great support while we were living on the road. She also discussed the court case with me and how to tackle being questioned and prepared me for anything. She said Mackey's barrister would say almost anything to throw me off. This was, at the time, the most frightening part of having to go to court. By Mackey saying to me, all those years ago, "Are you still screwing around with the boys in the bushes?" I was frightened there would be some reference to how he thought I behaved as a young girl. Pauline was extremely helpful.

# CHAPTER 19

## *LETTER TO JEREMY*

I also made contact with an old friend from school, Jeremy. Jeremy was a former school captain at Geelong Grammar School and was, at this time, the head of the school council. During one of our conversations, he enquired whether I would like to be involved with reaching out and helping other survivors. At this time, it was all too fresh again in my mind, so I was very vague in any commitment made to him.

## LETTER RE MACKEY PRE COURT 2018

*To Jeremy, head of GGS school council*

*Dear Jeremy,*

*Just thought I would touch base.*

*I have read the letter from the new head at Geelong Grammar School and you actually came to mind. She sounds like a very grounded and compassionate person.*

*About time we had a woman running the show.*

*I have started some sessions with Pauline Ryan and, although the worms are surfacing, I think it is best to be prepared for my court hearing in September. Another Mackey survivor actually told me, she would be good to talk to, because things may come up in court that are a little overwhelming. The entire experience may be a very big deal because I have never had to go to court before.*

*I figured also that the school is making a huge effort to help us out and even though I am travelling on the road, it helps me a great deal.*

*At this stage of the ordeal, we have all been given court dates, mine being in September. There are now 17 people, that have come forward to report and try to get Dr Mackey dealt with. The woman in charge of the royal commission task force, told me that with a case like this, there is every chance they will get a good result. Most cases of abuse normally only have a few witnesses.*

*The most devastating thing is that this man is still pleading not guilty. It is very distressing for me that he doesn't think he did anything wrong and it hasn't affected any of our lives.*

*We, unfortunately, live this almost every day. It affects our relationships and the entire way that we go about things. I know myself, nearly all my relationships have ended because of what happened beyond my control in my life. Others have expressed the same to me.*

*I am very lucky to be with a fantastic partner. He, however, understands because he is also a victim of assault. This, sometimes, makes things very touchy but we both battle through.*

*On a better note, we are having an amazing trip this year. Last weekend, we swam, with an eight-metre whale shark. Wow, what an experience. Recommend it to anyone. The tour was fantastic, as well as the information and research we were involved with just going out on the boat. The people that ran the trip were incredibly passionate about these amazing creatures and also involved with tagging and researching their existence.*

*Another bucket list for all of us to do. I am still buzzing from it. We also have spent time on a live fire army base (our friends were caretakers). We stayed when there were American and Australian* troops there. Choppers flying all night, a fly by from a jet fighter, that made the house shudder, and live fire 24/7 that makes you appreciate a war zone but we were safe.

We have visited Kakadu and Lichfield National Parks, in the Northern Territory and gone out on a billabong to fish for barramundi. Plenty of crocodiles too.

Heading back up north after Exmouth, as we don't want to go back to cold Mansfield, until we have to. Going back to the beach at Barn Hill (50km south of Broome) 29 degrees and a fantastic beach to walk along. Hopefully, for two weeks.

From there, we will head through the Tanami Desert to Alice Springs on the Tanami track. Staying north, until we need to return home in late August.

Watching the full moon come up tonight over the river that we are camped next to. And, believe it or not, watching the footy. Geelong versus the Bulldogs.

David is a mad football supporter and, I hate to say it, but he follows Collingwood. He does, however, have all of his teeth, no tattoos and does have manners.

Everywhere we travel, we take the Foxtel box and watch football. We can even get television at the King River Hut.

Anyway, nice to touch base again with you. Love to hear your thoughts on things.

Take care of you and your family.

Jo

# CHAPTER 20
## *COMMITTAL HEARING*

We arrived back in Victoria in late August 2018. We had timed things so I could be prepared for the committal hearing. I had spoken to Pauline Ryan again and we discussed how some of the other survivors had gone into court and told me of some of the weaknesses of Mackey's barrister. His barrister was particularly troubled when it came to discussing vaginas, clitorises and other female genitalia. She had told me he wasn't very well informed and found it very confusing and embarrassing to discuss the anatomy of females. During some of the previous testimonies in the committal hearing, he had experienced a great deal of embarrassment.

I prepared for my court appearance, making sure I was confident with the correct pronunciation of all female genitalia. I also made note of where each of our physical parts were and how far apart they were from each individual part of the female anatomy. In my case, my cyst was on my labia majora, not my labia minora and I knew Mackey was definitely looking and touching me in the wrong area, when he had assaulted me.

It was nerve racking for a few days before court. I was scared of what may be brought up and how I was to answer questions. I was also scared of Mackey's barrister's potentially gruelling questions. I remember telling my mother I was scared and as usual, she had just fobbed it off and said, "There is no reason to be scared, you just need to tell the truth."

Really? As if I wouldn't?

I think that a criminal court appearance, especially for the first time, would be difficult for any person. Not to mention as a victim. And also, it's important to mention, the sex offender was a qualified general practitioner and I was the one who was going to be drilled about my anatomy.

David and my daughter came to Wangaratta with me for moral support. I think my mother may have offered to support me but I declined. This was because she always found it difficult to show any empathy or sympathy at any time when it came to this subject. Her attitude had always been, "Just get over it." or, "It happened to lots of little girls." She always had a very contrary way with dealing with things like this.

We drove to Wangaratta, where I was met outside the court by a member from the Victim's assistance program. Louise was assigned to me to provide moral support during the court process. She wasn't allowed to talk in court; she was purely there as a physical presence in support of me. It was really nerve-racking, waiting to be called. Louise and I chatted between ourselves until it was my time to go into the court.

We were called in and Louise sat down behind me. I was given some water and then the proceedings started. I could see Mackey sitting there in the stand. I was so glad I wasn't in the same room as him. My testimony was done via a video link to the Geelong Magistrates Court. I tried not to look at him at all during my questioning, because even the sight of the man was disgusting. The court was introduced to me, including the judge, my barrister Kim, Mackey's barrister and then it was down to proceedings.

To begin with, I was read out a list of people and asked if I knew any of them or if I had been in contact with them in recent times. The entire idea of this questioning by Mackey's barrister was attempting to get a theme of a conspiracy theory by all of us against Mackey. It was somewhat absurd really, because I only knew three of the victims and only one of them really well. However, the person I knew, hadn't been in contact for years. Our contact wasn't until the royal commission and we had spoken only briefly of late.

We then got down to the nitty gritty of the female anatomy. Mackey's barrister became completely confused. He didn't know what was where and how far things were from the other parts on a female's anatomy. In the end, he finally gave up, because he couldn't deal with talking about clitorises, labia majoras and vaginas.

Because he was slightly confused, he started questioning my statement. He also tried his very best to make me look stupid. I had sworn I had never been back to see Mackey again, after the incident in 1981. There were some medical records kept for me and they were then brought up. Apparently, I had gone to see him about a cyst behind my ear, a couple of years later.

By the time we had finished my testimony, I did get a little rattled. Mackey's barrister had tried to tell me the cyst was on my left ear and not on my labia majora. I'm sure he was just confused about the entire deal and also rattled, because I made sure that the subject we were talking about again was my labia majora.

When we left the court, Louise told me most criminal barristers will try and rattle people on the stand. She also said I had done really well in keeping my cool.

## MY WRITING THAT EVENING

*Mackey committal hearing 2018*

*Appearance in Court Mackey sept 2018*

*Wow, what a day. I did my court appearance today, via video link in Wangaratta. It's been a bit scary for the last two or three days but I managed to sleep better last night.*

*Just tell yourself you need to be cool and talk slowly like your father. Slowly and collectively.*

*Had great support from the witness support system, provided by the government. Louise was great to talk to and great to spend some time with prior to my hearing.*

*Spoke to my barrister and she gave me the confidence I needed, post testimony. She said I was supremely knowledgeable about my anatomy and I did a great job.*

*By the way, he is still pleading not guilty but I don't care. He is guilty.*

*Can't believe there is a tactic by the defence to say there is a conspiracy. I would never dream of conspiring or conjuring up something like this. Something that has totally affected my life, in so many ways. I think of it more of an insult to my intelligence to even entertain that.*

*I think I did a great job too. I could freely speak about my experience without flinching too much and, although the hairs stood up on my back at some stages, it was merely because the barrister was trying to make me feel stupid and ignorant.*

*That, I am not.*

*I want to make it the priority to ensure that stops this happening in institutions. Children are children. Innocence is innocence. I was a child and things that happened to me were totally beyond my control.*

*Very chuffed and grateful I have had the support of many, my David, my children and my friends. Not to mention, the amazing support from the task force and independent people that have helped.*

The biggest highlight of that afternoon was my barrister, Kim and the SANO detective, both rang me separately, later in the day. They told me they had laughed about it after the hearing and how much of an idiot I had made of Mackey's barrister. They also said they both found it very hard not to laugh, during my testimony. The poor man couldn't deal with the word clitoris or labia and had a few issues with the difference between a cyst on the ear and the cyst on a labia majora. Clearly in two very different parts of my body.

Another thing that happened was also quite strange for me that evening. This was because my older sister rang me to congratulate me. She congratulated me for being strong enough to go to court and help to get some sort of justice. Then she ruined all the praise she had given me by finishing our conversation with, "But I just don't get it."

My thoughts were, *Don't get what? What is it that people don't get? How can you not realise, that when someone is sexually abused as a young person or a child, that it is an enormous breakage of adult trust? It is an enormous violation on an innocent child, that can also have a most devastating effect on that person's life. Not to mention, their life direction.*

A few days later, we had the result of the committal hearing. The judge's decision, based on all of our testimonies, was to proceed with the criminal case and progress to the County Court. The date was set for October 2019. This was going to be another twelve months of waiting to get a result.

The County Court in Victoria has jurisdiction in civil and criminal cases. It has the power to hear both types of cases and also has the power to make decisions.

I was kept informed by the detective at SANO and my barrister, regarding the future court dates. The detective had always assured me, because I was the only person Dr Mackey had kept medical records for, I would definitely be appearing in the county court to testify once again.

Dr Mackey had been assaulting children for years, but obviously, in order to mask his abuse, he wouldn't keep records of the times he had offended.

Interestingly, some offenders do keep records of abuse. Almost like a token of their experience. I have heard of another Geelong Grammar School paedophile kept a diary of all of his sexual abuse.

Another interesting fact is, the times I had appointments with Dr Mackey for my mental health and weight problems, he never made or kept any record of it. This also was the same scenario for the day he sexually assaulted me. Because that proof wasn't diarised, then it seemed it really didn't happen. This same situation would have occurred for all the other victims of Mackey too.

# CHAPTER 21

## *THE WORST NEWS EVER*

David and I were letting our house out with a property letting business whilst we were away during the last winter. We had decided that after my court case we would do our own Air B&B at the house. When the house was in use, we would stay down at the shearing shed in our caravan. From 8th September 2018, we let the house out. We had so many bookings, we were literally living down in the caravan. My daughter had a bed set up in the shearing shed. It was warm and she had a television and an electric blanket. She was close to finishing Year Nine at Mansfield Secondary College.

One evening in October 2018, David and I were discussing a subject to do with sexual assault and my daughter came out with the most devastating news I ever wanted to hear. This news was something I thought I would ever hear, with regards to any of our children. The worst fear in my life.

She had been sexually assaulted.

Earlier on in the year, when we had attended my girlfriend Shez's wedding, my daughter had experienced a truly horrible experience. It happened whilst we were in Warrnambool and it was the beginning of our big trip with her earlier that year.

The following was my response in writing. It was to try and process what had now happened to my beautiful 14-year-old daughter. For obvious reasons and for the protection of my daughter, the male who raped my daughter will be referred to a Fred Smith. This name is fictional.

**My fourteen-year-old daughter was raped.**

*My little girl was only a baby, snuggled up with a girlfriend in bed, in an unused parents' retreat at my girlfriend's house. We had been to Shezzy's wedding ceremony and had a fabulous night with old friends. Then, we retreated back to the house at about 12.30am, on 4th March, 2018.*

*Another girl, who was the same age as my daughter and also attending the wedding, was the daughter of an incredibly old friend of mine and Shezzy's - Paula.*

*Paula was larger than life and a great deal of fun. You would only look at her and be rolling around on the floor laughing. We had been friends for a long time and, likewise, my daughter and her daughter were inseparable throughout the entire day and evening. They also decided to sleep together in the same bed for the night. We organised for them to stay in an upstairs parents' retreat that was a separate part of Nick and Shez's house.*

*The girls tucked themselves into bed and we all thought nothing of it. They were safe. Safety in numbers. A good parent's concern is always the safety of their child. I have always said to my children and David's daughter that if anyone ever makes you feel uncomfortable physically, you need to tell David or myself immediately. We will believe you. It doesn't matter who has done it to you. We will always believe you.*

*Fred Smith had been a guest at the wedding. Sherryn and Nick were, in a way, compelled to invite him because he had been working for Nick. He had also played in the band Nick had formed long ago with a group of friends. He was part of the crew. Sherryn was against him attending the wedding, but he was invited, because it was the right thing to do.*

*Fred Smith and his girlfriend at the time, had also stayed for a period of time in the retreat upstairs. During that time, Smith was trying to make his life a little easier and get set up financially. He eventually moved out into his own place of rental with his girlfriend. His girlfriend also had a young daughter.*

*There were always strange events surrounding Fred Smith. He had moved to Warrnambool from northwestern Victoria and left a previous relationship that included a daughter. Apparently, his leaving was under strange circumstances. He also had a history of drug abuse. His drugs of choice included hard drugs, such as marijuana and methamphetamines. He was also a big drinker. He was 35 years of age.*

*At around 3am, my daughter was woken to find Smith assaulting her. She told me later, she just froze and he eventually stopped and left the room. Nothing was ever said about it until about seven months later. I don't know why she finally spoke about it then but I was absolutely devastated and found myself at first saying, "What am I going to do?"*

*Because I had been sexually assaulted and eventually told my parents about it, I definitely knew the only thing to do. It was something my parents, very sadly, never did. And that was to go straight to the police.*

The day my daughter told us this had happened, I contacted her father. He was in shock as well. I told him I was taking matters to the police. He totally agreed with that as well. He ended up being very supportive of my actions.

He obviously didn't want to see nothing done about it. It had really tormented him about me when we were married, because he knew matters had never been dealt with by my parents. He also knew the effects on me, of not having any reaction to my horrible experience. And the flow-on effects that had seriously made my life so terrible.

David and I were also absolutely devastated. We both apologised to her, because this had happened on our guard. We also told her, we knew how awful that this experience must have been for her and we totally understood. I told my daughter that she wasn't going to school the next day. And that we were going to the police in Benalla.

Benalla is a larger town in Victoria, about 60 kilometres away. The town has a larger population and a larger police station. It is also where any sexual abuse statements are normally processed. There isn't this facility in Mansfield or the qualified personnel, as yet, for dealing with this sort of crime. However, you can request a qualified member to attend the Mansfield police station for an interview.

As you can imagine, she was incredibly nervous but managed to talk to a police officer. The officer said we would need to be referred to the SOCIT member in Benalla. We were told that the suitable person wasn't available on that day but he would be informed as soon as it was possible.

SOCIT stands for Sexual Offences and Child Abuse Investigative Team and is the child sexual abuse task force in the state of Victoria. The SOCIT task force member in Benalla was a lovely man and was incredibly helpful and compassionate about my daughter's circumstances. He organised to come to our house to interview my daughter. This was so it was a more relaxed way of getting her testimony. Especially for a child or teenager.

Between my daughter and the task force member, they produced an audio/visual interview, which would stand as a testimony. This testimony was live evidence that had enough standing in a court of law. This type of interview had been set up for minors in the Victorian judicial system. It meant that it was less confronting and the victim did not need to physically appear in court.

A court appearance was also something my daughter was really concerned about. Probably because I was currently involved with the royal commission case involving Dr Mackey and I had to physically attend a court. I am sure that she was so scared because she thought she might have to appear in a criminal court. This was also another reason she took so long to talk about it. She let us know this when she first told us. She only ever spoke to one other person about this and that was a friend of hers called Claire.

It now made a little sense to me why she had kept to herself a great deal on our trip in 2018. My poor daughter was probably suffering silently on her own and too frightened to speak up. It sounded all too familiar.

After our visit from the SOCIT member, all the investigative motions started to roll out. I had to do a police statement in Mansfield to explain how things had transpired around the time of the rape. I had to identify other witnesses for the SOCIT detective. People who attended the wedding and the party afterwards, who may have been of some help. I was asked to find names of people and their contact numbers who were witnesses. I was asked to find out other details that may help him put a in the strongest case to get a conviction. The task force was very determined to get this result. Incidentally, the man who interviewed my daughter, was sworn to secrecy by my daughter. I never knew exactly what had actually happened to her on that awful night.

Shez and her new husband were absolutely devastated too. Their entire new married life was tossed up in the air over it. We all started getting a bit of clinical psychology to deal with all those indigestible feelings. It totally ripped our hearts apart. Nick and Shez also had two young children and there was a concern for their daughter as well, because, of course, Smith had lived in their house for a while. David and I were also in turmoil with the entire experience, due to our own experiences. There were raw wounds opening up and bleeding once again.

# CHAPTER 22

## *FINDING MY PURPOSE*

We continued to live down at the shearing shed over the summer and we let our house out. I had enrolled my daughter at a private boarding school in Albury for her final three years of schooling, year 10 to HSC. I felt she now needed a bit more structure in her life. And I wasn't sure she would get that same structure in Mansfield at the local secondary college. She was happy to attend and become a full-time boarder. It also meant David and I could travel freely around the country and know all the kids were involved in a stable and, more importantly, safe environment.

In late February 2019, David and I were sitting up in bed in the caravan, and I received a text from a lady called Kate Parsons, inviting me to join her for coffee in Mansfield. At first, I was scared to even entertain the idea of meeting her.

I had reported to the Royal Commission into Institutional Child Abuse in 2015. Gone to a committal hearing and testified. That was totally enough. I had done my bit, and I wasn't about to go any further. My contribution was really all about letting people know about the abusive people out there and reaching out if they needed help. I really didn't think Kate would make a difference to me at all. So why did I need to meet her?

Kate was on the scene for the entire royal commission. She had testified and was involved with the Mackey case and others.

Friends had said to me, "Why don't you contact Kate. She is amazing. She is great and she is out there for Geelong Grammar School people." And survivors.

From the time I was at Geelong Grammar School and up until this time, the entire school thing was totally taboo in my mind. I didn't want to have a bar of anybody from there. Geelong Grammar School was a toxic place, and I had certainly experienced enough of that.

Kate was still working as a matron at the Timbertop campus. She had heard of me through the royal commission and decided to try and be of any help that she could in directing me to channels of healing and other relevant processes that Geelong Grammar School had put in place for survivors.

I was really quite nervous about meeting her. I probably associated her with the normal Geelong Grammar people. Meaning, she would be all about saving face for the school. And not unlike some other people in my life.

The meeting went incredibly well after my nervousness and concerns had faded. We hit it off so well. Neither of us drew breath, neither of us ate any food and guess what. We were born on the same day. Well, wow wee.

Kate and I spoke very freely about the information she had learned about Geelong Grammar staff that was exposed during the royal commission. There was an incredible amount of sexual and physical abuse that had occurred throughout the school in the seventies, eighties and nineties.

It is sickening to think I had been exposed to so many paedophiles in my schooling years. Sexual abusers that were music teachers, heads of day student houses, deputy heads of school, doctors, and school assistants. These occurred at predominantly three campuses. They were at Bostock house which became Highton, Corio and the Glamorgan campus in Toorak in Melbourne.

From the day I met with Kate I became so highly driven. I suddenly wanted to know everything about everything. I especially wanted to know everything that had happened at what is supposed to be one of the most elite schools in Australia.

## A PIECE OF WRITING

*A week ago, I met a wonderful lady. We were to meet for a coffee and have a chat. Instead, we had coffee, nothing to eat, five glasses of water each and two wees. I think I may have had four. There was mention of food, but the conversation just flowed, and we were still in the cafe until closing. Our conversation continued for quite some time out in the car park.*

*Since then, our conversation has been completely on my mind, and I am still shaking my head at what we discussed and how we both got incredibly mixed up in the entire scenario.*

*The scenario of case 32, Geelong Grammar School Royal Commission into Institutional Sexual Abuse.*

*Because of all of this, I have made completely different decisions about what I was doing in the near future. I have doubted people and changed plans that involved these people, because I no longer have any respect for them.*

*I am touching base with old friends but not going to discuss too much. Everything comes under the banner of just processing.*

*I have also touched base with a girl from school who has changed her entire identity. This change of name was as a result of events that took place whilst she was in her final year at Geelong Grammar School.*

*I now know and feel her pain because I have had it myself.*

*We are the victims of a silent crime, that has been hidden and swept under the table. Our stories would be taboo back in the seventies and eighties. The secret men's club was totally in charge and their women* wholeheartedly supported them, even if they knew what was going on. It was something you would sweep under the carpet and my mother would say, "Oh well darling, that happened to a lot of young girls and we just need to move on."

She never once asked what had happened when I refused to spend time with an old friend of the family. She just thought I didn't like him. Then, when I told her about another man that was close to the family, her excuse was, "We just thought you were silly teenage girls making a fuss."

Many girls became sexually active at school and needed oral contraceptives. In order to do this, they would have to see the school doctor. He would routinely give any girl who wanted to go the contraceptive pill, an internal examination.

Oh, fucking really. What for? For his kicks of course.

There is no medical reason for a doctor to give a girl an internal when prescribing the contraceptive pill. If an internal examination was necessary, I am sure it would be a gynaecologist performing the examination. On another note, there were never any records kept, of course, for these ridiculous examinations.

# CHAPTER 23

## *CASE 32*

After I had met Kate, I was driven to look into more about the Royal Commission into Institutional Abuse. I was working for a lovely lady in Mansfield and we would talk from time to time when I saw her at home. In conversation, we talked about my involvement in the Mackey case and she offered to print a copy of the royal commission report Case 32 for me. She kindly printed off two copies and set them up in a binder for me.

I used one of the copies to write notes in the margins and I saved the other copy for my parents and other people to read. Hopefully, my parents would read it one day. After all, it was all about their friends and associates.

What I began to read about Geelong Grammar School made me recognise the environment I was brought up in. It was wicked, evil, and completely perverted. I was entrapped in a vortex of sexual abusive horror at Geelong Grammar School.

As I avidly read my working copy, I scrawled and scribbled my thoughts all over it. There were at times, and completely understandable, where I experienced uncontrollable tears of anger. There were also tears of pain and frustration. Another thing that occurred at this time whilst I was reading, was an increased occurrence of panic attacks. I didn't even know what they were or what I was feeling when I had them. However, they had been extremely vivid in more recent times. I now realised I had been having these panic attacks for years. For well over 40 years.

Another thing going on at the time was, Kate and I decided we needed to have aliases for a while. We thought, because we were uncovering so much truth and also some new truths we became extremely paranoid.

Kate told me we needed to be careful about talking on the phone. That made things become even more scary. Were we being bugged on our phones? This paranoia was predominantly during the build up to the Mackey county court trial.

My name became Jodhpurs, and Kate's became Parsley. Meeting Kate started off the most amazing friendship that I could ever have imagined.

A little history on Kate.

Kate had been employed by Geelong Grammar School as the nurse at the Highton campus in the late eighties. Because of her involvement in the school, Kate had born witness to child sexual abuse in the junior boarding house at Highton. She had also recognised other abusive behaviour that occurred at other school campuses. Kate had become a key witness during the royal commission Case 32 hearings into institutional child abuse. She had been severely drilled throughout the royal commission hearings and had an enormous understanding of what had gone on in those darker than dark years at Geelong Grammar School.

Kate was still employed by the school and had a lot to do with survivors of this abuse. Kate was there to help. This included giving mountains of support, even in her own time. She was extremely helpful dealing with my experience with Dr Mackey. She also knew a lot of the stories about other Geelong Grammar School paedophiles. It was astonishing to hear all these horrific stories.

Our conversations sent me on a rampage of trying to find out as much information as possible, about what had happened to other students that attended Geelong Grammar School. I started getting in contact with parents of children who had lived at the school. I was asking questions about their knowledge of this abuse. One particular mother had gone directly to the headmaster at the time. She reported that she knew of sexual abuse going on in the school day house, Allen House, by its housemaster.

The headmaster John Lewis did nothing about it. He just fobbed it off. This, unfortunately, was how the abuse was dealt with. Sweeping it under the table, as if it had never happened.

Kate and I would discuss more of these horrible abuses on a regular basis and she would tell me more home truths, about some of the people at the school. There were stories of how some of the abuse simply struck off because offending teachers did the abusive things at weekends and that wasn't part of school hours. No accountability, according to the powers that be, at Geelong Grammar School.

I also heard that teachers were frequently moved on to other campuses and shuffled about so they could never be found out. I have read this is similar to what the church had done with some of its dirty priests.

I began to really detest Geelong Grammar School more than one could imagine. Hate is a better word. I felt ill thinking about what had happened to so many innocent, helpless children in that time. Everything really started to hurt, all over again.

Every time I heard something new, or read it in case 32, I would relive that guilt, shame, and fear. All these emotions I should never have had to experience. And clearly, it was still all about the flipping Geelong Grammar School image.

On top of that, being a schoolteacher's child, we had to behave and act appropriately, because we couldn't embarrass our parents. This was constantly drummed into us. It was always about how our parents looked in other people's eyes. Always looking their best, no matter what.

I spoke to so many people that never came forward. It was because they were so scared they would not be believed. Others that didn't come forward were frightened to be mocked by others. Some students that did come forward were shunned by the school and expelled. Their life as a student was made extremely difficult for them. So difficult they had to leave. It was always all about the Geelong Grammar School image.

Keeping up fucking appearances.

## ANOTHER WRITING

**Reading Case 32 date May 2019**

*Wow.......*

*Not really sure how I feel about my reading today. An incredibly inspirational, yet horrific, inciting look, at the detailed paedophile ring that existed in the seventies, eighties and nineties at good old Geelong Grammar School. How on earth could this have existed in such a 'by the book' school?*

*Maybe because His Royal Highness, King Charles the third, attended the school, that no one could ever slander or report on it. Or didn't dare to question the school employees. Or was it just the good old fucking men's club in action? Looking after their fetishes and their penises.*

*Well, they did just that and we still suffer. This was the best way for certain men to slip to the shadows and never be found out. Or should I say, never be reported. The most painfully and hurtful thing when I was reading, was that every day there was another instance where someone had their entire innocence ripped away from them. And sadly, because of immaturity and vulnerability, they had absolutely no idea.*

*There are more stories to be heard every time I ask a question. That is the most devastating part of it. There are still things today that are new to our ears. I am so anti Geelong Grammar. My father has been involved in the school since 1969 and I guess, myself and four other sisters, have been totally entwined in the paedophile cult. Yes, I think it almost became a cult. And because of my abuse, I was caught in the vortex of it.*

During 2019, it was also my 40-year reunion at Timbertop. It was during the royal commission court hearings involving Dr Mackey that we had our reunion. For the first time ever, I had offered to be part of the committee.

I had always had feelings of entrapment when we lived at Geelong Grammar School, Corio. And because I didn't want to feel trapped at any Geelong Grammar School campus, I wanted my husband David with me. I wanted to try and organise a slightly different reunion. One that was not specifically tied down to Timbertop for the entire weekend.

An extra excursion on the Saturday night was also discussed just for a slight variation. We talked about getting a bus out to Sheep Yard Flat in the Howqua Valley. We had camped there, while we were at Timbertop, on numerous occasions. We were going to have a big fire and just hang out with a few drinks and some music on the Saturday evening.

But everything to do with the reunion, seemed to be organised stringently for the weekend and it all revolved around the Timbertop campus. In my eyes, it felt like a Geelong Grammar School set up. A little outside the square would have been nicer. It would also have been an opportunity to have my partner's support. Something I very much needed at the time. David was always an amazing support for me.

Getting closer to the event, I contacted one of the reunion committee members and retracted my involvement and participation in the event. I just simply couldn't do it. I was also very scared about any potential confrontation. Most old Geelong Grammarians knew there was going to be a court case later in the year. Some people in my school year were connected quite strongly to the man that did the abusing and there were also a number of us involved in the court hearings and in the royal commission.

Remembering I had just read the royal commission report case 32, I was so scared of being pointed out and mentally bashed, especially by the mean girls. Yes, we had them in my year. There was also a particular mean girl that surely would have known the names of people involved in the Mackey trial.

Maybe I was gutless, but I thought I would end up resorting back to my good old buddy, alcohol. I would be triggered into getting absolutely plastered. Only to make a complete fucking fool of myself.

I also rang another Dr Mackey survivor and explained the same thing to her. She was also involved in the committee, but she was still going to attend. She was obviously feeling a lot stronger mentally than me, at the time. Incidentally, the mean girls did have a go at her at the reunion. In their own special bitchy way.

I had been informed by a friend, the new Geelong Grammar School female principal, in conjunction with the school, was beginning to compensate survivors. This was a bid to make amends for the past. On advice from Kate, I was referred to a legal company in Melbourne and rang them on the same day I found out about this compensation.

I continued to keep researching Case 32. I also continued to ask more questions. I contacted former house mistresses and had a lengthy conversation with one in particular. She was extremely helpful. There were also other girls in the school I could make contact with and see if they also had similar experiences. I also knew of a girl in my year who had commit suicide and I contacted her younger sister.

This woman's older sister, Kate, had been a brilliant young woman. She did her VCE twice, was a school captain and had exceptionally high marks in all the 10 or so subjects she had chosen. She eventually became a lawyer. Then, sadly, she just could not deal with her life anymore. She suicided at an incredibly early age.

I remember, that whilst we were in our Timbertop year, that she had been bullied about being a slut. I am sure now, and so was her sister, that her suicide would have possibly been connected to something that may have happened whilst she was a student at Geelong Grammar School.

Another person that came to mind, was a brilliant man named Hugh Crole. Hugh lived near us, when we first came to Australia, at Cameron Close. Hugh was brilliant in the arts. He was dux of Geelong Grammar School and the state of Victoria in his final year. Most incredibly and unusually, he was dux in the arts.

Hugh was always unsure about whether he was Arthur or Martha. Because of the sexual confusion that potentially can come from being abused, I have often wondered whether Hugh may have had an untoward experience at the school. Unfortunately, Hugh was so severely affected by his life, he drank himself to death.

Reading the royal commission case 32 made me want to know so much more. I kept thinking of some people's behaviour that had been similar to what I had experienced and questioned why.

# CHAPTER 24

## *HOUSE AND FARM SITTING*

In late April 2019, we sold our farm at Paps Lane in Maindample. From then onwards, we house sat for various people and moved around Victoria and southern NSW with our caravan. Our first extended stay was during the winter in Mansfield. We sat at a local horse-riding operator's farm.

This family travelled each year to El Questro, in the Western Australian Kimberley region and conducted trail rides, during the dry season. They were set to leave for the winter and asked us to look after their place and feed a few horses that were left behind. We stayed there until their return, later on in the year.

During these winter months, I was constantly supported by Kate Parsons. Unfortunately, everything became incredibly confronting, so I started seeing my clinical psychologist again. I was incredibly overreactive from everything I was learning about the school and Dr Mackey. Flashbacks of the incident were in my dreams and even during times of intimacy with my husband. I just kept seeing Mackey's face. As a result, I started drinking more and using alcohol to sleep and block out all the memories and emotions.

A person, by the name of Petrina, from Victims of Crime Assistance also started appearing on the scene. This was because I was due to go to court again in October. Petrina visited me at the house that we where we were housesitting. She had replaced Louise, whom I had been in court with for the committal hearing. Petrina was lovely. She was incredibly supportive and great to talk to. She would even ring every now and then, just to make sure I was okay. We are still in contact.

After David and I had spent the winter in Mansfield house-sitting, we decided to start looking for houses in the spring, in both NSW and Victoria. In August, we travelled over to Eden on the south coast of New South Wales to stay with my long-time friend, Robbie.

Whilst we were there, I received a call from another Mackey survivor. She rang to tell me she had been notified; she wasn't needed to testify in the upcoming trial. I was quite amazed by this because there were over 21 people who had now reported to the police.

To add to this, the Office of Public Prosecutions had engaged different lawyers and a different barrister to prosecute on behalf of us at the trial. Remembering I was always reassured by the detective from SANO, I would definitely be testifying.

Unexpectedly and within a few days of hearing from this other survivor, I received a phone call from the public prosecutor's office from one of the newly appointed lawyers. She informed me that, due to lack of evidence beyond reasonable doubt in my testimony and statement, I would not be required to testify either. I was, as you can imagine, absolutely devastated.

I contacted Pauline Ryan, the clinical psychologist who was helping survivors and we composed a letter to the Director of the Office of Public Prosecutions in Victoria.

Here is my correspondence:

*Dear Ms ______,*

*Yesterday, I received a call from Ms D and Ms R, regarding the upcoming criminal case against Dr David Mackey.*

*I was informed yesterday, (21/08/2019) that despite being subpoenaed to give evidence at the upcoming trial on October 7th, I would no longer be required to testify.*

*I gave evidence at the committal hearing in September 2018. I was also informed that at the time, I would be required to testify at the case this October 2019.*

*As you can imagine, I was astounded, to be informed that after two long years, living in the wake of legal proceedings, suddenly the evidence in my case is no longer strong enough to test at trial.*

*At the committal hearing in September 2018, I was informed I was the only complainant to have medical records of consultation with Dr Mackey. Ms D and Ms R also confirmed this in our conversation yesterday.*

*It seems, though, that Dr Mackey only chose to keep some records of his consultations.*

*Just to put this in some context. In 1980, I returned to the Corio campus at Geelong Grammar School from the Timbertop campus and, due to my unexpected loss of weight, my mother sent me to Dr David Mackey. My parents, who were also employed at Geelong Grammar School, knew Dr Mackey and his wife Sue. Dr Mackey had consulting rooms at the Geelong Grammar School Medical Centre and it was convenient for me to see him.*

*I recall seeing Dr Mackey on a few occasions in 1980. Incidentally, there are no medical records kept for these consultations. I am sure my mother would be willing to make a statement to the police, to confirm these consultations.*

*The reasons given to me yesterday, for not attending as a witness, was because Dr Mackey kept some records of my consultations and none of them correlated to the dates I had provided in my police statement. In fact, I was treated for a sebaceous cyst that was behind my ear in 1983 (records provided) and the assault in 1981 was during the treatment of an infection on my labia majora. (No records provided). Somehow, it seems this would be ammunition for the defence, as they may assume I wasn't aware of my anatomy.*

*My police statement also says, after Dr Mackey's assault, I never went to see him again. I did, however, for the cyst behind my ear but obviously had no memory of those occasions when he didn't assault me. I was, however, only a child, and we tend to remember only very unpleasant experiences.*

*I believe that my case is definitely worth reconsidering and if I need to provide further evidence that Dr Mackey didn't having good record keeping habits, I can provide evidence of the above-mentioned.*

*I would appreciate it if you were to review all my evidence, including my police statement and court transcript from the committal hearing and the only medical records provided in this case.*

*I hope that you will reinstate the charges relating to Dr Mackey assaulting me.*

*While I have no great wish to be a witness in this trial, I believe the police and the OPP would not have pursued these charges being paid, if they believed they weren't strong enough to obtain a conviction.*

*I would appreciate a written reply outlining your thoughts on this matter.*

*Yours sincerely*

*Joanna Herbert*


I did get a reply from the Director of Public Prosecutions QC. Her reply was, my testimony wasn't good enough evidence to prove beyond reasonable doubt. That response, to say the very least, was incredibly disappointing.

David and I did a few more house-sits in NSW and Victoria, so we could have a look around and see some more of our country. We also camped on the Murray River for a few days in the lead up to the trial.

I was extremely out of sorts at this time. Flashbacks were vivid and I was very stressed. There was one particular night during this crazy time, David found me in the early hours of the morning, waist deep, sleepwalking in the Murray River. It was a large river with strong currents and quite often had floating debris from surrounding fallen trees. Not really a safe river, even in broad day light. From then on, David locked the caravan door so I couldn't get it open.

The rejection from the Office of Public Prosecutions and the four-year long involvement in the royal commission was extremely stressful. And it was stressful enough to start me sleepwalking again.

We were doing a house sit in Cobram at the time of the county court hearing. Only four witnesses were called. One being Kate, who had witnessed Mackey's conduct. The other three survivors weren't known to me. The trial was over a few days. I had a running commentary on what was going on, from another Geelong Grammar School survivor.

Interestingly, Dr Mackey's children, now adults, all attended court. The youngest daughter, apparently, was always in tears whilst in court. Did she know the real truth about her father? The question may be hypothetical but it does make you wonder.

The court case didn't go how we all expected. It was a disaster, as well as incredibly frustrating. The case was thrown out by an older judge. Obviously, typically old school and he felt sorry for Mackey. Dr Mackey, at this stage, was in his mid-eighties.

Another possibility I have considered now is, Mackey may have been too feeble to be in prison, because of his age. Protecting an old, sexually abusive doctor may also have been over and above the funding in the state's prison system. At the time, the result was extremely disappointing.

# CHAPTER 25

## *THOUGHTS POST MACKEY TRIAL*

**GGS Court result November 2019**

*Today being 8th November. Wow, where has this year gone. Staying on the South Island of New Zealand in a community park at Cusp. Have had at least 10 days travelling this beautiful island and going home to Australia next week.*

*Court case has been dismissed, due to fucking medical rules in the seventies and eighties. Rules that protect, perverted old dirty doctor offenders. I am extremely emotional and feel it has all been very futile.*

*Is my father going to say the old bastard is innocent? He wasn't convicted, so he didn't do it. He had better not go there, ever. He will definitely lose me once and definitely for all.*

*School principal has sent a sorry. I know that she meant it.*

*Does this absorb the potential liable? Not in my case, not ever.*

*Very disheartening and very heart full feelings, to think that another man is sheltered by a gown or the cloth. What has our society ever done to make sure our children are safe from these predators and heinous people?*

*To think that this man rubbed his hands together at the thought of violating young, beautiful, healthy, innocent human children.*

We had a great time in New Zealand at the end of 2019, exploring the beautiful South Island, but had to get the above news whilst we were away and, of course, had to write about it.

A week or so later, we were in Wangaratta and house-sitting again. I was informed by a friend that Dr Mackey had appeared in court again. He had pleaded guilty to two rape charges at his clinic in Vilamanta street in Geelong. He was let go again with a $200,000 bond. He had also pleaded guilty to two other sexual assaults in his Geelong clinic in the eighties. That was, in total, pleading guilty to raping on four different occasions. All of the crimes were committed in a doctor's surgery during a medical consultation.

At least, he was going to be put on the sex offenders register for the remainder of his life. And, at least, he was labelled as a rapist. Even if he wasn't ever convicted of abusing all of us at Geelong Grammar School.

Mackey was a professional offender. It always made me think he knew how to work the system. The entire system. Geelong Grammar School's system, the medical system, and the judicial system. Mackey was a very smart person, and he knew just how to get away with abusing anyone who was vulnerable.

Another strange thing created at the time of his court hearings, was the Dr Brian David Mackey fighting fund. The Mackey family members and a few ex-Geelong Grammar School people started putting funds together to provide Mackey with money for legal representation in court.

All these people were in denial about what Mackey had done for over 30 years at Geelong Grammar School. And they were willing to help financially. He was also delivered meals by some of these ex-Geelong Grammar School people. Casseroles for comfort for the dirty doctor.

## GEELONG ADVERTISER HEADLINES

*CRIME AND COURT*

*Geelong Grammar School's former doctor David Mackey guilty of sex offending, but avoids jail term*

*Geelong Grammar School trusted him as its live-in doctor for almost 30 years, now David Brian Mackey will spend his final years as a registered sex offender.*

*Former Geelong Grammar Doctor David Mackey leaves court.*

## MY WRITINGS

*Today and yesterday have been both emancipating and crippling.*

*He is now a registered sexual predator. Big.*

*But on the other hand, "What's the big deal?"*

*What difference is it going to make to his life? Not a bit.*

*He has been doing this to us for over 50 years and only now, when he isn't practicing, there is a label.*

*I have to ask myself, "Where is our justice?" The life, our lives that have been taken away. Then there is the wretched guilt, the feeling of dirtiness, the where the fuck do I go to now?*

*Always soaking in filth.*

*It's like when you get raped. No shower, not even for an entire day, can get rid of that filth.*

*The same intense panic I had experienced after Mackey.*

*I just ran away and kept running.*

*The criminal justice system in Victoria has let us down. At this stage, Geelong Grammar School has let me down and my family have too, apart from my younger sister, Lisa. She has been with me the entire way and was actually the only person in my family to identify there was really something wrong.*

We spent Christmas in Mansfield and did the usual Herbert thing at my sister and her husbands' house for lunch. We were staying at my parents' house on their lawn in our caravan, so it was easy to catch up with them. We met with other people whilst we were in Mansfield because we knew we were going to be heading off on another trip.

I did not feel comfortable at all about staying at my parents, because I knew I was planning to have a mediation with Geelong Grammar School. The mediation to me really felt like I was taking my parents to court, not Geelong Grammar School. Maybe it was because they were simply Geelong Grammar School. That is how they turned out, after all these years.

There was one occasion vivid in my mind. An old friend of the family was stopping by to see my parents. Lisa and I thought we may catch up for a cup of tea with him as well.

This old friend was the youngest son in his family. Both of his parents were doctors. They were also our doctors when we lived at Geelong Grammar School, Highton. His mother was a general practitioner, and his father was the gynaecologist who looked after my mother. All their children had attended Geelong Grammar School. This old friend had attended Geelong Grammar School for all his school life and happened to be in the same class as one of Mackey's daughters.

Before I entered my parents' house, there had been a discussion with my parents about the Dr Mackey court case. He told my parents and Lisa he had spoken to Mackey's daughter on a couple of occasions. He had spoken about his support for her and for her family. Being the children of medical practitioners was something they had in common. Obviously, he would have had a discussion along the lines that her father was targeted only because he was a doctor and dealt with people's bodies. Nothing seen wrong there.

When I arrived, not much more about Mackey's daughter was said. The conversation had suitably and quickly turned to other subjects. The conversation gradually returned to subjects regarding Geelong Grammar School and then, the royal commission and some of its findings. At this stage, neither of my parents would have read case number 32 and would only have discussed things on hearsay or what had been reported in the news.

I don't even think I had the chance sip my tea before I simply could not stay there any longer. I said with a panicked tone, "I have got to go."

I got up from my chair, and I walked out the door in distress. Lisa was closely following behind. She knew exactly what was going on in my mind and how I was absolutely horrified about the conversation.

She then proceeded to tell me about the previous conversation my parents were discussing with this old friend. The conversation had stopped suddenly and the subject changed when I appeared at the door. On hearing this from Lisa, I just went into panic mode. I went over to our caravan. And then I really lost it. David asked me what had happened and I couldn't stop crying. My body was electric once again, with extreme panic and adrenaline.

# CHAPTER 26
## *PANIC ATTACK JANUARY 2020*

*Had a panic attack today*

*Totally had to get the hell out of here, couldn't breathe, cried, but then couldn't.*

*Wow, absolutely panic stricken.*

*Couldn't breathe, couldn't get my breath. Couldn't breathe. Just walk and breathe.*

*Totally exhausted afterwards and needed a nap. I was drained physically.*

*I can't believe we are here, at mum and dad's. It's claustrophobic but good to spend time.*

*Does that make any sense?*

*I had a panic attack and cried yesterday when David said we were coming here. Is that why I panicked today. No, it's all Geelong Grammar School still. An old friend was here and the topic was about families involved in litigation. Criminal, legal. I just fucking freaked. I left. Lisa knew and followed me out. She told me the conversation was surrounding Mackey and his family, between the friend and my parents. He was saying how he was supporting Mackey's daughter and as a doctor's son, he understood it could have been all wrong. Meaning Mackey had definitely been falsely accused of abusing children.*

*There was nothing right about what Mackey had done. He hadn't at all been falsely accused. He was guilty. It was just so completely wrong.*

*When I appeared at the door, the conversation was completely stopped. My parents were too gutless and are gutless. They can't speak up and say it had happened to me. Why, why, why????*

*My sister Lisa does know and does get it.*

*All I wanted to do is run away, run away. Just get out and escape. It is smothering me and I want to breathe.*

*I want to be here because I want to see my parents but I don't want to be here, because I can't stand the Geelong Grammar School thing. Fuck Geelong Grammar School.*

*I am unable to function with them, because everything is the fucking cult. Keeping up appearances and also, I was never good enough. Never got a degree. Just a waste.*

*Is that me, or is it them?*

*Any advice I give has to be backed up by someone who has a university degree. David and I are both patronised regularly. We aren't stupid but we always seem to be treated in such a way. Only because we don't have a university degree.*

*Anything medical I talk about, is always shunned. I feel like I need a university degree to be accepted by them. Oh really. Why does it need to be measured by a university? I just don't fucking get it.*

I was continuing with my case for mediation with Geelong Grammar School with Right Side Legal. David and I had applied for a position on a farm near Coffs Harbour in NSW. We would be looking after this farm for a least 10 months. David had also read that the climate in this part of Australia was almost ideal. We were also going to get a good feel for the area and perhaps start looking at real estate.

# CHAPTER 27

## *FARM SIT HORROR*

We left Mansfield, Victoria on 2nd January 2020 and headed slowly north to arrive in Raleigh in late January. We were supposed to be doing a change over with the farm couple for about a week and then they were to head off on their lap of Australia. It was going to be the trip of a lifetime for them. However, they had problem after problem after problem and finally left in early February 2020.

My Writings at the time of the farm sit horror. Interestingly scary people.

*It never ceases to amaze me that there is this thing about small men who always seem to want to have the punch up, talk me up and pick a fight wherever possible with me. It's as if their mother or father has said to them as a child, "Whatever you do, always remember that you are a big boy and be proud of it," even if you are a short shit. Be bossy, be knowledgeable and make sure you push all people around.*

*They are always the control freaks and no matter what, a woman is a threat. Especially if she is an intelligent woman. Most men find me a threat when they are of a lesser intelligence. They try to bully and if they don't have a solution, then they will try to patronise me. They just can't stand a woman being bright and right.*

*There is an enormous feeling of being mistrusted at this place. Now, even the old ute is getting locked away and put out of action. Every vehicle promised to us is now going to be out of use.*

*So, it's now another week. His car has done a head gasket. I will have done my head gasket by the time they go.*

*She is lovely, however. She just loves to give directions in complete depth. A very drawn-out process most of the time. I have simply learned to just switch off from her. It is easier to rely on the GPS.*

*This morning, there was yet another comment made about us not being out of bed. Oh really? It's just none of his business what time we get out of bed. Far out. And really, at this stage, we have nothing to get out of bed for. They are still here and, until they go, we really don't have anything to do.*

*The horrible little man has, what I like to call, the Chihuahua syndrome- small, male dog constantly biting the heels of other dogs, in order to gain control and/or attention.*

*Finally, on the last Thursday in January, they make another attempt to leave. He had been swearing at her and she had burst into tears. He has also carried on with so much irrelevant bullshit. This included washing the car and the caravan.*

*When they had made their first attempt to leave, we moved some of our stuff to the house, finally. We were just settling in when we heard the van return. They were back. The car has still got overheating problems. David put it down to being overloaded. I'm sure he is right as usual.*

*We move back with what we need, back up to the dungeon (caravan in shed) and spent the night on our own, having a few quiet beers.*

# MY DIARY

*Friday*

*Managed to go to Bunnings and buy some seedlings today. Exciting stuff.*

*Saturday*

*Went for my usual walk and then had a lovely afternoon in the garden planting seedlings and seeds, before the big rain comes next week.*

*Starting to get a bit of purpose back in my life.*

*It is 1st February and guess what. They are still here. And what's more, it is everyone else's fault. And they are now, not leaving for another day or two.*

*Thank goodness, I love spending my time in a dark, hot caravan with a few outings. Just love the life. Not.*

*Monday 3rd February 2020*

*Well, today was supposed to be round three for leaving. Ho hum. Had to go into Coffs Harbour to get the Telstra booster thing changed over. Said he would be back in an hour and came back six hours later. Then we had a massive storm and it wasn't until about 4.45pm he started packing again. Then, there was a possible bush fire away on the mountain and that was going to be his next excuse for staying yet another fucking night.*

*So then, Mr Small Important Man is on the phone telling people what to do. Then because he has no firefighting gear anyway, he wouldn't be able to do a thing.*

*And to add to all of that, there is at least a foot of green feed in the paddock. There is absolutely no wind. Can't really understand how a fire could spread in this instance. Also, it would have to burn down hill, which is not a normal thing. And to boot, we have just had an inch of rain.*

*It would be exactly three weeks now we have been here. And they are still here. Then, because the power has gone out in the storm, the*

We eventually moved into the house after their many attempts at trying to leave. David and I spent about two days setting things up to suit the way we liked to live.

They had left us with a revolting, stained mattress to sleep on. So that was changed. We used our own linen because it was nicer and then we virtually spring cleaned the house. It was absolutely filthy. My commercial vacuum cleaner was emptied five times. Most of the filth was from the two working dogs living like humans. We made sure we moved the dogs downstairs. They had insisted the working kelpies slept next to each side of the bed. The bed we were sleeping in. The dogs snored as well as farted most nights. That was definitely a big no no for us. They slept very happily downstairs in the laundry.

Now we were set up in a place for a while with internet etc, I decided, straight away, to start a degree in nutrition. I had all intentions of using my knowledge to consult and help people we met on the road. This would be useful when we were travelling again. One of the reasons I chose nutrition was because of my life of terrible eating patterns and malnutrition. We had also, in our travels, come into contact with the ageing public over health issues. I wanted to educate myself enough so I could do some dietary consulting. I wanted to include diet to fix some of these problems instead of medicine. Or do preventative consultations by introducing food as a medicine.

Another decision I made was to be alcohol free for a while. It made it easier to study and remember what I was studying. I had also been through a stressful five years and consumed too much alcohol. My body needed a well-earned break.

I didn't drink alcohol for a period that was well over 10 weeks. I even attended a wedding and didn't have a drop. That was the first time ever that I had been sober at a wedding in my adult life.

Studying also gave me a bit of purpose whilst we were at the farm. Aside from a bit of gardening and looking after two dogs, it was something to fill in my day. It also stretched the old brain cells a little.

During our stay, we were permitted the use of the old farm truck. Initially, we were going to use the Toyota Prado but when everything went wrong whilst they were still home, they took that vehicle instead. This meant I could get out and have a little independence, when needed. We also took it out on occasions for dinner a couple of times. I could drive it legally. Our Ford F250 required me to have a truck licence, and I didn't have one of those. So, the ute suited.

Things weren't as good as they were supposed to be while we did this farm sit. So much more had been promised to us in the beginning but then changed. The little man's word was never kept on a lot of things. He was a complete control freak.

There was another occasion, mentioned above, that we were going down to Victoria for a wedding and needed someone to fill in for just the weekend. He totally lost the plot about it initially but then begrudgingly asked his daughter to come down from Canberra. Everything worked out fine in the end, but he always had a tantrum when things weren't going his way or he didn't have control of the wheel.

On another occasion, when I mentioned I may need to go down to Victoria with David for another legal matter, he got shitty again. This visit would be for my mediation with Geelong Grammar School. David and I were always up front from the beginning. The thing was, he wanted to be in complete control the entire time.

When they were away, we kept in regular contact. They knew how well things were going whilst they were gone but there always seemed to be a reason for him to dictate and try and take control.

In the first few weeks we were there, I had been walking the dog, Georgie. She was a bit overweight and had arthritis. Georgie's weight was not helping her at all, so I put her on a diet. She was improving by the day and was thoroughly loving the exercise. At the end of our stay, I would be greeted, when I had her lead, with leaps and bounds.

We also decided to do the neighbourly thing and introduce ourselves to a few of the neighbours. The direct next-door neighbour was a lovely kiwi woman called Fiona. Fiona had also studied nutrition and gave me an old reference book she had kept. She was lovely to talk to. Her daughter, Ariel, flew home from London when COVID hit Europe and Britain. From there, we heard more stories of how they had been very badly treated by the little man.

The couple we were farm-sitting for were also leasing out their farm to a local dairy. The people from the dairy were lovely and very kind to us and we really didn't have much feedback from them. Probably because they were in a business agreement with the horrible little man at the farm. However, the previous people that owned the dairy, had quite a few things go missing. All thanks to the farm owners.

They stole things like medicine and other items from the previous dairy farm owners. His wife had also worked there. David and I came across a few things down on the property definitely from a dairy farm.

He was not only a thief, but vandalised other people's property.

One day when I was out walking, a neighbour pulled up beside me on the road for a chat. The first thing she asked was how did we get mixed up with these people, especially that man. This was the first time things had really started to fall into place with the little devil and his wife. He had used and abused, sued and ripped people off, from Kempsey to as far as Grafton in NSW. He had mistreated his neighbours and done horrible things. He had filled in neighbours' cattle grids with soil so his stock could run all over their place. He was just such a horrid, evil little man. David and I have never in our lives, met such a horrible person.

One thing I must mention is, one day in the shed before they left, he had said to David how much his wife was giving him the shits and how she was just a "c..t of a root."

David was absolutely mortified by this. I was too when he had told me. What person ever says that about a life partner?

During this time, as well as dealing with my mediation with Geelong Grammar School, I was also dealing with the SOCIT task forces person and the police in relation to the case against Fred Smith. There were quite a few more investigations being done. Another phone call I received was about a plea. During the call, I was asked whether or not I would accept a guilty plea in relation to my daughter's abuse. It was whether I would accept a guilty plea for a child over the age of 16. She was only 14 at the time. This would mean a better and shorter sentence for Smith. I had no trouble at all in saying, "No flipping way."

In March 2020, COVID-19 hit Australian shores. We were happy where we were and settled into a great routine by now. Both dogs were well cared for and the garden was healthy and producing fruit and vegetables. I was enjoying my nutrition course and doing really well. We were really starting to enjoy our farm sit.

# CHAPTER 28
## *COVID HITS*

With COVID-19, the entire country started to go absolutely bonkers. There was talk of the country closing its international borders. And then, they started talking about closing the Australian state borders. It was a crazy time and really quite unbelievable.

Then, one day in March, we were informed by the dairy farmers down the road, the little man was going to return home to the farm as soon as possible. Interestingly, to begin with, he wasn't going to tell us when he was returning. Maybe to catch us on something we weren't doing right.

Later, he had called us and mentioned the Western Australian border was going to be closed and he didn't want to get stuck over there. We later found out the real truth. The little man had an enormous fallout with some of the other people they were travelling with and completely spat the dummy. Apparently, he had upset the other people he was travelling with, so much so, he had no choice but to return home. They probably didn't want to be with him, more to the point.

We were expecting them to arrive at the farm in a few days and really didn't want to be there anymore. This was because of the way we'd seen people treated and how he had been treating us. They offered for us to stay as long as we liked after they returned but we didn't really want to.

We organised a friend of theirs to come and stay with the dogs and just tidied up and got out of there as soon as we could. Incidentally, the friend actually apologised to me for what had been going on. She knew him oh too well.

We moved into the caravan park in Coffs Harbour for a few days because we were waiting on a part for the car. I really felt like we were running for our lives. We were always looking over our shoulder, because the little man became very nasty and threatening when he heard we had left.

He had also gone to the trouble of bad mouthing us to Farm Sitters Australia with a bunch of lies. David had tried to call him, but he was too cowardly to reply. We sorted out things with Farm Sitters Australia, and they understood exactly what our plight had been. They knew the sort of person we had been dealing with.

When we had received the car part, we were waiting for in Coffs Harbour, we headed down to Nambucca Heads. A town slightly south of Coffs Harbour. I said to David, I really didn't want to go back to Victoria, mainly because it was too cold. It was then we looked up a place we could stay at whilst the entire country went into lockdown.

Because of the COVID pandemic, my mediation case in Melbourne was also brought to a screaming halt. It had been discussed regularly throughout our time staying at Raleigh. Dates and further court action were also discussed with my lawyers. Part of these discussions also included the school asking me to help them with the idea of countersuing Mackey. This was because, there was a lot of money to that was going to be paid out to his survivors. A compensation to cover his disgraceful actions over the years. As you can imagine, I was more than keen to help with that.

We had booked our flights for the mediation but, unfortunately, they were lost because of COVID. Australian airline, Tiger Airways, did not survive COVID-19 either.

Because we wanted to stay in the north, David had chosen a place we could go. It was about 40 kilometres from Grafton. It was on the Clarence River in a large paddock and was called Lilydale Campground. We could stay isolated from people and because we were homeless, we were allowed to stay there whilst the entire country isolated.

My favourite river in Australia was the Clarence, and we couldn't have been in a better place.

## MY FIRST THOUGHTS AT LILYDALE CAMPGROUND

*What an extraordinarily beautiful place. We are forced to camp somewhere whilst the world goes mad in isolation, hiding from the Coronavirus, Covid-19.*

*We have been here now for two weeks and have found a lovely spot on the Clarence River, about 100 metres from the closest homeless people.*

*By saying homeless, I am not talking about destitute but definitely of no fixed address. We are all supposed to be self-contained (toileting wise) and are allowed to camp here as long as we need to.*

*We have a lovely young couple parked next to us, who have come from a farm and they are beautifully educating their two young children. Not only school but life and nature. Their days are spent going fishing, building gardens, digging for worms and playing soccer. They have built a makeshift pitch with wood and rocks at each end for the goals. No nets, of course. Beautiful people and amazing children. Worldly skills at the age of three and five years old.*

*Their immediate neighbours are Veronica (Ronnie) and Catherine. I know Catherine was a nurse. She told me when she fell over last weekend. I attended to her wound before she went into the emergency department at Grafton. David and I performed good old bush medical practice and cleaned her up and made her comfortable before she headed into the hospital.*

*Ronnie is quite an interesting character. I don't know if you remember a Mrs Jessop from the Sullivans years ago? Well, that's Ronnie. Very gossipy. Always in for a chat, very hard to peel yourself away. Most of the conversation is about a knee reconstruction (hers), Hashimoto's disease and emptying some urine from her pee bucket, to keep pests off her vegetables. She also told me putting urine on vegetables would feed them. Not a very intellectually moving conversation really. She did also happen to mention, the other day, we were all working class people. That, I found very amusing.*

*Then, there is another couple up on the hill, who we have met once. He actually mows his part of the paddock. She has kept to herself but was the one who carted Catherine into the hospital the other day. He seemed quite pleasant. Also very Aussie.*

*Then, up on the other rise, we have the Rocky Horror Show. Another very strange couple.*

*David and I headed into Copmanhurst, a small town with a general store and post office, a week ago to get some milk and organise our mail. Before we left, we headed around the community, asking everyone if they needed anything whilst we were in town. David went to one lot and I visited another and we met in the middle. The last couple we came across were very different. Bob and I'm not sure of her, or should I say his, name?*

*I really had to do a double take for a moment. In fact, I actually tilted my sunglasses, to have another look. She/he was definitely very hard in the face, with high masculine cheek bones, absolutely no breasts and with visible bones, yes ribs. Legs were like tent pegs and stuck out from under the dress this person was wearing. Just like a male completely lacking in testosterone. Quite a different being.*

*Bob is an older man, who seems to have worked hard, drunk hard and likes to do everything hard. He has both nipples pierced with sleepers and when he has clothes on, it's mainly shorts and a singlet.*

*Bob also has a habit of getting his pierced nipples out, every time the sun shines. Not really attractive but he probably thinks it is. Strange things seem to happen with The Rocky Horror Show living in our campground.*

*Last night, we were just keeping to ourselves, as usual. I was fishing and David was by the fire. We both heard the sound of someone running along the track above our place and, sure enough, Bob's partner was dashing around. He or she had run down through the middle of our camp, squatted by the river and then moved on quickly. Bob's partner made David believe he or she was going to jump in the water then took off again and was gone in only a matter of moments. Harmless to us but very strange all the same.*

*Today, when I had returned from my walk, I passed Ronnie's camp and said hello. Bob and partner were there too. I moved on quickly without anything more than a hello. I called in to see Mitch and Angela for a chat and Mitch then told me Bob's partner was a transvestite.*

*What do you call them? Male or female. I knew they existed and I knew the person in the dress was a man but what do you call them. Him or her? We nearly always manage to be surrounded by interesting characters. Some are boring, some strange and some completely painful. And some, completely out there.*

*Anyway, life is interesting and it's so lovely here. We couldn't be in a better space, just doing what we love and also being with each other.*

*The Corona virus really has had no big impact on us. We would be doing this anyway.*

*We will be living here for a bit longer than expected but I am sure we will manage.*


Apart from the above observations, Lilydale was a lovely time for us. David built a jetty made from scrap wood, that we found in the old mill up the road. Days were spent gardening and trying not to get my fishing rod tangled. Most days, there were no fish and plenty of tangles. It kept David busy anyway.

We, like everyone in Australia, started trying to improve our houses and gardens etc. In our case, it was our caravan. Because we were about 40 minutes in the car away from Grafton and trying to keep to ourselves, we started a vegetable garden. We lived from the produce after about a month and always had fresh vegetables. We also rigged up a fresh water supply to fill our tanks from the caravan awning when it rained. This meant we didn't have to buy drinking water. We also caught water for showering when there was a really good down pour. When it wasn't raining and we had run out of water, we would go into Copmanhurst and fill the 200-litre bladder in the back of the car. It was all about being as self-sufficient as possible. Living a simple life really.

I had great places to walk, as well as having absolutely everything we needed in the caravan. We had bought a Telstra booster, so we had good internet, and I could keep up with my study. I was really enjoying my course, and it was a good distraction from the upcoming mediation.

*Vegetable garden on the Clarence river during COVID lockdown*

# CHAPTER 29

## *MEDIATION AND VICTIM IMPACT STATEMENT*

I was in regular contact with my lawyers and we had a date set to do the mediation with Geelong Grammar School. Then that date fell through, once again because of COVID.

At this time, things were incredibly emotional for me. There were deep feelings of abandonment, even deeper feelings of guilt. I had quite a few panic attack walks during this time. I spent a great deal of time on the phone, mostly with people who were supportive of me and also other survivors who were going to mediation with Geelong Grammar School. I was trying to find new survivors as well, so we could open the criminal case up again. It was extremely disappointing that Mackey got off completely scot-free from his Geelong Grammar School career. A career of molesting and sexually assaulting children.

Another thing that kept me busy was reaching out to other survivors. I had told my neighbour, Angela, about my case impending and she asked me if I could be of help to her niece. This was also something I intended to do when this was all over. I had plenty of friends who had been abused and wanted to try and help them to repair and heal from that dark part of their childhoods. Get some sort of redress and, more importantly, some reparation.

With a mediation of this sort, there were discussions of compensation in partnership with a formal apology. This then led me to have further thoughts. Just how much is my life worth in monetary terms? How can someone put a figure on the pain and emotional abuse I have put on my body as a consequence of another's action? How can anyone pay me back for what happened as a child? Also, considering this has been 40 plus years of absolute confusion and self-abuse. The lack of income from being emotionally debilitated. For a while, I found it quite insulting to think of any monetary figure. I could never get the chance to live it over again. I would have loved my life so much, if I could have done it differently. And things would have been so different!

Money is no replacement at all for the loss of anyone's life.

Getting back to the reality of things, prior to mediation, we had a few tasks to fulfil. With my lawyers, we drew up my victim impact statement. The statement I was going to read out at my mediation hearing.

A victim impact statement is incredibly important in this scenario and can dictate the figure you are potentially entitled to. It is a recollection of either your pain, lack of progress as a human being in reaching your goals and an interpretation of how your life has turned out because of the historical events. It is an incredibly emotional soul-searching exercise. Unfortunately, you may still not always be able to find that soul.

My victim impact statement brought me to tears. Even when I was just reading it out to David, on the day prior to my mediation.

## MY VICTIM IMPACT STATEMENT

*My father accepted a position of employment as a teacher at Geelong Grammar School in 1969. Who would have thought his decision would have such an enormous impact on me, one of his five daughters?*

*He continued to live and work at the school until 1997. He held* teaching positions, was a junior headmaster at Bostock House and later GGS Highton and finished his career at Corio as the administrator.

It was the ultimate dream fulfilled. Introduced to a close net community, with all the lurks and perks to go with it. A schoolhouse with power and phone included and reduced school fees for each of his children.

The exciting prospect of a life, full of immense friendships, opportunities, and an incredible education benefit for his children. Also, a social standing of respect that he would retain for his entire life.

My parents had an enormous circle of friends, generated by, not only the school community, but an incredible and always expanding network which even extended overseas.

This was Geelong Grammar School. It was considered an elite school and a school for the elite. The Prince of Wales, now our King, had attended Timbertop, which was always a good conversation starter.

However, amongst the school, and its highly decorated employees, there was a dark side that existed. A group of men that had preferences for children. They all had good credentials and came highly recommended. There was one man, in particular, who changed the direction of my life. He was a trusted and respected member of the school staff and had the position of school general practitioner. He was a former school head prefect and was trusted and respected by most of the school community. He was given unsupervised access to children and, under the guise of performing medical treatments, was allowed to do whatever he wanted to them.

Nothing was done to supervise him or chaperone the students to make sure he wasn't abusing that power, even though, everyone had heard the rumour that, no matter what was wrong with you— even if you had a sore finger, he would make you take your clothes off. Everyone knew what he did: unnecessary internal examinations, playing with students' genitals. He felt safe to do this, because he was safe to do it. In places like Geelong Grammar School, where reputation and hierarchy were protected at all costs, the students knew who would be believed and whose reputation would be protected. Who could I have complained to, given that a lot of the staff at Geelong Grammar School knew about the other paedophiles on staff? Nothing was being done at the time, about it.

Because of my parents' work and involvement in the school, there was also no escape from the reminders of the abuse. I couldn't get out of that horrible place and away from the horrible predators lurking there. They were part of the school community and my parents even socialised with them.

While my parents and sisters thrived at Geelong Grammar School, I grew distant from them. I couldn't explain to them why this place had been so good to all of them and was poisonous for me. It's still a source of enormous sadness and distance between me and my parents, that we can't see eye to eye about the school.

I had been assaulted by a family friend as a child and my experience with Mackey made me think that this was just my lot in life. Was this how it was going to be? The stress of what had happened at school made me constantly ill, from about the age of 15. I caught every flu going around. I have battled an eating disorder for most of my life, trying to control and punish my body. I have lost most of my teeth because of this. I've abused drugs and alcohol for most of my life, to try and wash away my feelings of dirtiness and uselessness.

I did poorly at school and watched my sisters, who had the same genetic background and opportunities as me, go off to interesting and challenging careers. I got into teachers' college and was even given a second chance to make it work but couldn't – I made a bad decision and left.

I felt so worthless and low that I made a lot of bad decisions. I made bad relationship choices, I developed alcohol and drug dependence and the consequences of all of those just confirmed the ideas I had, that I was worthless, useless and unsuccessful.

*I still felt trapped by Geelong Grammar School. I wanted the success the school had taught us would deliver happiness and fulfilment. I even got married at Timbertop, as if that would give me the acceptance and approval and success I craved.*

*I have three wonderful children who have been deeply affected by my alcohol abuse and Post Traumatic Stress Disorder.*

*I hope the school is different today but I still couldn't bring myself to send my children there. It was like a cult in the eighties where the safety of children like me, was sacrificed to save face.*

*It has taken me years to get the confidence up to just talk and associate with so many people in my year. I have always looked at myself as a loser. And I thought they all did too. It wasn't until the royal commission that I could start to relate to any of my peers. I was and am so against my experience at Geelong Grammar School.*

*I am still very much in need of a clinical psychologist. My first psychiatric help was at 20 years old and that was 35 years ago.*

*It was only one step to where I am now. Living in silence or denial for so many years has taken an enormous toll on my life. I wish I could just be who I was supposed to be but I have realised it is too hard to work on my own. I am a smart and capable woman but I have to fight all the time against the feelings of worthlessness that make me want to self-sabotage.*

*I am now finally on the right path with my career. A little late at 54. I still live the event at 15 years old as if it were yesterday. I am still having days of tears and feelings of not wanting to live anymore. This has been a life sentence. I just wish it would go away.*

*I know that it never will.*

In order to prepare for my mediation with Geelong Grammar School, my lawyers needed to include a few other relevant reports. These included a former employers report and one from my clinical psychologists.

The employers report was a questionnaire from a former Target colleague which would review my loss of potential income after resigning from the company prematurely. There was no need to include this questionnaire.

My clinical psychologist's report is as follows.

**TREATING CLINICIAN'S REPORT**

**Re: Ms Joanna Herbert DOB: 16/09/1965, Your Ref: MM:TB:190285**

As Ms Joanna Herbert's treating psychologist, I write to provide an outline of assessment information, treatment history and clinical opinion, as per your request (dated 25th September, 2019). Please note that the information I have available to me was collected solely for the purposes of providing psychological treatment, as outlined below.

**1. How long have you been Ms Herbert's treating psychologist for, and how frequently does Ms Herbert see you?**

Ms Herbert was originally referred to me under a GP Mental Health Treatment Plan, prepared by her General Practitioner, Dr Daniela Friday, on the 16th May 2013. This plan cited binge drinking and eating as the primary triggers of the referral, and requested psychological therapy to "develop strategies to deal with events that remind her of previous misfortunes". I first saw Ms Herbert on the 24th May 2013, and I have seen her on 13 occasions since. Ms Herbert attended an initial course of treatment comprising five sessions in 2013, and she later re-engaged in 2017.

While she attends infrequently, dependent on travel and life events, she has maintained her engagement since.

**2. Please identify the condition/s you treat Ms Herbert for, including a brief summary of the symptoms.**

I have been treating Ms Herbert for symptoms of Post-

Traumatic Stress Disorder, with associated Alcohol Use Disorder and recurrent (although infrequent) binge eating behaviour.

Note that she has a history of alcohol and cannabis misuse, and she suffered severe Anorexia and Bulimia Nervosa from the age of 15 years old until her early-30s.

During our time together, Ms Herbert has reported experiencing recurrent, distressing memories of two sexual assaults in particular: the first perpetrated against her at eleven years of age by a friend of the family, the second perpetrated against her by Geelong Grammar School doctor, David Mackey, in 1981. Ms Herbert found these memories utterly repulsive, and she went to great lengths to avoid their emergence, including by misusing alcohol to suppress memories and to soothe associated emotional distress. At initial contact, Ms Herbert's self-esteem was brittle, and she was frequently tearful and emotionally distressed. Her sleep was often poor, and she would have nightmares of the sexual assaults. Ms Herbert engaged in self-destructive behaviours, including binge-drinking and less frequently binge-eating, and she was often interpersonally reactive and irritable with her partner.

I have found Ms Herbert to be a motivated and insightful client, who has worked hard to reduce the impact of her symptoms on her day-to-day functioning. Using trauma-focussed cognitive behavioural strategies during our sessions, we have been able to identify and promote healthier alternatives to food and alcohol as tools to suppress memories and ease distress (e.g., exercise, relaxation, journaling, social support), and she is now better able to turn to these strategies when feeling vulnerable. We have also addressed Ms Herbert's memories of traumatic events from her past, allowing her to better identify the emotions and distorted beliefs tied to these events. In doing so, Ms Herbert has been better able to come to terms with these events, and as a consequence, she has had periods of being less preoccupied with them. That said, the recent Royal Commission and court cases involving David Mackey have been utterly destabilising for Ms Herbert, exacerbating symptoms in recent years.

**3. In your view, did the sexual abuse while at Geelong Grammar cause or contribute to Ms Herbert's illness or condition?**

It is my opinion that the sexual abuse perpetrated by David Mackey at Geelong Grammar School had a significant contribution to Ms Herbert's condition. Although Ms Herbert had been sexually abused prior to the assault at Geelong Grammar School, and this event alone could give rise to chronic mental health problems, it is my opinion that aspects of the GGS assault were particularly deleterious in terms of Ms Herbert's mental health and her potential for recovery.

Ms Herbert's father was a teacher at the school, and the family resided on campus throughout Ms Herbert's schooling. Not only was she surrounded by reminders of her assault, thereby amplifying her distress, Ms Herbert felt unable to report what had occurred for fear of jeopardising her family's position within the school. She was also keenly aware that her parents were friends with the Mackeys, and that her disclosure would surely cause pain and conflict for her parents on a social front. Indeed, these circumstances prevented Ms Herbert from receiving timely therapeutic intervention following the assault, and they acted as triggers to memories of the assault throughout her entire adult life.

**4. Please describe how Ms Herbert has been and is affected by the illness or condition, including her symptoms, and the impact on her work, within her family, and on her social relationships.**

The impact of Ms Herbert's trauma history has been wide-ranging. Her sense of self and capacity to regulate emotions and behaviour were significantly compromised, and this has prevented her from achieving personal goals and forming healthy and protective relationships.

Indeed, throughout her adulthood, Ms Herbert was drawn to work that was less personally demanding of her, and she prioritised relationships that allowed for her avoidance of negative emotions (e.g., those that permitted substance abuse). She also ultimately withdrew in her relationships with her family of origin, primarily because she could not expose herself to their positive recollections of GGS, as this was far too triggering.

**5. In your opinion, is it likely that the abuse by Mackey, and Ms Herbert's reaction to that abuse, have led to lower career achievements and earnings than would otherwise have been the case?**

Although Ms Herbert impresses as having above average intellectual capacity, she has not been able to capitalise on her natural aptitude in terms of career success. Indeed, in the absence of trauma, Ms Herbert appears to have had the capacity to pursue a career as a health professional, an area that has been of interest for quite some time (e.g., Ms Herbert completed a short course in sports dietetics in 2013). Of course, David Mackey's abuse of Ms Herbert occurred at a critical time in her education, and gave rise to prolonged mental health problems that would have compromised her overall performance in her secondary school studies. This not only affected her options with respect to tertiary studies, but more profoundly, it affected her self- belief. Furthermore, as noted above, as a result of her trauma history Ms Herbert's capacity to regulate both her emotions and behaviour was compromised, and this affected goal-directed behaviour and resilience. Her attempts to ease her distress via a range of compulsive behaviours also interfered with these areas.

## 6. Please provide your assessment of Ms Herbert's likely prognosis.

As noted above, Ms Herbert is a motivated and engaged client. She is receptive to feedback, and she practises various psychological strategies between sessions. I suspect that she will evidence residual post-traumatic symptoms for much of her life (e.g., a vulnerability to anxiousness and broader psychological distress; intrusive memories when triggered in some way), but that she will work hard to limit their impact.

## 7. Please provide recommendations as to Ms Herbert's future treatment, if any, and the duration and cost of such treatment.

I would recommend that Ms Herbert have access to five to six sessions with a clinical psychologist per year for the next five years. If she were to attend my service, the cost of this treatment would approximate $5,000.00. I also note that the research literature points to a vulnerability to chronic physical illness in survivors of childhood abuse, and ideally, Ms Herbert would be supported in engaging with preventive medical care as well (e.g., regular medical review, allied health and screening initiatives).

Please don't hesitate to contact me if you would like to discuss her circumstances further.

Kind Regards,

Dr Kate McSweeney

BA (Psych.) (Hons.) DPsych (Clinical) MAPS

Clinical Psychologist

# A LITTLE INFORMATION ON PTSD

Post Traumatic Stress Disorder is associated with altered activity and structure in the Amygdala and Hippocampus in the brain.

The Amygdala is responsible for processing emotions like fear, and aggression and also contributes to memory, social cognition and decision making. It acts as a central hub for emotional response and links emotions to other brain functions like memory and learning. With PTSD, the Amygdala tends to be highly overactive. This disruption to the amygdala can cause anxiety and over heightened emotions. Panic attacks were my main symptom.

The Hippocampus is primarily involved in learning and memory. It is involved in the formation of new long term memories and spatial navigation. It plays a crucial role in converting short term memories into long term memories and also retrieves those memories when needed. PTSD causes the hippocampus to become smaller and less active.

These changes contribute to the characteristic symptoms of PTSD, such as heightened fear responses, intrusive memories and difficulty with memory and emotional regulation.

People with PTSD frequently experience nightmares, which are often vivid and distressing re-enactments of the traumatic event. These nightmares are capable of disrupting sleep and contribute to the overall impact of PTSD.

I have included this in my story so that it gives people a better understanding of how this has directed my life and also to understand the physiological changes that occur in the brain with Post Traumatic Stress Disorder.

Around this time, I was in contact a lot with Kate Parsons, still discussing the royal commission and my upcoming mediation. On 2nd April 2020, Grace, my lawyer, telephoned to say my mediation had been put off once again due to COVID. I was incredibly upset and felt let down once again by Geelong Grammar School.

Within a couple of days and, after talking to Kate, my mediation was back on again. Kate had contacted the school and facilitated a new date of mediation. She had told them I was extremely vulnerable and anxious about my mediation and the sooner it occurred, the sooner I would find some sort of closure.

On 20th April 2020, Grace contacted me to prepare me for my mediation the following morning and to tell me about her game plan. I knew, prior to this, Geelong Grammar School had a ballpark figure they were going to offer a Mackey survivor. I felt this to be quite unreasonable because everyone's case was different. We talked over how the mediation would pan out and when I would read my survivor's letter and, the above victim impact statement. Grace also explained how the process would continue from there.

I'm not quite sure how I slept that night. Most likely with a mixture of nervousness, flashback dreams and mixed emotions and thoughts about what I was really worth. How can you give anyone back all those lost years of hurt, missed opportunities, guilt, lowering confidence and lost time trying to block it all out? What was the right monetary figure?

The morning came. I was the first of Dr Mackey's victims to have mediation with the school. When I think about it now, it was extraordinarily strange. I was sitting in the middle of a cow paddock, in a caravan, with an iPad set up to take a conference call. That call that would potentially begin to change my life. It was quite unusual to say the least.

My mediation was the first ever with the school to be held on zoom. This was the new world of COVID. Grace said she had never done this before either. She said this was very strange for her, because she would normally have been able to support a client in person. I think it was a first for all of us. We were all the first COVID mediation experiment.

There were formal introductions and then the legal jargon began. It was very strange meeting people on an iPad. I tried not to fidget out of nervousness and concentrate on what was going on. It was then time to read my letter of survival and from the first few words, I started to well up with tears. Then a few deep breaths and I was in control again until the last part. The part where I had said I was worthless and useless.

The mediation made me feel for the first time ever, that I was appreciated by someone at Geelong Grammar School. I was also apologised to by the school. They apologised for their lack of knowledge and also the actions of what went on, all those years ago. And on top of that, they were going to compensate me. Try and give me back some of my lost life. It made me feel like a human being again. An appreciated human being. Someone had finally said sorry to me for my stolen childhood and life. They believed me! And I willingly accepted their apology.

That was how my mediation transpired. Following the zoom call, my lawyer and I talked through some figures. The rest of the day was spent waiting. and Grace apparently went back to the school on a number of occasions. That evening everything seemed to be all settled.

To celebrate, David and I drank a bottle of Verve Cliquot champagne. I had put a post on Facebook saying I had had an educationally beneficial day. I was studying at the time, after all, and only people who knew what had happened during the day, would my gist.

The following day and quite unexpectedly, my lawyer contacted me with an even better offer from the school, which I happily accepted. Within a day or so, I was contacted by the Geelong Grammar School legal consultant. She asked me if I would be interested in having a conference with a member of the school council, who was also a leading women's psychiatrist at the Royal Women's Hospital. The psychiatrist was extremely interested to hear about how a resident child coped with living in an institution like Geelong Grammar School. The current school principal had a young daughter and was very concerned about potential scenarios etc. We had another zoom meeting and I spoke to her for about an hour.

I started to get the fantastic feeling that I was being needed by the school and needed by other people. This also started to make me feel like I was appreciated. It was the best feeling I had felt about Geelong Grammar School in over 40 years. They wanted me to help them. They wanted me to work out how to deal with this horrible time. They wanted to include me to help other victims become survivors. They gave me an incredible purpose, which I will now have for the rest of my life.

*Celebrating my mediation with GGS on the Clarence River during COVID lockdown*

Since then, I have made personal contact with the school principal. I also have regular phone meetings, regarding the school's handling of past and future potential abuse. We talk about helping survivors heal and potential policies to be put in place to prevent child assault.

I have had a couple of survivors contact me for advice on the civil and criminal sides. I have also suggested a confidential and private reporting program to be put in place. Stymie, a confidential reporting scheme, has been introduced on my recommendation to be implemented, so children and students have someone to go to, to report any sort of abnormal behaviour. Totally confidential.

I also believe, on my recommendation, that is now being used at the Mansfield Secondary College. I made mention of it to Lisa, who worked as an assistant teacher. Lisa made the school aware of the scheme as well. The day my mediation was settled, I rang Kate Eggers. Kate had set me on a life changing challenge and I told her Geelong Grammar School had apologised to me and compensated me for my appalling treatment. Finally, for what had happened and they totally recognised the impact it had on my entire life, from living at the school. I couldn't thank her enough. It had been a long journey but incredibly worthwhile, emotionally.

# CHAPTER 30

## *WRITING THE DPP*

After my mediation with Geelong Grammar School, my life improved so much. I began to have the feeling I was finally worth something. I started helping others regularly with similar experiences and learning more of how the different systems worked in the country to help people. I wanted to put in to practice everything that I knew, and to help those who really needed it.

I was still bitterly disappointed about the Mackey result. I would also, from time to time, come across people in denial of how he abused us, the way he did. Then there was also the denial by his own family. All of this denial, when it came to actions he clearly performed at Geelong Grammar School, was questionable. This especially when considered that he pleaded guilty to two other rape charges. These first two cases Mackey was let off a prison sentence because his wife was very ill and he was her carer.

With final two rape charges that occurred in his clinic after he had left the school, he pleaded guilty and received a slap on the hand, because he was too old to go to prison. He was also put on a good behaviour bond and registered on the sexual predators' list for the remainder of his life. Not really any sort of punishment for all of the damage he had done.

In the Geelong Grammar School case, we were mentally and emotionally paralysed from the case being kicked out of court. Apparently, the judge at the County Court was old school and people who attended said he was typical old school man that would look to protect someone like Mackey. His entire Geelong Grammar School chapter of sexual abuse was written straight out of a sexual predator's book.

After the Mackey trial ceased, I wrote a letter pleading for a retrial. It was devastating to have our case thrown out of the courts. It was excruciatingly painful for every one of us. He did do what we said he did. He totally got away with it. As a survivor, you have no idea how horrible it was. After all those years, all our never ending pain was all in vain.

This result prompted me to contact, once again, the Director of Public Prosecutions office:

*I am absolutely crippled, when it comes to an historical case, uprooted by the Royal Commission into Institutional Child Abuse.*

*This case involved a general practitioner, at the highly regarded Geelong Grammar School who, in his role as a resident doctor, violated and sexually abused children.*

*I, amongst another 21 individuals, have been involved in this case. I know this, because the defence barrister tried to suggest we colluded but this was the first time I knew about other victims.*

*I believe there are another three people who have come forward since the Royal Commission and even more since our case got thrown out of court. So, that is an excess of 24 people and I am sure there will be more.*

*I reported to the Royal Commission in June 2015 and I made my statement to the police in January 2018.*

*Our case was heard at a committal hearing in Geelong in 2018. The committal hearing was staggered over a couple of months beginning in August.*

*My testimony was on 6th September 2018. It was an incredibly confronting experience but worth it as it then proceeded to the County Court in October 2019 in Melbourne.*

*I was served with notice in July 2019 and was told by police and the barrister involved, in the committal hearing, that I would definitely be called into the court to testify. The barrister for the committal hearing was Kimberley Swadisir. The detective in charge from SANO also told me, due to my being the only complainant with any medical records, I would have to appear in court again.*

*This team was an incredibly dedicated group and I was confident we would finally be heard and the outcome would be everything we needed to hear. The truth and justice served.*

*In August 2019, I was informed by a lawyer from the OPP, that I wouldn't be needed, as my testimony wouldn't be enough to prove beyond reasonable doubt. I was absolutely mortified. I also believe that of the 21 people who testified at the committal hearing, only three were going to be heard.*

*I sent you a letter regarding my concerns and was informed that, because the prosecution may not be able to produce a result from my testimony beyond reasonable doubt, I wouldn't be required.*

*Please tell me, if 21 people said this man did this, does no one believe us? It was nearly 40 years ago. Why would we make this up? Part of the defence's idea in the committal hearing was, it was a conspiracy theory and we all had colluded.*

*I only knew of two other people that were assaulted by Mackey, out of the entire 21. One of which I heard out about when I was cross examined at the committal hearing.*

*Dr David Brian Mackey was at Geelong Grammar school for 31 years and the complainants span this time and both girls and boys were violated.*

*The hearing in the County Court in relation to our case, involved* only three students who had been assaulted, with no medical records at all and a matron/ nurse, who worked at the school for a long time.

After about 10 days the jury was dismissed and the judge asked the defence and the OPP to present their cases. The judge ultimately made the decision to throw the case out. We were all terribly upset about this result and felt let down, once again.

It was so extremely distressing to find out that two weeks later, he pleaded guilty to raping two people at his clinic in Geelong. He was sentenced with a $200,000 two-year bond and his name was permanently placed on the Sexual Predators register.

Why was our case so hard to prove? What is the problem? What is the problem with our judicial system? Why are we looking after horrible old men with sexual obsessions towards helpless, defenceless human beings, including children? Why is it that any decision made would have to rely on historical cases concerning doctors? And how hard is it to prove that he was examining us in an unacceptable medical fashion?

If 21 people, who hardly knew each other, make the same complaint, doesn't that mean, that it is our word against his? I would understand it if there were only four of us and we were best friends, but some of us hadn't even heard of each other.

There were no chaperones because he didn't want them and we didn't know if we had a choice to have one or not. We trusted a man who was a doctor. A doctor who was under an oath "Heal Not Harm". He did internal examinations every chance he could. He even invited one of the two males involved to have a consultation with him. In other words, he groomed and selected one of them, seemingly an easy target. The harm this man has done was totally inconceivable and he will never be found to be guilty of his crimes at the school.

I was also the only child, out of 21 people, that this man managed to keep medical records for. Of course, he wasn't going to keep records when he assaulted children. Why would anyone keep a record of a sexual crime? He never kept records of the two times he assaulted me. One of which, he implicated I was a little slut by asking me if I was still screwing around with the boys in the bushes, and the other was stimulation of my clitoris for a considerable amount of time, when I went to him with an abscess on the outside of my labia majora.

My mother sent me to him for an eating disorder and he was asked to help me psychologically. Instead, he intimidated me with smutty remarks.

I am sure my mother would testify that she sent me to him in desperation, because I was suffering with my eating disorder. Unknowingly and entirely trusting Dr Mackey, who was a close family friend. My mother actually sent me to a sexual predator.

Please note, he was also convicted, after pleading guilty of two rape charges in 2013, and was excused from serving any time, as his wife was ill with cancer and multiple sclerosis. He was her primary carer. The rapes occurred at his Young Peoples clinic in Geelong. The conditions of the rape were very similar to experiences we encountered in his medical centre at school.

If you had a sore finger or toe, you were asked to take your clothes off. One appointment, I have been told, was for a sore toe and he took the opportunity to rape her. He apparently dismissed her as a slut from Leopold and he just wanted to get it over with and look after his dying wife. He pleaded guilty for this reason.

I understand this is not typical of a letter you would ordinarily receive, but I do think there are 21 people that have been let down by the judicial system. And I am most definitely sure this isn't the first time a man has walked free but was guilty. And he is still out there. And with his record, he will still leave a trail of collateral damage.

Looking forward to your response.

Yours sincerely

Joanna Herbert

I did receive a response from the DPP but the case was never going to be opened up again.

# CHAPTER 31

## *MY LETTER RESPONDING TO DPP ON MY PLEA FOR A RETRIAL*

*Dear SANO detective,*

*Just a quick note to thank you for all your support during the arduous Mackey case versus Geelong Grammar School's students. You have been extremely informative and very supportive throughout the entire process. It is an enormous emotional and mentally tangling experience going through what we have gone through and your help has been consistent all the way.*

*These last few days have been like living the entire nightmare all over again. My first reaction to being dropped from the case, was similar to the loneliness and abandonment that occurred in the eighties. Is it that we can't be believed enough. That was always the way I felt then. And then to finally be able to have a say and make a difference for future students at Geelong Grammar School and other institutions is very mind and soul building. Only to have the entire stability ripped away again.*

*I know my evidence is strong. I am very aware of what happened. I live it every day. I see the window and the smirk on that horrible man's face knowing he has hit the right spot. I too, am completely frustrated that a person can come in and play God again. Who decides that we have been incredibly damaged and hurt? We do. Why can't we all testify? Who has the right to say that this didn't happen? That is exactly what it feels like. We are nothing. We don't have the final say.*

*I remember being in a state of panic and just running when I got out of there. Then there were the dreams for years of not being able to get away. Being trapped and not being able to move. I still feel trapped in that time. This is what it is like for a child. You just freeze. And maybe you hope it will all go away.*

*11/09/2019*

*I guess you received my email from the DPP.*

*Now that I have no say at all in the conviction of Mackey, I guess I will, like everyone else who has participated and not been included, just keep on processing it in our own way as the unheard victims. It is a shame we have all had to struggle through two years of waiting to be heard. And now we are silent again.*

*It is by no fault of the police and the task force that this has occurred. I have gained a great deal of strength in myself and totally understand it is as frustrating and upsetting to you, as it is to all of us.*

*Thank you so much for helping me through this journey and being as supportive as you could possibly be. You have personalised things to help me and you are an absolute credit to the police and the task force.*

*Hope to catch up with you one day in Melbourne.*

*Cheers Jo Herbert*

*(Miss shoulder pads and big fringe 80's girl.)*

The detective and I became great phone friends. She was an eighties girl and we would quite often have a great old chat on the phone besides talking about the Dirty Doctor.

It is amazing to have such great experience in our Victorian police force.

# POST MEDIATION THOUGHTS AND WRITINGS

*It's truly an amazing thing when you get to a place in your life when you all of a sudden you stop beating yourself up. What happened there?*

*I told David last night, I finally like the person that is within my skin. I am so happy being me. It is still very hard to accept the praise and acknowledgment. I have been told recently, I am truly an amazing person. I am constantly told how beautiful I am. What is with that?*

*In the last few years being with David in the outback has been incredibly emotional. I have cried. I have actually sobbed listening to music and then I feel absolutely elated and calm.*

*What the flip does this all mean?*

*Two years ago, I was really still hammering the grog. I was going to a live music situation, botting a cigarette and totally singing to my heart's content. Way out of tune. What head space was I in? Totally out of control.*

*I have also said, I haven't had the urge to write with panic recently. But instead, it's with passion. It's so systemically settling. I am not angry or aggressive or basically pissed off anymore.*

*Why does it take so long to get to this special space?*

# CHAPTER 32

## *REFLECTIONS ON GEELONG GRAMMAR SCHOOL*

These are some of my thoughts about Geelong Grammar School growing up as a child and how truly things worked when I lived there.

My parents' socialising was always done with either other teachers and families or families who had children attending the school. My parents made many friends over the years, and Geelong Grammar School became their home and their entirely comprehensive life network.

Another especially important feature to my parents was the fact the school paid for nearly everything when it came to existing. My parents paid highly discounted school fees, no rent, no power, and no phone. My father was also involved in enrolling students from overseas. On trips to other countries the school also paid all the bills for travel, meals, and accommodation. It was a very extravagant life that my parents could probably have not otherwise had.

We were told regularly that we had the most wonderful place to live. We were constantly reminded that it was totally about our wonderful education and we should relish in it. Apparently, all my sisters did, except for me.

My parents could also afford to buy a house of their own as a holiday house because they only ever had that mortgage. The fringe benefits were immense. I think there was a retirement fund of some description.

Anything to jeopardise these living conditions was always instilled in us as a veto and taboo. As children we also knew, we had to be seen and definitely not heard. Even if there was something terribly wrong. We definitely could not jeopardise their financial or their employment situation.

Mackey was a trusted and respected member of the school staff and had the position of school general practitioner. He was a former school head prefect and was respected by most of the school community. It would seem, there would be no one who could fill this position any better. And who would ever doubt or question a doctor's conduct? The ethos for a doctor is supposedly, to heal, not harm.

Because we were children, if we said anything, it was always fobbed off. Hormones were always blamed. Or we were silly little teenage girls. Any inkling of sexual abuse was always scrapped by these excuses. It was always brushed off and never, ever taken seriously.

Mackey had everything planned. The nurse at Kennedy, Carol Mallet, was so in love with him, he could do no wrong. Therefore, there was never any need for a chaperone. So, it was open slather for the Dirty Doctor.

With every opportunity, girls and boys were asked to take their clothes off. He would fondle boys' testicles and say he was cupping their balls. Every girl that went in for contraception, he would give them an internal examination. In addition, he would tweak their clitoris and help identify it for them. Young girls could not say anything about his abusive manner. More than likely the most stand out reason was because they were frightened, he would tell their parents they were sexually active and needed contraception. You could say it was a case of emotional and physical blackmail. Mackey was absolutely having the most fabulous time of his life. And we were all so sexually dispensable.

# CHAPTER 33

## *DEALING WITH SEXUAL ABUSE*

People have said to me, you just need to leave this all behind. What they don't seem to understand is, you can't leave it behind. It is totally with you for life. It is something you have to learn to try and deal with and find happiness in yourself.

Child sexual abuse, or any abuse, never leaves you. And it haunts you for ever. No matter what we do to block it out, like drinking copious amounts of alcohol, or drugs, or taking sleeping tablets etc, you still wake up the next day and it's there. The memory is like a raw and opened wound. The same emotional wound that was there the day before.

It could be said we have been scarred for life and we don't heal completely. It is a scar, and it is always there. Sometimes it fades, but mostly, it is still there.

Even if you wanted to leave it behind, you can't. Nearly every week you dream. Nearly every week you have a flashback and nearly every week you are haunted. Certain events that happen can trigger those memories. It's being able to deal with those memories and treat yourself. I see that is the only solution. But it doesn't necessarily stop it happening

So next time you think about saying to somebody get over it or it's about the future now, just remember the people who have been abused as children have suffered some sort of post-traumatic stress disorder and it is not just a matter of getting over it. It is going to be present in the rest of their life.

271

# CHAPTER 34

## *THE OLD MAN'S CLUB*

The old man's club is an informal system in which wealthy men with similar social or educational background help each other in business or in personal matters. In other words, it is the toxic masculinity that was and probably still is, extremely present in some Australian boys' private schools. The same toxicity also rolled into boys' private schools that went coeducational.

Geelong Grammar School had this toxic culture too. Not only amongst the male school students but also amongst the male teaching staff, not to mention the male medical staff.

More incidents of this were revealed during the Royal Commission into Institutional Abuse. Incorporating, of course, case 32, which was our own Geelong Grammar School's volume of abusive horror.

Some of the men who were heads of school were even involved. But because they came under the umbrella of the Old Men's Club, they were never detected or dealt with. Incidences that were reported also had a blind eye turned on them.

A certain headmaster was known to have not involved police in some of these sexual offences because he thought he could deal with it himself. The man is quoted as using the beyond reasonable doubt line, when it came to hearing about some of the abuse. That to me is, very arrogantly, putting oneself above the law. There were many letters of complaint by parents about this abusive behaviour. They were simply ignored and filed. Or just destroyed.

Other school campus headmasters were also known to have covered up sexual abuse in the junior schools at Geelong Grammar School, including the Highton and Glamorgan campuses.

This toxic Old Man's Club behaviour was also amongst male students. The two boys that digitally raped me, did so because they felt entitled.

I contacted a girl from school recently, because I had noticed that she too, wasn't attending Geelong Grammar School reunions. I was inquisitive because this girl was extremely popular at school in our year group. I wondered if something sinister might had happened to her.

We chatted about a few things, and she told me she had an eating disorder post her school years. This intrigued me more and I did ask the question about abuse. I explained what had happened to me. She was shocked and, after a few expletives, she told me she had experienced a couple of uncomfortable appointments with Mackey. We all know about those uncomfortable experiences.

She did, however, say she also found physical contact was very confusing with boys at the school. Her words were, that her major issue was with the totally entitled and horrible boys, especially in our year group. She said she was still astounded by their entitlement to say and do anything to women or girls at school. She had let it happen because she thought this was normal.

There is that normal behaviour mentality again and not knowing, as a girl at Geelong Grammar School, what normal behaviour was. Yet another alliance to the old men's club.

It was extremely hard to come to terms with this particular story because I did believe this woman was sexually abused by Mackey. She just didn't know the difference at the time between normal practice and sexual abuse in a medical clinic. Let's face it, none of us knew. In hindsight, feeling uncomfortable in a medical appointment sounds a lot like sexual abuse to me.

Because of the old men's club, we were also silenced. In saying that, we didn't complain because firstly, we thought it was normal and, secondly, who would hear us or believe us anyway? It was also as if, this was a Geelong Grammar Schools male's entitlement.

Other upsetting incidents that happened at the school campuses was the sexual harassment of female staff members. This was also not reported or acted on because of the Club. They were just mere women and allocated a second rate title.

One of the worst cases of all, was the conviction of my school housemaster, Johnathon Harvey. The man did his time in jail for sexually abusing boys at Geelong Grammar School. But when he was retiring a year early, he was given a monetary golden handshake by the headmaster at the time. A full year's salary. Another toxic old men's club gesture.

It was totally horrific what happened to all of us at such an elite school. It was also hideous, in the way that it was shadowed over by the headmasters of that time. And that old men's club was Geelong Grammar School's protective shadow.

# CHAPTER 35

## *MORE FUEL TO THE FIRE*

Amidst the COVID lockdown, existence at Lilydale campground and my Geelong Grammar School mediation, there was also the criminal case for the conviction of the rape of my daughter in 2018.

Just like adding some more fuel to the fire, this was always on my mind. Understandably, I was still trying to come to terms with what had happened to her. Aside from the communication with lawyers, police and bouncing off and rejecting ridiculous pleas, I was also keen to get my daughter some mental help by means of counselling. Counselling that I never had, until Lisa instigated those meetings with Elizabeth. And, in my case, because it was far too late, a great deal of damage had already been done.

I was always totally committed to the idea that my daughter had psychological help from the very beginning. From the very first moment she had told me about it, we started making plans for counselling. I really did not want the horrific experience to fester any more than it already had.

The man from SOCIT had told me about how I could get some help through the Victorian government. He also introduced us to a group, known as Victims of Crime Assistance Tribunal. Abbreviated to VOCAT. This organisation in Melbourne was established by legislation, to provide financial assistance to victims of violent crime, committed in Victoria. The financial assistance was to be used for any mental health issues. In addition, it also processed claims for crimes compensation.

There were other organisations available, and I had already mentioned engaging the lady, Petrina, from Victim's Support Services. My daughter had met with Petrina when we were house sitting in Wangaratta, in December 2019. Petrina was a great back stop for her if she needed support to appear in a court situation.

My daughter was boarding at a private school in NSW, doing her Year 11. I had spoken to the school about what had happened to her in 2018. From there, I entrusted the school boarding nurse, Elsa, with my daughter's care. Because we were living a long way away and because we were in the midst of the continuing COVID chaos, Elsa was the perfect choice.

Elsa was just like a mum for my daughter. The mum, while I couldn't be there physically. We were in conversation regularly. Apart from normal physical health, this also included her mental health. I was very keen for her not to have the immense ocean of problems I have had to suffer with.

I was recommended a counsellor who was registered with VOCAT. She was based in the same town, and she also had children attending the same school my daughter attended. My daughter started seeing this woman, prior to, during and post the criminal court hearing.

Just like my mediation with Geelong Grammar School, we did a zoom call for the committal hearing for Fred Smith. Another court appearance, set up in the caravan, in the paddock at Lilydale campground.

David and I sat in on the court hearing from our end, Elsa and my daughter were in a private room in the school boarding house and the actual courtroom setting was in Warrnambool. Shez and Nick also sat in via zoom because they were witnesses.

It was extremely painful for both David and me to watch. Just the memory of what had happened. Not to mention, my daughter having to go through the one thing she was scared about doing from the start. A criminal court case.

David and I cried quietly together during the hearing, in our caravan. The worst thing about it all was Smith's face was constantly being focused on by the camera. I would hate to have thought about how my daughter was feeling. From my own experience, whenever I saw a photo or face of a predator, I started visually flashing back to that time. And she would have been flashing back constantly to the horrible incident throughout the entire proceedings.

Another thing that was extremely difficult for me was, I could not physically be there in person for my daughter. I wanted to be there to hold her hand and cuddle her. COVID, unfortunately, had destroyed all that contact.

There was one thing we who attended the court remembered vividly, and that was the judge's words. His exclamation was, "How outrageous!!!".

The judge was referring to the act that had been committed by Smith. Outrageous, for a 35-year-old man to premeditate and then do what was carefully planned and then brag about to someone. He knew exactly what he was going to do to my 14-year-old daughter.

After the back and forth with trying to get a better sentence through a lesser plea, which happened during our awful farm sit, Smith eventually pleaded guilty to what he had done. On closing the case for the day, we were informed there would be a sentencing court appearance in the not-too-distant future.

I spoke to the lawyer who had been involved in my daughter's case that evening and thanked him for the result. We had spoken about maximum penalties etc and he informed me; the sentence would still be a few years in jail before any parole. The guilty plea, of course, lessens the jail term slightly.

On 11th of June, we zoomed into the sentencing hearing. We were all there on our iPads once again, because of COVID. After the usual formalities, Smith was sentenced to five years in prison, for the digital rape of a child under the age of 16. Smith was eligible for parole after three years of serving his sentence.

I was advised at the time, to make sure I was on the victims register, so I would be aware of Smith's release from prison. This would enable us to take measures, so my daughter would always be safe and hopefully never found by him. Another thing that was extremely comforting and supportive was the communication that circulated amongst everyone involved in the court hearing and policing. The lawyer wrote to us separately hoping the result was good for us. There were letters and phone calls of thanks.

We were extremely lucky to have such a fantastic system in this country, to help victims and survivors of sexual abuse.

# CHAPTER 36

## *TRAVELLING ON FROM LILYDALE*

In the last few weeks we were at Lilydale, I had made many new ties with legal people associated with Geelong Grammar School and with my civil lawyers in Melbourne. I spoke to an amazing legal representative for Geelong Grammar School who, incidentally, was the coordinator at my mediation. During some our discussions, I had said I would be very interested in helping survivors at Geelong Grammar School and help the school with any enquiries they may have.

We had some very funny phone calls after my mediation. The legal representative had an incredible sense of humour and was also very endearing. She was also very much on my radar because we had talked about David's experience with the priest. I was then informed by her, she had been involved in setting up the redress scheme in Victoria with regards to the Anglican Church. She knew where I needed go to from there and how to get in touch with the right people.

She put me in touch with a fabulous guy. His name was Trevor, and he was a New Zealander. Trevor was fantastic from the start and, apart from also being very entertaining, he knew his stuff, and we started to work on a result for David. Not specifically a monetary outcome, however, that was discussed. We discussed an apology. The same sort of result I had experienced with Geelong Grammar School. Actually, the result could be described as more like a life-changing experience. I was so grateful to the new age Geelong Grammar School for that. I really wanted David to have that incredible experience as well. Like with any survivor, it is essential to facilitate a more normal life.

Trevor helped me to guide David with his victim impact statement and then helped me to go through the entire application process. He was brilliant. He too, was an incredibly sympathetic person. It really amazed me how many of these fantastic people were around for sufferers or survivors of sexual abuse. Pity it wasn't dealt in the same way all those years ago.

Most of our correspondence was done via email and phone calls while we were still at Lilydale campground. However, it wasn't until we were further north in Queensland, that David managed to do his statement.

We left Lilydale in July 2020, heading into Queensland, the day before the border opened. We said our goodbyes to Angela and Mitch and their two lovely boys. We had a few hours to travel before we got to the Queensland border, and it was raining.

Before we left, entertaining the fact that we had Victorian number plates, we decided we needed to prove where we had been and where we had lived during the first lockdown. We printed out all our bank statements from late March and highlighted all our purchases in Grafton. It was really about proving we hadn't been in Victoria since COVID began. Or had not escaped during a lockdown. Victoria was pretty much a no go place to anyone north of the NSW border. At that time, Victorians were under a lot of pressure with restrictions, because of the pandemic. You could have easily made the broad statement that every Victorian in the rest of Australia's eyes, was diseased.

We sailed to the Queensland border after having a very average meal of chicken nuggets from McDonald's. It was the only place open on the highway, and it was getting late. We also were not familiar at all with the newer layout of Ballina, so we decided to stay on the main highway.

When we eventually reached the border, we were directed into a lane to be processed. We simply produced our highlighted statements. The policeman was lovely and really more interested in the van and our travel plans at the time. That, of course, was after seeing our highlighted bank statements.

We chose to go across the Queensland border on the evening prior to the border opening, because we knew there would be a long queue. We were absolutely spot on with that assumption. Apparently, there was a queue for nine kilometres the following day. We didn't have to sit behind a single vehicle. We drove to Brisbane and stayed at a campground in Beenleigh.

The visit to Brisbane was to have a new lithium battery system fitted and solar panels put on our caravan roof. At the same time, we installed an adjustable mattress bed.

Incidentally on this visit, we were going to stay with an old friend from Target Geelong but that was knocked on the head because of COVID. My ignorant friend thought we would be carrying COVID because we were Victorians. The country's reaction to COVID put a great deal of silly thoughts into some people's heads.

After our caravan was nicely upgraded, we headed towards Far North Queensland. We decided to visit some old ground on our way up. We returned to the Bowen River Hotel, inland from Bowen and stayed at a place called Terrible Creek. It was actually a beautiful spot on a cattle farm and situated on the river. We revisited Brisk Bay for a few days and looked around where we had done some work for Helene and her family.

Our next stop was Balgal Beach which is about an hour's drive from Townsville. We caught up with another old friend, Rhonda, from Target Geelong and stayed at the local golf club. We even had a special reserved spot because Rhonda was a member and she also worked at the golf club.

It was here that David did his Victims Impact Statement. This was one of my writings about the day David wrote out his statement.

*It is 2nd September 2020. We are in the midst of COVID-19 in Australia. David and I are in far North Queensland and staying at Balgal Beach at the Mystic Sands Golf Club. We chose this place to stay because I wanted to catch up with a former Target colleague, Rhonda Earl. We were also looking at property around this area.*

*We started off this morning as usual and I set off for my walk, in need of a good stomp on the beach. I listened to music instead of talking on the phone because it was too windy. I was a little cranky this morning and needed some JoJo time.*

*I sang to my heart's content, all my favourite songs and removed all the shitty emotions and brought out the endorphins. What a great way to spend over an hour and cover over nine kilometres. I also walked along the beach and that always puts me somewhere else.*

*When I strolled in, David had mentioned he wanted me to read something and said for me to eat my breakfast before I looked at it.*

*Before I could do anything, I received an untimely phone call from the legal representative at Geelong Grammar School who was nearly in tears. In gratitude for all her help, David and I had sent her a present. She had just received our hamper from Bill's Farm.*

*Bill's farm is a delicatessen in the Victoria Market in Melbourne. Our good friends own it, and I had organised a gift to be delivered to her at home. What an amazing and deserving woman. She had bent over backwards to help us in any way she could with everything legal. She deserved it and I told her I was absolutely chuffed with her response.*

*After my phone call finished, I sat down at the bench and started to read the letter David had composed and wanted me to read.*

# CHAPTER 37

## *DAVID'S LIFE STORY AND VICTIM IMPACT STATEMENT*

*To whom it may concern*

*My name is David Payne. I was born 6th March 1950. I have two sisters and a brother. My father attended school at Beechworth, before graduating as dux, at Dookie Agricultural College. My mother finished her education at a boarding college in Wangaratta.*

*My parents married after my father finished serving in 1946. I was raised on my parents' farm, near the small country town of Bonnie Doon. My parents were very strict and were very respected members of a close-knit community. I was born the third child and had a younger sister and an older brother and sister.*

*Most of our social time as a family was spent attending church. Being on a farm, it was really the only day we would congregate with other people. We were all expected to attend every week and did so. My parents weren't close friends with Canon R.J. Brown but held him in high regard because he was the local priest.*

*In the summer of 1959/1960, both my parents were attending tennis practice at Brankeet, not far from Bonnie Doon. Whilst they were practicing, my brother and I decided to climb a large pine tree* adjacent to the courts, just near the entrance gates. We were told to get down immediately or else. So, in hurrying down, I stepped on a rotten limb and crashed down, hitting my leg on the entrance gate, which resulted in a broken femur.

I spent the next three months, lying in traction, in the Mansfield district hospital. I was still there on my 10th birthday. Once stabilised, I became more comfortable and was very well supported by my mother, who never missed a day visiting my bedside.

I am unable to recall whether my parents organised it but was having regular visits from our local Anglican minister, Canon Robert John Brown. Because my parents were regular church attendees, I thought his visits were normal.

After several visits, he became very familiar with me and asked one day if he could take a look at my right leg. In traction, my right leg was in a cradle but covered by a split sheet as the lower half of my leg was open and supported by ropes, with a weight out over the end of the bed frame.

Because of my situation in traction, I was unable to move at all. I was completely bedridden for the entire hospital stay. Because I was in a peak growing time, it was paramount I didn't get out of bed or move. I literally couldn't move anyway.

I remember being very uncomfortable about this because I couldn't wear any underwear or pyjamas. On looking, he made a 'hmmm' sound and then commented on my penis. Then continued on making that 'hmmm' sound. After a few more visits, one day he grabbed my left hand and put it on his penis, then continued making that 'hmmm' sound again.

This then became a regular occurrence. And no one could see what was going on. This was because each time he came to visit, he would make the nurses pull the screens around my bed for privacy, so no one could see what he was doing. I am sure the nurses didn't have any idea *about his intentions and thought he was visiting for religious reasons. As he was a respected man in the community, it was never questioned.*

*He never prayed for me and his visits, in hindsight, were purely grooming me and testing trust with my mother and staff at the hospital, before he began sexually abusing me.*

*I knew this wasn't right but, being so young, I was so frightened to say anything and I also knew no one, especially my parents or my siblings, would believe me. I am not sure of the exact amount of times that he abused me but he visited me weekly during my three month stay in the hospital. His visits were like an eternity. I didn't see him visit any other children whilst I was there.*

*Once I was released from the hospital and was ready to attend school again, I became so worried that if anyone found out what had happened to me, I would be the laughing stock and the subject of harassment and ridicule from my peers. In fact, I left school as soon as I could start work, so no one would ever find out. It was incredibly difficult to deal with, even on a day-to-day basis after I left the hospital.*

*What if someone found out? It had to be my secret and no one was ever to know. I knew if anyone did find out, I would be ridiculed constantly and called all sorts of horrible names.*

*On another occasion, one day during primary school, after a couple of months, I was beckoned over to the minister's house. His house was in the church grounds (as the resident priest at the time, Brown occupied the house). The house and churchyard were next to the primary school playground, where we were playing.*

*He asked me inside his house and, once inside, he made me take my pants off, lifted up his black robe and pushed his engorged penis up against me. I panicked, pulled up my pants and ran back to the school yard. I believe if I hadn't reacted the way I did, he would have definitely tried to penetrate me.*

*I made sure I never played in that area again, which my friends* couldn't understand, because that was where we always kicked the football. Ever since, I have been so closed and always kept to myself.

Later in high school, I became a form captain, house captain and a prefect. I was captain of the cricket team and competed in the football, swimming and athletics team in our interschool sports. I was always worried the whole time and would think if anyone knew, or something was said, I would rather vanish. This has continued throughout my life.

It wasn't until I met Jo, my partner of 14 years, that any of this came out. Jo is the only person I have ever told. Possibly what prompted me to talk to her about this, is there were times when Jo would seem to be hiding behind something, then would start drinking excessively for no apparent reason. I explained to her I had had previous relationships that were alcohol fuelled and they never worked out. One especially which ended because of excessive alcohol on my wife's part.

When I put that to Jo, she then opened up about being assaulted as a young girl, and I felt comfortable to confide in her about my abuse. Jo was the only one to ever know.

Although Canon R. J. Brown is no longer alive, if the church were to admit to his behaviour and be accountable, it would be some sort of closure for me.

You would have probably heard it a million times, that not a day goes by when you have been sexually assaulted as a child, that you have flash backs and visions. I am still concerned about my family and friends knowing about this.

My skin still crawls to this day, every time I have to attend a church and certainly when a case like Pell's or others come up in the media. In circumstances like these, I just disappear out of the conversation.

The reason for my disclosure is because I have now been diagnosed with cancer and want to finish the rest of my life knowing I have finally spoken up about this and hope the church will acknowledge what has *happened to me. And hopefully put things into place to protect other vulnerable people's lives.*

    *Yours sincerely,*
    *David Payne*

## DAVID'S IMPACT STATEMENT.

*Education-due to my fear of being found out, I left school at the end of form five and proceeded to get a job in the work force. I was an A student and wanted to pursue a career as an airline pilot. I had the potential to reach this goal but lacked in confidence and really just wanted to get out of school as quickly as possible, for fear of being found out.*

*My schoolwork, results and enjoyment, changed after the abuse. I was no longer enthusiastic or committed to becoming a pilot. I did, however, go on to become a house captain and a prefect in my last year but it really didn't improve my confidence level or change my self-shame. I was always shameful and have still had those feelings for my entire life.*

*My home life was very limited as I felt guilty and didn't want my siblings to find out. My brother, even though he never knew, used to stir me up about Bummer Brown as he had seen his hand on my bottom one outing when we were attending a harvest meeting organised by the church for the needy.*

*Canon Brown was known by most of the boys at school and at church by the name, BUMMER Brown. I guess he was always grabbing boys on the bottom, not just me. I don't know if any of the adults at the time knew of it. There certainly wasn't any restrictions put on him when interacting with children.*

*My relationships always suffered and I became involved with the wrong people for security. They never worked. I was married very young, for the wrong reasons. I chose my partners badly and too quickly.*

Sexual relations were always rushed as a sense of security. My sexual manner was based on my acceptance and security.

I believe this was a result of my abuse which negatively impacted on my relationships as I didn't know how to build normal ones. There was never normal.

My friendships were strained as I was always scared of being found out and ridiculed. If the blokes were carrying on down at the pub about a homosexual or a priest, I would feel a sense of panic and always leave the conversation. Just in case they knew.

My mental health has always suffered but I have never had any counselling. I have self-medicated with alcohol. I couldn't ever seek out counselling in case I would be found out and wasn't comfortable with that. I couldn't tell anyone anyway, until my now partner, Jo, told me about her abuse as a child.

My whole idea of a sexual relationship has been based on guilt and insecurity. I have made some poor life choices. I can still hear that horrible groan as he touched my penis and made me touch his. It makes me feel ill every time I think about it.

I am still quite estranged from my family, apart from my younger sister and, to this day, none of my three siblings have known about it. I have never wanted to get too close to them, just in case the truth came out. And I am always concerned about how they would judge me.

I have made poor work choices from time to time as well.

## RELIGION

I attended church, up until the abuse happened. My mother would tell me I had to go and I had to attend church every Sunday, until I left home.

I detest, to this day, setting foot into a religious institution. I am unable to attend friends' weddings and funerals as a result of my abuse by the church. I have turned up late to these occasions and made sure I couldn't enter the church.

Canon Brown was the only church I ever had and I am totally against any religion as a result of my abuse by a man of the cloth. Every time I hear about priests interfering with anyone, I am sick to the stomach.

This has been a lifelong impact. Not only was it child sexual abuse but it was a spiritual abuse. My entire outlook on life has been changed and my ability to react to people has also changed.

Now I have cancer and it is starting to progress again. The last two test results have shown that my cancer is starting to step up in pace. I have had to deal with the stress of this experience in my life and, I am sure, contributed to my mental and physical health.

I believe I need to be heard and apologised to as I was a little boy, lying in a bed, and I couldn't get away from this horrible priest. I wish the church would acknowledge the fact that I and all other children, who had been assaulted, were young and innocent with no one to go to. Nobody would ever believe us over a priest.

If I had gone to my mother about this, when I was young, she would have grabbed a switch from the orchard and given me a beating and told me I was a liar. I was totally trapped as I couldn't go to anyone. A priest had status in our community and I wouldn't have been believed.

Canon Brown was known as a great community leader amongst the adults. A highly respected man. No one would ever have believed me. So, I was left helplessly alone and isolated from everyone. I couldn't come forward with my horrible secret. This has been one of the hardest things to live with for my entire life.

It has had a huge effect on my family life. Our family were well respected people. What would have been the ramifications if I had spoken up? My parents would have been shamed by the church had their son come forward with the truth about Canon Brown.

*It has taken a great deal of courage to finally bring this to any authority as I was scared that I wouldn't be believed. This has ruined my life spiritually, my education, career choices and my relationships.*

*I trust that due to health reasons, my claim will be considered as an urgency, so I can enjoy what is left of my life.*

# CHAPTER 38

## *MY REACTION*

I proceeded to read the letter of abuse David had written and all the horrible experiences. I found myself in tears. I could feel the helplessness of his innocence. Reliving my personal child abuse once again. As I typed out his words, I found myself agonising again with my own past.

The uncontrollable alcoholism as a result, the guilt and the pain of being hopelessly young and defenceless. Then the running away and the panic afterwards, along with the guilt and the shame that followed. Almost so you were not believing this ever happened. But then, it did.

I have made sure I have congratulated him on doing such an enormous task. It was a huge feat even to write it down.

And then he sent it off in an email.

# CHAPTER 39

## *FIGHTING FOR MY DAUGHTER*

Back to compensation and the application processes for my daughter. I engaged a lawyer, who was also paid by VOCAT, to apply for a crime's compensation for my daughter.

The first lawyer I was recommended turned out to be another horror event, for both my daughter and me. David and I were in far North Queensland, in a small town called Rollingstone, not too far from Balgal Beach. My daughter and I had an appointment to do a zoom meeting with the lawyer in Victoria, so we could get started on her claim. I was in Queensland and she was at boarding school in Albury.

We set everything up, made the call and then the conversation started. After a few minutes into the call, I had to terminate it. This meeting was quickly cut short because the lawyer had the audacity to ask my daughter to describe exactly how and what had happened to her. Her tone was also very contrary, and this added to our build-up of emotion. I just could not believe what I was hearing.

My daughter looked at me through the screen and simply said "Mum?" Her tone was inexplicable. There was just so much emotion in that simple word. She would have been absolutely mortified with what she had just been asked to describe. I know she would have immediately flashed back. The thought of that absolutely mortified me. Fortunately, for all of us, Elsa was sitting with her at the time.

I was not only extremely upset but incredibly cross. How dare she make my daughter live through this experience all over again. I immediately told her we would no longer need her services and I would find another lawyer. I gave her no explanation and no opportunity to justify herself. I just finished the meeting with her before she could say any more or do any more damage.

I was so very unsettled with what had just happened that I needed to speak to someone about it. The first person I called was Petrina. I was in an absolute blubbering mess for a while. How cruel, how cruel? How cruel can some people be? It was none of her business what had happened to my daughter. It was extremely invasive to even entertain asking my daughter such a thing. Petrina and I talked our way through it all and I managed to calm down.

All I needed now was to find another lawyer to help me with the compensation claim. I contacted the lawyer from Geelong Grammar School I had spoken to a great deal after my mediation. She gave me the name of a very reputable firm associated with VOCAT in Melbourne.

When I contacted this firm, things started to roll nicely and smoothly. Compensation and all the other benefits that my daughter needed were dealt with a fantastic girl called Kim. She was extremely helpful, very efficient and an absolute delight to work with. I told her about my experience with the other firm. Kim told me she was astounded by the question my daughter had been asked. She was also incredibly sympathetic and supportive to both my daughter and me.

We muddled our way through all the legal paperwork and then everything seemed to flow from then on in. All my daughter's psychological counselling costs were to be covered and her claim for crimes compensation was set in motion.

My daughter was compensated by the state of Victoria with a sum of money that would help her buy her first car. She was awarded the sum on her 18th birthday.

Not a huge award but enough to help her have some independence. There was also an amount awarded for ongoing mental health care. If necessary. Because my daughter was also in the midst of doing her last years of school, I was able to get some extra tutoring for some of the subjects she was struggling in. This cost was also reimbursed by VOCAT.

This part of my story is also in place as an information point for survivors to go to. The police throughout Australia are always the first good starting point. Not just for reporting this violent behaviour but to enable victims and survivors to find the right direction, for the best possible outcome.

# CHAPTER 40

## *GOING OUTBACK*

For the next couple of months, David and I enjoyed our travels. We travelled to the tip of Australia at Cape York, and we explored beautiful country all the way. We then decided to take what is called the longest short cut in Australia: the Great Central Road. The Great Central Road started at Kata Tju_t_a, known to most Australians as the Olgas. And finishes at Leonora in Western Australia.

Because of COVID and the lack of travelling people from most states, we hardly saw another car, unless it was on a state border. During COVID, we were just so free and really had no idea about what was going on in the other Australian states.

Our first state crossing into the Northern Territory from Queensland, we came across a couple of typical territory police officers. Wonderful sense of humour, wearing hats with corks to keep the flies off. Their attire was simple, and they wore shorts and thongs. When I asked about OH and S, they just laughed and said there wasn't anyone around really to instigate it. They were great guys, and we just chatted about COVID and our travels and then off we went on our merry way.

The scenery along the Great Central Road was amazing. You really wouldn't believe it was outback Australia. There were rock holes fenced off along the roads which were a natural ground water source for anything living out there. Including the indigenous people of the past. There were also wild camels, dingoes, emus, kangaroos, and various bird species.

*Sink hole on the Great Central Road*

We had a rest stop halfway through for a couple of nights. It was incredibly hot during the day, around 43 degrees Celsius. On the first night, David got into our shower. He had turned the temperature right down to cold. Even when he turned down the water temperature in the shower, it was unbearable, because of the heat. We had to decant water a few times to cool it before we could put back in the tank and run it through the shower.

This heat in the water was due to the iron content in the gravel that the roads are made of. David always describes it beautifully. It was just like driving over a hot plate all day.

When we arrived at the Western Australian border, we didn't feel particularly welcomed. After looking at our license plates, the police officer asked us where we had been. I piped up and said cheekily, "We've been everywhere man."

The next moment we were asked where we had isolated and how long we had been out of Victoria. This was because there had been yet another lockdown in our state, a week previous to that. David said we had been in Queensland and the Northern Territory since June. He also said to the police officer, it is not physically possible to drive from the Victorian border to the Western Australian border with a 17-metre car and caravan rigged up, in just three days. We weren't driving a jet, as David put it.

The police officer cooled off and was quite friendly in the end. He then proceeded to give each of us our first mask and a couple of pairs of gloves. However, these stayed in our car's centre console for a long time because they were just never needed.

We drove into Kalgoorlie in Western Australia and stayed in a caravan park for a few days.

# CHAPTER 41

## *DING DONG THE DIRTY DOC IS DEAD*

**DECEMBER 5TH 2020.**

Early that morning, I received a text message from my civil lawyer telling me she wanted to let me know some news. She wanted to speak to me before it had leaked out in the media. The news was, the Dirty Doctor was dead.

This, of course, brought back every living visual memory since I first realised what he had done to me. It was also another hideous reminder of all the information I had found out about in reading the Royal Commission. So much for that amazing year, once again.

I really did not know what to think. I was not happy about it because I had always wanted him to really suffer. Suffer, like we all had. He deserved to have a horrible cancer, where he was in unthinkable pain. Without any analgesics or morphine. Just hurt so much that it was like a long living hell for him. Death was an incredibly easy cop out for Mackey. Like it is for any sexual predator. The death of a predator doesn't ease or erase any memory or pain.

My emotions were peaking so much so, that I wrote this letter:

# MACKEYS DEATH WRITINGS

*The dirty doctor is dead. And, if the world is right, for over 40 years' worth of victims of this man, he will be rotting slowly in hell.*

*The only benefit in this, is there is one less person in existence on the sexual predators list. He earned that title eventually, in October 2019. Finally, after decades of sexually abusing children, both male and female. Yes, the dirty doctor liked both girls and boys. Didn't matter to him. We were groomed and then the subject of his dirty deeds and his evil sexual greed.*

*I hope he is slowly festering, like we have had to fester with fear, shame, guilt, flashbacks and feeling dirty for our entire lives since he arrogantly and evilly took it upon himself to touch us. The horrible man played with our innocent bodies and our innocent minds.*

*The man hid behind the gown. Because of his medical title, he played with boys' testicles, stimulated girls' clitorises and gave internal examinations at every chance he could. Doctor of sexual deviancy.*

*When I was assaulted, I warned my sister and she wore bathers when she went to see him. Every chance possible we had to remove our clothing. Even a sore finger would mean get your clothes off. The man even pleaded guilty to four charges of rape. Apparently, one of the women he abused had a sore toe. It was in the papers as proof.*

*His excuse for pleading guilty was because he just wanted to get back to his ailing wife. She had multiple sclerosis and was dying of cancer. At his wife's funeral, he gloated about how much money he had made out of the school. His children all had lovely houses and his grandchildren have been looked after at the best private schools. His wife's eulogy was all about him. He had ripped off more than his victims. He had totally ripped off Geelong Grammar School as well.*

*People's medical records were scanned, so he could find a reason to touch and then see if he could get a reaction. I know of one guy who* had a pre-existing ailment and he zoomed in on it. He even held his testicles for over four minutes, to see if he could get a stimulated reaction from the boy.

In another case that I am now familiar with, a girl was given an internal when she secretly went to get the contraceptive pill. Of course, she wouldn't have questioned his contact over her parents finding out. Digital rape with blackmail.

No chaperones, meant sexual delight for the dirty doc. He could do what he liked. And he did.

Now, the real story is 21 of us came forward during the Royal Commission in 2015 and made complaints against him. Yes, 21 people said he did what he did and went to the police independently. Interestingly, most of us didn't realise so many of us existed. I was shocked at how many people had reported and I only really knew two of them.

We then appeared in a committal hearing between August - September 2018. Our testimonies were heard and believed and the hearing proceeded to the county court in October 2019. At the committal hearing, the dirty doc had to listen to every testimony. Twenty one of us were heard and 21 of us were believed by the court.

The problem with these types of offences is, historically, it has been incredibly difficult to prove beyond reasonable doubt that he, or any doctor, had done anything wrong. There was also no policy in place for chaperones for minors. So, no witnesses. As a result, only four of us were asked to testify. Then, because criminal law bases all results on the strength of beyond reasonable doubt, the jury was let go and the decision was ultimately left up to the judge. The case was thrown out.

The dirty Dr David Brian Mackey did assault all of us and, without any doubt, many more. There are people so damaged from this abuse, they just can't face proceeding further. The last count was over 25 people had come forward. There would definitely be more.

Unfortunately, in our case, the law let us down. He was guilty and is guilty of hurting all our lives.

This is where Mackey was in protected seventh heaven. He also probably knew he could get away with it as well. Apart from being a doctor, he had been the head boy of the GGS senior school in his final year. He was very bright and a well-respected member of the GGS community.

As children, we didn't know whether this was right or wrong, we couldn't speak up about it because who would believe us? All of us, our parents, and the school we attended, people in Geelong who attended his young people's clinic, trusted a doctor but, unfortunately, he was a paedophile with a stethoscope. An evil, perverted predator. He continued undetected for years.

I just hope that everyone who has been so deeply and emotionally hurt by this man, will find some sort of closure in their life, now he is dead. I hope this is remembered by everyone who came into contact with the Dirty Doctor.

I know how much I have hurt from all this and I hope everyone else is slowly changing their lives for the better. I know I have started enjoying mine. Life is too short. Believe in yourself and forgive yourself. You were only a child.

Believe me, this was written now, because the dirty doctor is dead and, finally, we can speak without being denied our story. Our story is real. We can't change the past but can slowly learn to live with it. I also hope we keep a close eye on our children with people we are meant to trust. It is still so easy for these evil people to operate and prey on the innocent. They have our trust always.

This is by no means an attack on Geelong Grammar. The current ethos in the school is incredible and this entire situation has been dealt with and policies put in place, in order to protect future children attending the school.

The news wasn't comforting, whatsoever. He just got away with his horrible life and all the despicable things he did. I had the identical emotions when Geoff Hines died. My mother had told me about his death one Christmas Day a long time ago. The feelings experienced were a total and incredible pull of being emotionally ripped off. They got away with their evil lives and somehow took an enormous part of my innocent life away. All my innocence.

Death was just too easy for a sexual predator. Prison would have been a better option, even though these types of offenders have to be protected there. It's not safe for them to mingle with others, because everyone in jail either has a brother, sister, daughter, son or mother. More reason why they should be put in mainstream prison. So, they get to experience everything we as victims and survivors had to experience.

My ultimate wish would have been that Mackey and Hines had both gone to jail and been attacked by others. Hopefully, painfully sodomised and possibly made to feel the way the people they abused feel. Dirty and helplessly confused.

Mackey's death stirred up a few more worms, with my thoughts and feelings for my mother as well. I sent her a copy of that letter on the day I wrote it. At the same time, David was really starting to get annoyed over the entire handling of events by my mother, in relation to Mackey and her obsession with the church. So, he wrote her an email and explained quite a few things.

The church was never a topic David liked to talk about understandably.

I believed the church was a completely ridiculous and utterly hypocritical place. That was my opinion anyway but I did respect people if they have their own beliefs. They were just not mine. And I was definitely not interested in hearing about the church, either.

Not surprisingly, David never received a reply to his email. However, my mother sent me an email. She was sympathetic to start with but then started going on about lighting a candle in church for me. She knew I thought very differently about the church than she did. A candle? A candle would do what? Make my life, that was horrible, just simply disappear without a trace? Erase all of those horrible memories? Maybe it was a get-over-it candle.

Then, she also expressed, because I had chosen to retire early and travel, I was a nomad and too hard to comfort. My mother never ever comforted me, even in my desperate times. Then she decided, I may need to have some counselling. I have had a clinical psychologist for over 10 years. And I am still seeing one! She was now really starting to patronise me. Treating me like a child.

Then she started trivialising about other subjects. All about their moving house. Change the subject sort of stuff. So, there it was again, just "the get over it" tact.

This is one thing I will never be able to come to terms with and neither will she. I cannot get over it, ever. I will never fully recover from it.

# CHAPTER 42

## *ANOTHER LETTER TO JEREMY*

*Dear Jeremy,*

*I guess you would know the news by now, that the dirty doctor died on Friday. Hopefully, he's rotting in Hades.*

*Another awful chapter for the school finished. However, I think his estate may be under threat. I am happily helping out with that one. I know the school had a certain amount they were going to pay for Mackey's actions. I would estimate it to be well over the four-million-dollar mark. His property at Point Lonsdale sold for around three million.*

*I also know he bragged about the amount of money he had made from the school and how he had set up his children with property and their children's education. He really ripped everyone off.*

*Apparently, his family still claim absolute innocence about the claims against him at Geelong Grammar School. That makes it so much harder again, for all of us. It also gives me such enormous determination to make sure the truth comes out and the school is reimbursed for all the money he has cost it.*

*Yesterday was difficult with lots of mixed and twisted emotions. At least the old bastard is dead and can't harm anyone anymore.*

We left Kalgoorlie after a week but had a good look around the goldfields area. Then we headed to Wave Rock in the east of the state, then headed south to Esperance and Albany, visiting the pink lake and admiring the stunning beaches in the south of Western Australia.

We did the tree top walk in the Valley of the Giants near Denmark. Located in Tingledale WA, the tree top walk is suspended at 40 metres above the forest floor in the canopy of the ancient Tingle Forest. It was an amazing experience and the Tingle trees have been aged at up to 400 years old.

Another highlight of our trip was staying at a limestone quarry in Myalup. The quarry was still working but the separate accommodation and camping was really quirky. There was a Hobbit House where we put our camping payment. They had a large chook run but instead of fences, there was a moat around it, to keep the foxes out. And coming out at the front of the house, there was an Ansett aeroplane, including wings. We met the man who ran the show. What an eccentric! Definitely worth a visit.

Heading towards Perth, it really started to look a lot like Christmas. People were making their driveways and front paddocks look very Christmas-themed. It was lovely to see the festive spirit.

*Me at Wave Rock Western Australia*

For Christmas this year, we had organised to do a house sit in the Perth Hills. The family were heading south in their caravan for a few weeks into the new year. The house sit included looking after three dogs and we also had access to a swimming pool.

We had also booked flights to travel to Victoria in January, so it was easier to stay in Perth. A few days before we were supposed to fly, we decided we would cancel. We didn't want to get stuck out of Western Australia or didn't want to do a ridiculous isolation in a hotel in Perth. As it turned out, the day we were going to be in the air, the Victorian premier announced another immediate COVID lockdown.

At that stage, we had decided to start doing house sits in the hotter months, down in the south of Western Australia. The next sit we applied for and were accepted, was in Geraldton.

# CHAPTER 43
## *MORE REFLECTIONS*

I don't know whether this may explain a few things I have written about my mother in this book. But there is evidence, that emotional trauma experienced in pregnancy, can lead to mental health issues for both a mother and a child. My mother had the trauma of losing her only sister when I was in utero.

My grandparents on my mother's side both died around 18 months to two years before I was born. My grandmother gassed herself with a coal gas oven. She had been unwell, as far as I knew and I was told she had a blockage in her carotid artery. This blockage apparently would alter her mood on a regular basis.

My mother said she would be fine in one instance, then completely different in another. I knew she smoked but not a lot. Another thing that always puzzled me was, there was never any mention of my grandmother having a mental illness. Normally, a suicide would be the choice of someone with a mental illness. My mother always referred to people who choose to suicide, as being incredibly selfish.

Really, if she only knew what it was like to totally detest yourself and then not know how to live with yourself anymore. It was so awful to feel this way and not selfish at all. You just can't bear to take another breath or another step because you hate yourself so much. Believe me, I know it. Fortunately, I wasn't very successful at it.

My grandfather died of leukaemia. In that era, little was known medically about most cancers. People just died and there was nothing that could be done about it. My Aunt Patricia died of an inoperable brain tumour. My mother cared for her for a while but then she had to go into care, because my mother couldn't cope when she really deteriorated. My mother also already had my older sister and, at the time, she was under 18 months old. My father was quite often away because he played international rugby union. On top of all of that, she was pregnant with me.

My mother lost her entire family in a matter of two years. Gone. She was 25 years old when I was born. My mother has always said, just get on with it and just get over it. That's probably exactly what she had to do. She went into a form of survival mode.

I can imagine that when I was born, she just fed me, changed me and put me into bed and then got on with it. Perhaps like a robot doing its job. Think about nothing but the tasks that needed to be done. She was on her own. That was a woman's job, just to be at home while dad worked and played rugby. Stand by your man and family. Chin up and get on with it.

I really think, as a result of my mother's family trauma, she just could not bond with me. And whether the emotional trauma she suffered affected me, I will never really know.

I can't really blame her but, I guess, that is why she never really wanted to even try to understand what was going on with me. She wasn't prepared to look outside the shallow square she was living in. She never asked for any advice about it. She expected everyone to get over it and didn't want to be any part of it.

A close friend once told me she and my mother visited her sister in a nursing home and it was around the time, when her sister's life was running out. When they had finished their visit and left the nursing home, my mother instantly said to the friend, that they should go and do some shopping. She didn't talk about her sister and shopping seemed to be more important. Talk about strange priorities.

During the times of incredible depression and through some of my healing episodes where I desperately wanted help, my mother still couldn't support me. I asked her once, "Why didn't you ever do anything when you found out what Geoff Hines had done to me?"

Her answer was, "We didn't know what to do and we didn't want to upset their family."

Wouldn't you find out what to do?

Also at that time, I was apparently ripping my family apart and my mother was more interested in protecting someone else's wife and children. Someone who had digitally raped me and sexually assaulted me, as an 11-year-old. Someone who was supposedly one of their friends.

A few years later, Geoff Hines split with his wife and there had been some story of a little incident in the family unit. I never knew what that was but he had obviously done something untoward and possibly been caught red-handed.

My mother also told me once, it wasn't surprising to hear the story about him, because my father had said, he was always a womaniser when on tour playing rugby. So why wouldn't she entertain the fact, he might do something to one of her daughters? Why was I made by my parents, to kiss a womaniser good night? Why was I left as a young girl, in a sexual predator's house?

I did wonder sometimes, did you need a totally out there sister, in a large family of girls? And is this because it helped everyone else feel normal? Why was there always one? Always a black sheep? And I'm afraid, it was me. But I was glad I was different, even if sometimes, it had been embarrassing.

But I have to say, that was all in the past and I was okay. In fact, I could now say I was amazing, fantastic and everyone loved me. Oh, except some of my family. I was a total embarrassment to them. A total waste of intelligence.

My sisters, with the exception of Lisa, just rolled their eyes and would say, "Oh Joanna, what a mess and what a waste."

Or another sister said, "I thought you would have gotten over it by now."

A family wrecker is what my older sister referred to me as and that was quite recently.

These sorts of comments made me believe some of my sisters were heartless. It was also apparent there was extraordinarily little understanding or compassion in their emotional acumen. It seemed, they thought I had intentionally behaved this way and intentionally hurt all the members of my family and there was no reason at all.

Why couldn't people realise, being sexually abused was like having a compound emotional fracture in the brain. There was an incredible amount of mental scarring.

This had been one of the hardest things to swallow in my life and there was only one sister that understood me and why I was the way I was. That was Lisa. You could probably say Lisa was the one who initially got me help. She had gone through binges with me. She protected me. She told her friend's mother, the child psychiatrist that I was in a lot of trouble with my body image and what I was doing to myself. She was my catalyst for help. Lisa was my saviour. She knew and understood Jojo.

Sadly, this was very unlike my mother, who had sent me to see Dr Mackey for my eating disorder. Epitomises the taking of lambs to the slaughter. Except, that I was more like a sexual sacrifice.

# CHAPTER 44

## *AUSTRALIAN OF THE YEAR*

On 26th January 2021, I had another monumental panic attack, one of the worst attacks I have ever experienced. David and I were in Geraldton, house sitting for a young couple and staying at the back of their property. We were looking after a couple of dogs and a cat, for about three or four weeks.

I had found suitable places to walk and David was busying himself with jobs in the garden and a little bit of maintenance. I was watering the garden and caring for trees that had just been planted. These are the sorts of jobs we did, in return for a place to stay with water and power. It suited us because we needed to run an air conditioner in the summer in this area. I also busied myself by doing a spring clean and windows etc.

We had been there for a couple of weeks in January, and it was very hot. On this particular morning, the news had been on and we were watching the evolution of the Australia Day awards on the television. The Australian of the Year was announced and her name was Grace Tame.

My initial reaction was, "Who the hell is she?" I had never heard of her in my entire life.

She was a young woman who had stood up and spoken about her dreadful sexual abuse suffered as a young girl at school. As usual, I found this knowledge of her experience to be totally confronting. It sent me into yet another a horror reflection moment. I was extremely empathetic to the damage Grace had experienced but there was something really insulting about the way it was portrayed. It almost felt like there was a bragging by the current government for giving her this award. I also found the media's comments almost unsympathetic and reporting it as a horrible truth. But there seemed to be an unusual underlying theme, as if it was just a normal thing that had happened to a young schoolgirl. Another Old Men's Club reflection.

I would never want the hype she has received, and I do not believe at 27 years of age she is the right person to be given attention. She was still so young and incredibly inexperienced.

At 27, you are only just an adult. Because she was so young and inexperienced, I decided to be in contact with her via messenger and offer as much support as possible. It was always stories like these that I relived the struggles of some of my early life. They were triggers for me, as well as wanting to help someone else through it. I never received a response.

It raised questions of why were we putting this sort of responsibility on a woman who had only just evolved as an adult. She has had no experience with life and the consequences of abuse. She was probably still having an incredible amount of psychological help to understand what was going on. And needed about another one or two decades to deal with it.

She would have no idea about the confrontation that comes with processing this awful abuse as an adult. I was not stupid and, as an incredibly intelligent woman, it had taken me a hell of a long time to be able to enable others to heal. It was not in a 27-year old's empathy acumen.

I was absolutely insulted she was made Australian of the Year for being sexually abused. I was sure it was due to the sexual harassment going on in politics at the time. It was the political party leading the country showing their way of dealing with the in-house problems. This was to make a child sexual assault victim the Australian of the Year. We needed to confront these things, of course, but to do this in this way, made a mockery of anyone who has ever been sexually abused.

The panic attack was really a crude reminder for me. At 55 years old at the time, I still had these horrific moments of panic, despair, and I just didn't want to live anymore. What did someone half my age have?

I went for a walk and sent David a text to say I was safe and needed to exercise to get over this. I cried for most of my six kilometre walk and returned home absolutely exhausted. As usual. The rest of our stay was mentally even flowing and I had no more flashbacks or triggered panic attacks.

Interestingly, it was stories like these, even now, that I would be triggered a little. The life of an abused child, I guess.

## MY WRITING POST PANIC ATTACK

*I am absolutely exhausted.*

*I have just had the most enormous panic attack.*

*I have been for a six kilometre walk to try and recompose myself.*

*I am now lying on the bed and feel like I need another eight hours sleep.*

*I cannot explain the energy low I am feeling. I can't believe how drained I am. Someone has taken away all my iron stores in one morning.*

*At least, I can breathe again.*

*I kept thinking of the black American, George Floyd saying, "I can't breathe." That is exactly what it feels like when you are having an episode of panic. And then when you come down off the ultra-level, you are totally exhausted. Maybe my body is telling me I need to rest now.*

*I also realised I have these attacks, but they have been not so vivid as the last few. They have been often and gone on for over 40 years. Even running away as a child was really me experiencing panic attacks.*

*Running away from what and who? Whenever you feel uncomfortable or frightened, you run away.*

*I remember it happening at Christmas at Highton once and I ran out of the house and out into the paddock. I was trying to escape. Sometimes you just need to escape and sometimes you can't break free. Sometimes you are tied down or just can't run. You are stuck.*

*Some attacks are mild, and some are absolutely massive. Just like today. I just kept flashing back today. I eventually told myself; I was safe.*

# CHAPTER 45

## *WESTERN AUSTRALIA AND A CHEEKY PARROT*

At the end of January, we did another house-sit after the young couple's place. It happened to be Kate's parents. We were invited over one afternoon to meet them, and they were lovely people. We hit it off from the word 'go'. Their names were Jamie and Di. We thoroughly enjoyed our stay there and were asked if we would like to do house-sits in the future.

It was whilst we were at Di and Jamie's house that David finally received an apology from the Anglican Church for his child sexual abuse by Canon Brown. He mentioned to me, he experienced a strange feeling and said he felt differently instantly about a few things.

I assumed he felt the same way as I did when Geelong Grammar had believed and then apologised to me. It is a strange feeling. Being believed finally and realising it really was not your fault. You were an innocent child and confused about what happened and why.

When we had finished the sit at Geraldton, we headed north for the winter. We began with a house sit in Dampier for a couple which had been referred to by friends. Lizzy and Chris were going to Perth for a six week visit and Chris was having both his knees reconstructed.

We did a changeover with them for a couple of nights and got to know the run of the house and animals. There were a couple of dogs and a parrot called Molly. Molly ruled the roost in this household and definitely kept us busy. She would be let out of her cage in the kitchen every morning and have a good walk and fly around. Then she was to be put outside in a larger cage for the day and fed. The food was very exotic, and she ate the best of the best fruits and fresh vegetables on top of her normal parrot food. However, we nearly always seemed to have some sort of drama with her, getting her into the outside cage.

*The parrot at Dampier*

Lizzie had told us she was easy to move by letting her land on your shoulder. David tried this and ended up with an enormous bite on one of his ears one day. I had a glove on, on another occasion and she drew blood through that as well. She was an absolute bitch of a bird.

One thing that was absolutely hysterical happened to us whilst we were there. One morning David had opened the cage door, and Molly had got out of her cage and was freely doing her thing in the living area. David and I had got out of bed and David forgot to close the bedroom door on his way out. David has been on circulation pills since the removal of his prostate in 2017. These circulation pills, commonly known as Viagra, were on the bed side table, along with some paracetamol.

I had gone out for my usual walk and David was outside doing something to the caravan. On returning from my walk, I went into the bedroom and, to my astonishment, Molly had not only helped herself to some Panadol but had hooked into the Viagra as well.

You can imagine what was going through my head! Oh, my goodness, I thought we had killed the bird. Immediately, I started googling parrots consuming Viagra and Panadol. I wasn't sure how long I had been away, but I waited a further half an hour, to see what happened next. Fortunately, nothing did happen and Dr or Vet Google said it would be relatively harmless.

By this time, I had also come across a joke on the internet that involved a parrot taking Viagra. It went something like this:

*A parrot accidentally swallows Viagra and starts sweating profusely. His owner does not know what to do to settle him down, so he puts the parrot in the freezer to cool him off. Later, when he opens the freezer, the parrot is panting and still sweating. The owner then says, "How come you are still sweating?"*

*The parrot replies, "Do you know how hard it is to open the legs of a frozen chicken."*

I went out to David and told him what had happened. Then I started to tell him the joke. We kept roaring with laughter for quite some time. We incidentally told these people what happened when they returned. And as far as I know, the birds still exists.

Another horrible incident happened whilst we were staying in Dampier.

My youngest sister was an equine vet and was attending as the vet on duty at a horse meeting at the Mansfield show grounds. David's daughter, Nichola, was an experienced horse rider and event-or and was competing in the event. She had been riding a very green horse who was doing its first event. They were on the cross-country course, Nichola's mount had baulked at a jump, and Nichola had taken a fall.

At the time, she was wearing a helmet and an air vest, that inflates when triggered, for spinal protection. As she fell, the air vest inflated and frightened the horse. The horse kicked in fright and seriously damaged Nichola's face and teeth. She was airlifted to the Royal Prince Alfred Hospital in Melbourne.

The first we knew of it, was when my sister rang me at once to tell us the shocking news. We wouldn't have found out about it so quickly if it had been left to Nichola's mother or her mother's partner. They simply wouldn't have cared if we didn't know immediately.

I went out to the garage and told David to sit down. I then told him that Nichola had been air lifted to Melbourne and was in a serious and critical condition. He made a few phone calls and organised flights to Melbourne via Perth so he could be by her side.

We were both in shock and extremely worried. Nichola had also been placed into an induced coma to restrict brain activity and hopefully reduce any brain damage. The horse had swiped out 11 of her teeth on the left-hand side of her head. Later, they found a tooth had been lodged in her gums in her mandible.

David spent a week in Melbourne with Nichola and then spent a further weekend camping with his grandsons before returning to Dampier.

It was a nice bit of time for me to be on my own whilst he was away.

I did some writing to iron out my mixed emotions about how the entire reporting of her accident had been. As usual, David was being treated badly by Nichola's mother and was kept out of the scene. Another thing I did to busy myself, was research into liable issues. This was so we could help Nichola rebuild her teeth and live as normally as possible.

From Dampier, we headed north as it got cooler. Also, at this time of year, it is nearing the end of the wet season, and the chance of cyclones was lessening. Fortunately, no cyclones hit us in 2021. They would hang around off the coast but never came to anything whilst we were in the north. However, on the day we left, we had a fantastic thunderstorm during the night, and it was quite wet in the morning. Something Dampier had not seen for a while.

After visiting Barn Hill outstation and Broome respectively, we headed to Derby. From there, we spent about five weeks on the Gibb River Road which was amazing. We sat on the bank of the Gibb River crossing for over two weeks. During this time, we met many travellers, including families, doing the lap. We were the caravan sitters whilst people headed up to Honeymoon Bay and Mitchell Falls. Three young families left their caravans with us so we could keep an eye on them, because the road was too rough for large vehicles.

We had a visit one day by an extended indigenous family. They all arrived, loaded with children in the tray of the ute and grandma in the passenger seat. The children swam and played loudly in the river. Another young man fished in the river. They had their lunch and afternoon fun, then tidied up and bundled the kids back into the ute and left no trace. Most indigenous we met along the Gibb River Road were polite and well behaved. Very different from how we have noticed the toxic behaviour in some of the towns.

We finished our Gibb River Road trip with a stay at El Questro. We house sat in 2019 for a couple that ran the El Questro horse riding gig, so we were allowed to camp with them as guests. We stayed for over a week and saw a great deal more of the station. A very worthwhile station to explore on the Gibb River Road. After the Gibb, we visited Lake Argyle and Kununurra.

We explored more new places to us on our way south, including Marble Bar. Marble Bar is noted as the hottest place in Australia. We had visited once before but never really looked around the area. We visited an old gold mine and did a tour with a lovely, old gentleman.

Then we made our way through the wildflowers, south of Meekatharra, towards Three Springs. This part of Western Australia comes to life in the most spectacular way in the spring. If the rain has been considerable in the winter, the highways and back roads are in full bloom. It is one of the most wonderful sights I have experienced in Australia. The red dirt comes alive with pinks, oranges, purples, whites and the amazing wreath flowers. We thoroughly enjoyed the wildflower season in spring 2021.

Our next stop was at a farm called Kadathinni. The people we house sat for in Geraldton, had a farm and we offered to stay there before we headed back to Victoria for a Christmas visit to our families. Our stay was only a couple of weeks but we said we would return to farm sit at some stage in the future.

# CHAPTER 46

## *CHRISTMAS IN VICTORIA*

Our trip back to Victoria, unfortunately, was not without incident. Whilst we were still in WA, we were on a quiet country road looking for a camp later in the day. Usually, we would try and finish driving at around 4pm. We were poking along at the usual 80 kilometres per hour looking for our camp. Out of nowhere came a service vehicle. The vehicle started to overtake us driving towards a crest on unbroken lines.

David commented to me, "Look at this bloody idiot."

Fortunately, we didn't get into trouble with his vehicle or any others at the time.

About 10 minutes further up the road, we both noticed there had been a multi vehicle accident. We continued slowly to the scene. I firstly jumped out and ran back down the road to stop any traffic behind us. Another man then took over from me with the traffic control, and I returned to the scene. There was another vehicle in front of us, stationary, and then there was a car and caravan stopped on the correct side of the road coming from the opposite direction. The passenger side of the SUV was completely smashed in. Another towed caravan had run into the back of the SUV and caravan as well.

Further along, on the opposite side of the road to us, was the service vehicle. It was upside down. David went over to the service vehicle, and I attended to the driver of the car and caravan who was sitting on the road. David saw the dazed driver of the service vehicle come out from underneath the car.

The gentleman that I was attending to on the road, had damaged his shoulder and was clearly in a state of shock. His wife could not be seen at all in the passenger side. There was absolutely no passenger side left.

I covered the gentleman with a coat to keep him warm. He said to me, in a bewildered fashion, that he didn't know what had happened. I told him he didn't need to know and he was okay. I told him the emergency services were on their way. By this time, there were a lot of people there and David and I decided there was not much more we could do.

To leave the scene, we needed to turn our car and caravan around. I had to stop the traffic back down the road in a wider spot, so we could turn our 17-metre rig around. We managed to get away safely and found our camp.

Sitting at camp that night was a little confrontational. We discussed what had happened around the fire. It is really quite an awful feeling when someone dies in an accident you have attended. There is an emotional numbness that overwhelms you. Based on the way the service vehicle was driving, we thought that we should definitely make a statement to the police, as soon as possible.

David made his statement over the phone the next day. The police also informed him the driver of the service vehicle had been noticed driving erratically by other motorists that day. Because the statement could not been formalised by the police over the phone, we were told it would be emailed to the COVID Eucla checkpoint, and he would sign it when we crossed the border.

This was the first time we were really hit by the COVID omnishambles. David waltzed up to the police officer on the border and introduced himself and the reason why he was making contact. He was immediately instructed to sit on a bench seat, until he was told he could move. Then, because we had never really had to wear our masks during COVID, we didn't have any. David was provided with a mask and told to sanitise his hands. Then he was allowed to sign the prepared statement. While he was dealing with the police, I said I would go into the roadhouse to see if I could get some food.

*Beautiful golden gums found along the Nullarbor*

On the Nullarbor, at every border crossing, you go through a quarantine. This protects farmers in each of the states. We always eat most of our fresh produce, so we don't have to surrender it to the bins. There is always a considerable distance between Eucla and a decent shop with fresh produce. Sometimes the roadhouses have fruit but not very often. As I wandered in, the roadhouse attendant asked me where my mask was. Then I was told by the same attendant that I if I wanted to buy anything in the shop, I would have to be wearing a mask. I simply walked out. There was nothing in there that I wanted to buy anyway. The COVID restrictions were quite a shock to both of us because we had been so free in Western Australia and for well over 12 months.

We headed across the rest of the Nullarbor, catching up and camping with good friends along the way. We caught up with them a few times in South Australia as well.

We headed east after Port Augusta and took our usual route through the Clare Valley. We stayed at our favourite spot in the area, at a town called Watervale. Finally, heading further east to visit David's sister in Harrow. Harrow is a place we often stay on our way to or from the west.

On the night before we were to head into Mansfield, we decided to stay at a camp at Axedale in Victoria. I went for a short stroll after our drive and felt a little wobbly. During the drive back to Victoria from Western Australia, I had often had the usual fears associated with seeing my family. I was very sceptical about going back. David and I had not seen my family since we had left in early 2020 to do the horrible farm sit. It was 22 months since then. COVID had interrupted so many visits and disabled any chance at all.

We sat around a fire on 25th October just chatting and having a couple of beers. Because of my nervousness, I was feeling quite nauseous and had thrown up a bit of fluid. We retired to bed early.

I woke in the morning, still feeling quite nervous. I made the usual tea and coffee, and we sat in bed, played cards, and checked emails etc. I really wasn't feeling myself at all. I was seeing flashes in my eyes and my iPad screen also seemed a little kaleidoscopic from time to time. I told David I did not feel like going for a walk. Something very unusual for me. I just didn't feel up to it.

*Wreath flowers found in Western Australia*

On 26th October 2021, we headed to Mansfield. Whilst sitting in the car, I was getting a combination of strange, mixed emotions. I really didn't want to go back there at all. I was on the edge of panic for most of that early part of the drive. I didn't feel right. I started to take really deep breaths to try and keep calm. This is something I have learned to do, to hopefully, either prevent a panic attack or take the edge of it and make it less exhausting. We were driving into the town of Seymour, which is about an hour's drive from Mansfield. The last thing I can remember thinking was, I feel so awful and feel really ill and I just want to go to a hospital.

At this moment, David had said I started groaning and then started thrashing about in my seat uncontrollably. I was unconscious and had bitten my tongue. I was drooling blood and kicking the door and the dashboard. David had to try and find a spot to pull over with the car and the caravan. When he finally managed to park, he came around to my side of the car to check my pulse and hold me upright. Then he had to try and call for an ambulance.

Apparently, I didn't become conscious until I was inside the ambulance. I woke up lying down on a stretcher. One of the paramedics was tending to me and he asked me what day it was. I had absolutely no idea. I remember asking if I had had a trans ischemic attack. Then apparently, I passed out again. David said I was in a complete daze.

The next thing I remembered was waking up in a hospital bed. The ambulance had taken me to the Northern Hospital in Epping, a suburb of Melbourne. I had no idea what I was doing there, and it was very strange to have lost so much time. Apparently, I was there for observation for a few hours. They gave me a CT scan and took bloods to see what may have been the cause. David said I had experienced a seizure.

David returned to Mansfield with the car and caravan from Seymour. He then picked up my daughter's new car and some clothes and drove back to the hospital in Melbourne. I was released from the hospital later that afternoon. We stayed in a motel for the night and returned to Mansfield the next day. The entire 24 hours had lapsed, and I was still in a swirly state. Exhausted from the ordeal, I slept for three hours that afternoon.

In hindsight, I am sure the seizure was caused by enormous stress. The stress of going to Mansfield. The stress of seeing my family after 22 months. As well as everything else that was jam packed into the last two or so years. I think it may have been caused by having an enormous panic attack. When I had a conversation with my mother about the seizure, all she could say in her usual patronising fashion, was she hoped I was eating properly.

One of the reasons we had returned at this time of year, was because my daughter was graduating from year 12 at the Scots School in Albury. She came down to Mansfield to pick up her new car, and we all returned to Albury for the graduation. Because my daughter still wasn't eighteen and didn't have her driver's license, she drove me back to Albury. David took our car up separately. I remember getting back to Albury with Molly and not really remembering who had driven the car. The effects of the seizure lingered for quite a few days.

My results came back from the Northern Hospital, and I was recommended to have an MRI on my brain and an echocardiogram done on my heart. I had both tests done in Albury. Nothing showed up really, apart from low sodium levels which were picked up in a blood test. Apart from that, I was pleased to report my brain was fine and I had a good healthy heart.

We returned to Mansfield on 27th November after spending some time camping on the Murray River at Barnawatha. My daughter's graduation was held on 4th December 2021. It was a lovely night and great to see my youngest graduating. After the graduation, we returned to Mansfield to do a house sit for Kate Parsons at her house in Merrijig. We stayed at Kate's up until just before Christmas.

Apart from mediations and applications for redress and crimes compensation, I had applied more than three years ago, for a further crime's compensation for me. Because of COVID, everything was on a big go slow when it came to historical crimes compensation. This compensation was as a result of my statement to the police for the sexual abuse by Geoff Hines. On 21st December 2021, I was awarded a compensation payment for the sexual abuse I had suffered as an 11-year-old. I had applied originally for $5,000 and was delighted when I was awarded twice that amount. This compensation did give me a little more closure.

On 23rd December, we headed out to one of our favourite camping places in the Mansfield high country - the Upper King Basin. David and I have spent many Christmas seasons here. We have the place to ourselves which we really enjoy and there are lovely walks in the area for me. Sometimes our friends and kids come out and fish for a couple of days. We return to Mansfield after the new year normally. This is because we like to avoid the crowds that come to the district in the summer.

We returned to Kate's place in Merrijig early in the new year and then set off on our next adventure on 17th January 2022. Before we left, we made time to catch up with family and close friends.

# CHAPTER 47

## *TRAVELLING THROUGH NSW AND QUEENSLAND*

**2022**

From Mansfield we headed north towards the border and then into NSW. Our first chore of the year was to get new airbag suspension put on the caravan. This was booked in to happen in Brisbane, in the last couple of weeks in January.

During our trip through New South Wales, we came across a flooded area around Gilgandra. One incident to mention was when we were driving slowly through flood waters, a truck decided to overtake us. It would not have been an issue at all if we hadn't had the windows down. As the truck passed, an enormous wave came through the driver's window and absolutely soaked both of us. I thought it was quite amusing, but David was furious and the discussion over the two-way radio that followed was very expletive. At least there weren't any fish in the cabin.

Apart from that one drama, we had a pleasant trip up to Brisbane. We had also caught up with an old friend from school as we went through Dubbo. We hadn't seen each other for over 30 years. He joined us for coffee where we camped, and it was lovely to see him again after all that time.

We had organised to stay with some friends in Brisbane whilst the caravan was being upgraded. They were relatively new friends we had met on the Gibb River Road during the previous year. Along the road, we kept meeting up with them and David and Yoshi would have a banter each time we met, about our F250 and his Chevrolet.

We had our own little section at the end of their house and spent some time with them out on their boat. We tried to get to Stradbroke Island but ended up getting bogged in the channel. So, most of the boat trip was getting unbogged and making it back to the mainland. We also helped around their house, especially in the garden.

We also did a couple of weekends away exploring Mount Tamborine and at the Bunya mountains, just to break up the waiting time for the caravan. We had recently set up our car so we could make a bed where the back seat used to be. It was quite comfortable and okay for a weekend now and then.

In early 2022, there was a great deal of rain which affected areas in both southern Queensland and northern NSW. Most of our trip, at this time of the year, was spent avoiding these rain events in Queensland. This meant more exploration in western Queensland. In February, we found ourselves at a place called Lake Victoria. A lovely spot with plenty of clean water, west of Rockhampton.

After passing a large bus on the road into camp, we set up in a nice spot on our own. There were other vans in the distance, but it wasn't too busy. I remember sitting outside by the lake with David and around 4.30pm, six children arrived on bikes. They all resembled the children out of the 1980s movie, Mad Max Beyond Thunderdome. Their hair was long and scraggly and they were tanned. They also weren't wearing on the top of their torso. They looked like free spirits. It was quite difficult to tell if they were boys or girls because of their clothes and obviously not anywhere near puberty. They spent some time in the water and then returned home to their bus.

The next afternoon, to our amazement, the number of children increased to 10. Two of the children were teenagers and the others would have been 10 years and under. They were also with a woman who looked around 40 and she was obviously expecting another baby. Not only was she pregnant but she was also breastfeeding the youngest girl.

I started talking to her, intrigued by their existence. Her name was Bec and she let me interview her. It was fascinating. She had two older children that no longer lived with the family. Dad was at work during the week. She was expecting her 13th child and had been pregnant for over 11 years. After her third child, she was told she would not be able to have any more children. Her fourth child she birthed with her husband in the bus and every child after that as well, with the family all in another room. I asked how she monitored her pregnancies and she said she was looked after by a doctor and midwives. Incidentally, no medical team was needed during the births, and she delivered her placentas around an hour later without any help at all.

I asked her how she managed to feed the children. She said they caught fish in the lake. As well as a shop each week in town. She also told me she decided to stop giving the children rice because they were eating a kilogram a day. Instead, she fed them sorghum which she bought at the local stock agents.

There was also no toilet roll and cut up cotton was used and washed after use. I couldn't believe, in this day and age, that this family could live so simply. The children were also home schooled. They had this beautiful relationship with each other. Part of the family were the carers for the youngest ones. The children played beautifully together and, in the entire time we were at Lake Victoria, they were very well behaved. I had beautiful places to walk as usual, and it never got too busy with other vehicles and caravans. A highly recommended and pleasant place to stay.

From Lake Victoria we spent some time at friends of friends in Mackay. They were going away for a week or so and needed someone to look after their animals. We obliged and it was nice to have a good look in and around Mackay. There is a fantastic botanical garden and I really enjoyed my walks around them. We also did a day trip to Sarina, a town further south and did a tour of the sugar factory.

West of Mackay there were also some beautiful places to visit, including a place called Finch Hatton. We did a few day trips from the house sit exploring new places. We always asked the locals of any town, what are the best places or best outings to do?

Whilst we were in Mackay, we noticed there was more rain coming, so we headed southwest again. We had picked out a free camp called Boynedale and headed there to avoid the rain. Boynedale was a great spot and had plenty of places to explore. There were also only a scattering of people so we had our usual privacy and no annoying neighbours.

It was also here that, out of the blue on messenger, came an unexpected and unrecollected incident. I wanted to include this because it said a great deal about my behaviour when I was in my early twenties.

## A LESSON FROM TRUDY, APRIL 2022

In early 2022, I received a message on messenger from a girl who I had managed with as a casual staff member at the Geelong Target store. I was a retail sales manager and worked in the hardgoods section of the store. Hardgoods were items for sale that weren't clothing or footwear.

At the weekends and also evening trading on Thursday and Friday nights, we had a group of young people to help with trade outside normal retail hours. They were mainly school students who worked after school on Thursday and Friday nights and Saturday morning, until close.

During my ridiculously nasty and cruel stages, due to my mental state, I was a bully and had no idea how to treat people. I don't ever really remember behaving that way but, unfortunately, I did. This poor young girl, some 33 years later, could no longer deal with the way I had so cruelly treated her.

This is the letter she sent to me.

*Hi Jo,*

*Not sure you remember me.*

*Many years ago, I was bullied by you, working as a 15-year-old after school casual at Target Geelong.*

*I'm now 48 and, as I think back to that moment in time, when I was a vulnerable teenager trying to navigate the world through my parents' divorce, I am still wondering why I was treated the way I was.*

*I can recall with clarity, you sending me home mid three-hour shift to change my pants because they were not black enough.*

*And you handing me your still burning cigarette to extinguish out in the back loading dock. When I didn't know how to do this, you snatched it back off me, threw it on the ground and stepped on it. Humiliating me in front of others.*

*Then there was the time at Geelong Golf Club when you pointed and mocked my dancing. After that night, I would only attempt to dance when I was drunk. To this day, I still feel incredibly self-conscious when dancing.*

*I do not know whatever happened to you to behave like this or how many other vulnerable people you bullied.*

*Looking back, your behaviour towards me had a profound effect on my self-esteem which, thankfully, has now been dealt with.*

*I hope that life has been good to you and you have found happiness in your life without the need to belittle and humiliate others.*


Her words stopped me immediately in my tracks.

My first reaction to this letter was to delete it and try to put it out of my mind. I was so sure I never knew such a person and I wasn't going to believe a word she had said. Or, that I had ever behaved in such a way.

Over the next 24 hours, it started to really bother me and I kept thinking how I would never have behaved like this. I can't ever remember being so mean to another person.

But then I began to reflect about that particular time in my life. It was probably one of my extremely darkest times. I was painfully addicted to food and purging all the time. I was addicted to slimming tablets that might as well been amphetamines. I had recently split up with my boyfriend of five and half years. I had also been raped by one of his friends. There was absolutely no emotional clarity and I was hopelessly insecure. I had absolutely no self-respect and no respect for others.

I had hated the world and I hated everyone in it. I hated myself so much that I couldn't care one bit about stepping all over vulnerable people. The total insecurity was probably what led me to put someone down. It would make me feel better. But only for a little while.

There was no excuse for my behaviour. Being the person I am now, I would never dream of being so cruel.

This was my initial reply:

*Hi Trudy,*

*I was quite shocked to receive your message yesterday morning. I don't remember you or any of these things, I was supposed to have done to you.*

*Thirty years ago, I was in an unbelievably bad place. Who knows how I may have behaved.*

*I am so sorry, to have been so nasty. It is not at all in my nature now.*

*I wasn't going to text you but it is bothering me so much that I could have been so horrible. I hope this can help you to forgive me and make a better difference to your life. Jo*

*Then another message*

*Hi Trudy, you are still in my thoughts since you contacted me. Not in any negative way.*

*I have seen that you are in Brisbane. I hope you are safe and dry. We are currently hanging out near Gladstone and staying above the rain.*

*Can't believe that we were in Brisbane last month and how your timing was impeccable, in contacting me.*

*Anyway, thank you so much for helping me to reflect on some of my horrible behaviour in my torrid and nasty times.*

*No doubt honesty and fluency helps us to cleanse and heal.*

*Take care Jo.*

Whatever you go through in life, there is no need to behave like I did. If you don't like yourself, then try and get help before you make someone else's life a misery. If you can't get help, because you are too frightened to come to terms with you, that's okay too. But if you have the opportunity to make amends like I did, then please do it. It will make a difference to someone's life if you can apologise and, it will make a difference to yours, because you will have the ability to forgive yourself.

I wrote to Trudy in July 2023 to see how she was and also asked permission to include this conversation in my book. I wanted desperately to include it, because it showed my tormented state of mind at the time. It also needed to be included because of my apology and her acceptance too. Trudy forgave me. I just hope I wasn't like that to anyone else. She was happy to oblige and was happy for me to include this in my story.

From Boynedale, we headed further north at the end of April making our way up through the precious stone mining towns. Most of the mines were in people's back gardens and they would dig and mine their precious stones to sell from home. The towns' names were Rubyvale, Sapphire and, of course, Emerald.

While we were travelling anywhere in the country, we always made sure we had a fully comprehensive weather channel. So, storm and rain events like these could be easily avoided.

In the middle of May, we were finding higher ground and travelling west again to avoid another big rain event in southern Queensland. This was where we found ourselves in a funny little town called Alpha. Funny in that it was one of the most laid back, slow rolling towns we had ever visited. We made a camp for over a week at a railway ballast, situated right next to the railway line. There was plenty of old railway sleepers to burn and we kept ourselves entertained by waving to the passing trains and vehicles on the railway. One morning, a police car came to warn us the Alpha creek would flood if the rain event came. Fortunately, we wouldn't have got wet anyway because we were on higher ground and the rain expected ended up not being as grand as it was first predicted.

David and I had visited Cape York in 2020 but we really wanted to go back there in 2022. After avoiding the last of the wet weather in eastern Queensland, we made our way back to the Cape. We had some lovely stops along the way and spent some time at a place just near Charters Towers. And just for something different, we were on a railway line.

After my mediation in 2020, I tried to stay in contact with the people that had encouraged me to help and guide survivors through the healing process. I spoke regularly to Kate Parsons and I had contact with a psychologist who was also associated with the school.

I had a conference call here with the psychologist and we covered a few new ideas about helping survivors. I also put together a grounding paper for the school, to deal with avoiding and coping with panic attacks.

From Charters Towers, we stayed at mostly free camps along the way until we stayed at a 72-hour rest area in Gordonvale just south of Cairns. It was here we had a new awning put on the caravan. Along with that, David was bitten by the next door neighbour's blue heeler and I also had to help another lady who was bitten by a nasty dog. Never a dull moment on the road.

We reached Cape York on 6th July and we camped in the exact spot we had stayed in two years before. It was at the Liberty Beach caravan park. We were on the sand and had a view across the sea to the Torres Strait islands.

Instead of going out to the Cape York tip again, we decided to do a three-island boat trip which included Horn Island, Thursday Island and Roko Island. On arriving at the start of our island tour, we were greeted at our boat by a few Torres Strait Islanders. One of them was to be our guide. He was a lovely young man and very informative.

On the way over, we sat on the boat opposite a young family. David has vitiligo, a chronic skin condition that causes pale white patches on the skin, on both of his legs and because he was wearing shorts, one of the children was staring at him. His mother told him off. David then piped up and, with his strange sense of humour, told the child he had been in the war and stepped on a land mine. He then reassured the child and mother about the story and explained it was vitiligo.

Our first stop on the journey was Horn Island. This was a significant target in WW2 for the Japanese and there was a war museum there. We had time to look around and watched a short movie about its involvement in the war.

When we boarded the boat again, we were on our way to Thursday Island. On arriving at the island, our guide walked us to the local taxi stand and allocated us all a driver and vehicle. David and I sat in the front of the vehicle, so we could hear his commentary. The fellow that drove us around was absolutely hysterical. I don't think I have laughed so much. Apart from a fabulous sense of humour, he was highly informative. He told us all about death ceremonies for Torres Strait Islanders, which were quite fascinating.

The death ceremonies were known as Sorry Business. These ceremonies involved a range of practices that honoured the deceased and supported their spirits' journey. Finally, after a few years, there was what was known as a significant ceremony. This honoured the deceased and marked the completion of the tombstone. It signified the family's goodbye and was a celebration of the person's life. This final celebration brought the community together in song, dance and feasting. Very different to how we celebrated a life.

The next part of the tour was to visit where all the military weapons were on the island. Most of them were never used. Another interesting fact about Thursday Island was, because Japanese pearlers were buried there prior to the war, the island was never bombed in WW2.

After the tour, we had a little free time to look around. We had lunch at Australia's most northern hotel and then returned to the boat to set off towards Roko island. The tour around Roko island was done on foot and we were met by a bloke in his late sixties. He was the only permanent resident on Roko island. The island is privately owned and was once a pearl farm that cultivated South Sea pearls.

Apart from glamping that was offered now, it was also infested with estuarine crocodiles. The bloke that took us for our tour, had a dog with a few chunks missing. The dog had managed to escape one of these crocodiles. All in all, the tour was worthwhile doing and I would recommend it if visiting Cape York.

David and I also decided this year, we would attend the southern hemisphere's biggest rodeo. It was to be held at Mt Isa on the 11th until the 14th August. We also knew a young Mansfield man who was going to be competing in the bull riding. His name was Will Purcell. Will had been successful throughout Australia and competed abroad as well, in the United States and Canada. We were looking forward to seeing him compete and also take in the atmosphere at such a big event.

We travelled down south through Lakeland, Gordonvale and then cut across towards Mareeba.

One memorable place we stayed at was Rocky Creek War Memorial Park. It was located at a place called Tolga and was on the way to Mareeba. We checked in with the caretaker lady and set up. Because of my love of walking and exploring, I wandered up to the lady who had checked us in and asked were there any notable places to visit apart from the war memorial. I also said I loved to walk and asked were there any paths that I could follow.

*Sacred Aboriginal birthing place in QLD*

From our chat, I got the feeling she was quite spiritually connected and this intrigued me. She then told me there was a very special place to visit in the area. She told me about an Aboriginal birthing place that was quite hard to find. After she gave me some instructions, she told me not many people find this place. Then she went on to say, those that did find it were meant to and would appreciate it for what it was.

I set off with her words and directions and, within 10 minutes, I came upon this incredibly beautiful and spiritual place. It had the most calming energy. I had never seen anything like this. It could be referred to as an amazing birthing oasis. Yet another incredible place in our country.

Prior to going to Mt Isa, we stayed at a ghost town called Mary Kathleen. It was once the town of a nuclear mine in central Queensland. It was great to walk around the old town and imagine what was there once and how people lived. There were no buildings as such but there were foundations in the ground and the streets were all still there. There were also updated information boards which talked about the history of the place.

Many caravaners stay there in the dry season and, even though it is popular, you can set yourself up, so you have your own space. Whilst we were there, David contacted a friend in Mansfield who knew people in Mt Isa. We needed to find accommodation during the busiest weekend of the year. We also needed to find somewhere safe as well. Mt Isa had a bad reputation for crime and violence.

We were put in contact with Heather and Peter and organised to stay in their back garden. We arrived in Mt Isa on 11th August and met them. They were currently building a new house in the Mansfield district and were moving down there at the end of the year. Peter worked at the copper mine in Mt Isa. After we had set up, we needed to get some supplies, so we went down to the local Woolworths.

It never ceased to amaze me when travelling in this country, as large as it was, you would meet someone, who knew someone you knew.

We were standing at the checkout in Woolworths and there was a woman in the queue in front of us. David was intrigued by the contents of this lady's shopping trolley. It was loaded with a stack of chocolate bars. He couldn't help but make a comment about it. Then the conversation started.

"You seem to be very fond of chocolate," said David.

The woman explained they were from the UK originally and it was exceedingly difficult to find this flavour of Cadbury chocolate in Australia. So, when she did find that particular flavour, she would always stock up.

Her accent was British, and the conversation turned to asking where she was from etc. I ducked back up into the supermarket to grab something I forgot and when I returned, the conversation came up about this lady's mother buying a horse from Mansfield. When I asked who did the vet check, the woman mentioned the vet's name.

I replied, "That particular vet is my younger sister."

It was such a small world.

That evening was the opening of the rodeo and there was a street party being held in the centre of town. Peter and Heather asked us if we wanted to go and have a drink and a bite to eat. We were happy to do just that. The only condition was, we needed to be home before 8pm. The reason for this was because the crowd would get drunk and nasty after that time. And as a result, it would become very unsafe. As we left the street party, there were quite a few people drinking and yelling out at each other. We were glad to be home safely.

Peter had told us a few stories about his growing up in Mt Isa. He also told us he himself was indigenous. In recent years, there had been a large transient movement of indigenous from the Northern Territory into Mt Isa and the violence and crime levels had escalated. Incidentally, this seemed to be a common reason for increased violence and crime in the larger towns in the outback.

Peter kindly took us for a drive the following day to look at some of the sites of Mt Isa and its surrounds. We visited Lake Mary Kathleen and drove around it. At the end of the lake were hundreds of dead fish. The smell was quite ordinary. There were machines piling them up in heaps. We asked Pete about this.

Apparently, in some years, there is an early wet season and extensive flooding. In other years, there have been extreme heatwaves and this also causes stress to the fish and leads to their death. This wasn't the first time Pete had seen this in his lifetime. We had a thoroughly interesting day.

As I have previously mentioned, the locals of a town are the best to ask about local attractions. That evening, we drove to a disused granite mine and had a couple of drinks whilst we watched the sun go down. It was magic.

On our way to Mt Isa, we had also organised to go out and see our friend, Judy, and stay at a large station in the territory to see what station life was all about. She was also coming to Mt Isa to watch another Mansfield friend, Will, compete at the rodeo.

On the Saturday of the rodeo was the best time to see Will compete. There were heats on and if he was to get through to the final, we could go on the Sunday as well.

David took our good camera with a lens to the gate at the rodeo grounds. When he approached the counter, he was asked to leave the lens behind. I asked the lady at the counter why we couldn't take it in. They were not permitted inside because of the animal liberationists, PETA. The People for the Ethical Treatment of Animals were a group that would turn up at these events and film whatever they could to stop the sport.

In all my years of attending rodeos, I had never seen an animal so badly treated or injured that it needed to euthanised. PETA was yet another group currently that were very extreme.

We went in without the lens and found Judy. From there we watched a few events before Will came on to compete. Unfortunately, he didn't have a good ride and he injured himself very badly. He was taken off in an ambulance to the Mt Isa Hospital. We caught up again with Judy to organise when we would go out to the station and we left pretty soon after that.

I rang Will that evening in the hospital. He had rebroken his neck. This had happened once before, and he forbade us from ringing his mother or telling anyone about it. He was going to be alright, but he didn't want his mother worrying. I did what I was told, for once.

345

# CHAPTER 48

## *DAVID'S HEALTH REVISITED*

After a couple more days, we left Heather and Peter's place and headed towards the Northern Territory. We had lunch In Camooweal and then turned off at Ranken and headed towards the Northern Territory's Alexandria station. We stayed along the road that night, camped on a dry creek and then arrived at the station the following morning.

Alexandria station is a pastoral lease that operates as a cattle station. It is the largest pastoral property in the Northern Territory and Australia's third largest pastoral property after Anna Creek station and Clifton Hills station. Alexandria station is 16,116 square kilometres of open plains and wooded Sandhills and is situated on the Barkly Tableland. It was established prior to 1877.

Our first glimpse at Alexandria station was incredible. I had never been to any place like this before. We had driven through station county in central Queensland, but this was out of this world. You could see absolutely nothing for miles, yet it had an immense aura about it. About that outback obsession!

There were many buildings and ablution blocks for the 50 or so employees that worked there. There was also catering staff, including Judy, butchers, ringers, machine operators, bore runners and more. We met the managers on the first day. Kate was expecting her fourth child and was a registered nurse.

We parked the van outside Judy's house and had use of the ablution blocks etc. We didn't dine in the evenings with the staff but caught up for drinks in the mess room and played a bit of pool.

I enjoyed my walks and loved watching the workings of the station. I was lucky enough to go out for a full morning on a bore run. This run is to ensure that the water supply to the cattle is maintained. The bores, Turkey nests (dams) are checked regularly and bore pumps are run to top up if required. Bore runners also check pumps and equipment, keep a daily maintenance diary and report any issues to the management. It was all very interesting and very new to me.

Around 20th August, David told me he wasn't feeling too good and was having trouble breathing. He was producing bloody sputum when he coughed. I went to see Kate, to ask about what we should do. She suggested David have a phone appointment with the Royal Flying Doctors. We went ahead with that later in the day and David was diagnosed with a respiratory infection and was prescribed antibiotics. Kate had some on hand and he started his course. The following morning, he said he felt a little better. Possibly a placebo effect because of the antibiotics.

While we were staying there, we had offered to help fix up the chook house and run. There were holes in the roof and sides of the netted run, and our main aim was to repair it so the crows couldn't get in and eat the eggs. The chook yard was about 100 metres from the caravan. David had struggled to get there on that morning. The following morning, there was more blood in his sputum, and he had complained of a sore calf. When he went to visit the bathroom on the Sunday morning, he had struggled again to get there. We were both starting to become quite worried.

Kate was due to go into Mt Isa, about 410kms away for a doctor's appointment on the Monday morning. David and I had a discussion about him going in with her. I said he needed to make the decision. He decided to go into Mt Isa with Kate.

They left quite early on the Monday morning and without breakfast. Kate decided to have a break at Camooweal and get a coffee and breakfast then. David went off to the bathroom and really struggled to get back to the car. By the time they were on their way again, David told me he was even struggling to talk. He was so out of breath.

They finally arrived at the emergency department at Mt Isa hospital and Kate dropped him off at the door. As David approached the window, he was asked what was wrong. Without uttering a word, the nurse knew immediately what was going on and disappeared, then reappeared with a trolley. David was hooked up to oxygen and was seen to immediately by a doctor. The doctor asked him if he had had any pain in his lower leg. From David's reply, he told David he had a pulmonary embolism. The clot had travelled up his leg, gone through his heart and ended up blocking his pulmonary artery.

He was transferred to intensive care and put on thrombolytic needles for three days. These thrombolytics would help to dissipate the blood clot.

After David's initial diagnosis, because of COVID, he had to take a rapid antigen test. The nurse confirmed he had COVID, so he placed into isolation for the first night. During the night he had to take a proper test for COVID. That came back negative.

When he first contacted me and told me what was going on, I was concerned I had COVID too. So, until I could test myself, I didn't spend any time with anyone at the station. I put myself into isolation. Along with the dread of having COVID, I was really scared about what might happen to David. He was in good hands, but he was in intensive care and was critical for a couple of days until the thrombolytics kicked in.

I spent most of my days researching his condition and other associated conditions. Since doing my nutrition course, I had enjoyed researching medicine and ailments in people my age and older. It was another useful hobby whilst we were travelling. My rapid antigen test came back negative as well. Thankfully.

By Wednesday, 25th August, David had improved considerably and was able to start walking further without being out of breath. The hospital was going to release him on 26th and we needed to find a way to get him back to the station. Judy needed to go into Mt Isa on the 25th and was coming back via Camooweal to go to the annual rodeo. She was going to stay in a swag on the Thursday night after the rodeo.

Because I didn't have a light truck licence, David did all the driving in our F250. I could drive it if I had to but it would not be legal. When I spoke to David, the only option was to send a swag in with Judy, and he could stay at the rodeo grounds. Not really suitable for a man who had just got out of intensive care with a pulmonary embolism.

I had liaised with Judy about the time she was due in Camooweal so I could pick David up. I also didn't tell David. I was a little nervous to start with when I got into the truck. I hadn't driven for quite some time and hadn't driven the Ford this far. I had put a couple of things in place before I left as well. One being, that I was on the local two-way radio channel in case I had a flat tyre. I would have struggled to change the tyre on my own. I also had plenty of water with me. Another important item in the outback.

Driving on my own in the outback was one of the most amazing experiences I have ever had driving. I was alone, I was free and there were miles and miles of red dirt, rocks and an eternity of space. It took your breath away.

The road into the highway was all dirt and I just stayed on 80 kms per hour all the way. Once I hit the highway, I had become a lot more confident. However, there were exceptionally large road trains, and I was a little nervous to start with. By the time I reached Camooweal, I was sitting on the speed limit. The speed limit in the Northern Territory is 130kmph.

I rang Judy when I arrived and she told me that they were sitting at the cafe in the service station. David had his back to me, and I just walked up behind him and gave him an enormous cuddle. It was emotional because, for a while, I had thought I was going to lose him again.

David drove back to the station, and we watched the sun go down with a couple of beers once we were on the dirt. Another adventure on our travels.

# CHAPTER 49

## *ADVENTURES ON THE ROAD*

David fully recovered and was now on medication for the rest of his life to take out the tackiness in his blood. The medication is not blood thinners; they were anticoagulants.

The rest of the time we stayed at the station was for David's recovery. We were included by everyone out there. Station life was an amazing experience.

Another circumstance that ensured we stayed longer, was a rain event that closed some of the routes out of the station. We were going to go out through Brunette Downs, but it was too muddy. So, we had to head back out to the highway on the same road we came in on. From there, we organised to go up to Darwin and catch up with friends. We weren't in any hurry, so we decided to take some of the back roads. Our first brief stop was at Barkly Roadhouse. A local girl from Mansfield managed the roadhouse, so it was a good excuse to catch up with a familiar face.

From Barkly Roadhouse we decided to go out through some more stations in the outback. We took the Central Tablelands Highway and headed along past some of the stations we would have been through if it hadn't rained.

About 4pm that afternoon, driving on a single strip of bitumen,

David's side of the car dropped down and we hit the road on the brake rotor. My exclamation was, "What the flip was that?"

David said calmly, "We have lost a wheel."

Before we came to a halt, we had crossed over a cattle grid and found ourselves on the edge of the verge but, fortunately, still intact. David is an exceptional driver, thank goodness.

Adrenaline was streaming through me and, as usual, I started to shake. I leapt out of the car and said I was going to find the wheel. David got out and assessed the damage. We had also lost the wheel guard and that was sitting back up the road before the cattle grid. The wheel studs had sheared off and there was no sign of any wheel nuts anywhere. When I was walking up and down looking for the wheel, two four-wheel drive vehicles stopped and asked if we needed help. Typical station hands in the outback. They are good country men that just want to help out. These boys were from Brunette Downs station. We eventually found the wheel. It was a couple of hundred metres ahead of the car.

The boys hung around for a while, and we had a beer with them for their help. One of the guys offered to go and get some wheel studs from the station, so we could limp off and find somewhere until we could order parts. He returned later with some Toyota studs and wheel nuts. They would do but David needed to modify them a bit so we could fit them to our F250 rims that weren't standard. Because of our position on the road and the lack of a wheel, we couldn't move either the van or the car. We needed to spend the night on the side of the road. So, in order to be seen, we lit a fire out in front of the car. David also left some parker lights on.

There were cattle road trains that travel along the Central Tablelands Highway quite frequently. They were over 50 metres long and we were only just off the road. I remembered waking in the night with a road train passing beside me close to the bedroom window. About a foot.

The following day, I went for a walk to see if I could find any of our wheel nuts. For the four and half kilometres I walked, I found nothing.

David started tirelessly modifying and putting in the wheel studs and new wheel nuts. Halfway through the morning, he had made phone calls to Melbourne to organise the parts. This was on a satellite phone. One of the guys in Melbourne had wanted photos of the wheel nuts. This was not possible on a satellite phone. After we had organised the wheel studs, they were going to be posted to Barkly Roadhouse. The wheel nuts were still a dilemma.

After a few more hours, three carloads of guys with boats turned up and asked if we needed a hand. They had been fishing in the Gulf of Carpentaria and were Victorian. After further discussion, David told me about the dilemma with the wheel nuts. David explained to a guy that he needed to order them from a Mister Lugnut, who was situated in Lilydale. You wouldn't believe it but this guy knew the business and the person who ran it. Small world yet again.

We asked them if they wouldn't mind taking a photo of the wheel nuts and sending a text through to Mister Lugnut when they arrived at Barkly Roadhouse. It was no problem at all. Before they left us, we were offered about three kilograms of frozen Spanish mackerel. Did not resist that at all. The travelling public, especially in the outback, were extremely helpful and would go out of their way to help. Another wonderful thing about most travelling Australians.

Because of the time frame and our travel schedule, we needed to get the wheel nuts posted further up the highway than Barkly Roadhouse. David organised these to be posted to Tennant Creek. After the car was fixed and the wheel was back on, we headed slowly to another outback station called Anthony's Lagoon.

The Brunette Downs station manager had recommended we went there to wait until our parts arrived. We were given a place at the back of the homestead and we had access to washing machines and ablution blocks. It was satisfactory.

On that weekend each year, there was an inter-station competition which included activities like barrel racing, calf wrangling, and other horsey events. They were quite busy.

David needed to have the use of the internet and some reception, so he could follow up our parts orders and have a date when we could get back to Barkly Roadhouse.

We were introduced to the station manager the next morning and, interestingly, the first thing she asked was, whether we had been to Bali recently. It was totally out of the blue. Apparently, there had been a foot and mouth outbreak in Bali. Paranoid station managers, I guessed. We ensured this woman that, no we had not spent any time in Bali. Well, not since 2014. The rest of our stay there was just okay. We kept to ourselves because we really didn't feel as comfortable and welcome as we had at other earlier stations.

We left Anthony's Lagoon on 5th September and headed back to the Barkly Roadhouse. We looked along the Central Tablelands Road for our wheel nuts as we back-tracked. We found quite a few wheel nuts along the way but they weren't from our Ford. On arriving at Barkly, we were welcomed by Sally and her staff and set up the caravan for a couple of nights.

A few days before we arrived, a dreadful strip storm had gone through the centre of the caravan park at the roadhouse. It was in one hell of a mess. There were trees squashing cars and large heaps of tree debris in the back of the park. This is not uncommon in the outback. Storms are damaging and fuelled with heavy rain and incredible winds. The wind was measured, during this storm, at 175km per hour.

I am glad we weren't there. Fortunately, no one had been hurt but some of the staff said it had been extremely frightening. One staff member was noted to say they couldn't open the door of their accommodation because the wind was so strong.

My morning walk, the next day, was around the park. Most days when I walked, I nearly always found something that could be useful to us.

I tended to find plenty of D shackles without the pin and when I produced them to David, he normally asked me to go and find the rest of it.

I was up at the camping site end of the campground, which had already been vacated for the day. I walked around the path outside the camp sites, and, to my delight, I found a leather-man, a multitool device with scissors, screwdriver, file and pliers. A very handy tool. I looked at it and thought, *I know what you are* and picked it up. The strap that attached it to a belt was broken and must have fallen off. Whoever had lost it had long gone, so when I returned to the van, I gave it to David. What a wow find. I remember buying one for my sons and it was not cheap. They are an exceptional tool to have.

That afternoon, our parcel turned up at the roadhouse. We set off for Tennant Creek the following day and found a paid safe camp at Tennant Creek station. It was a lovely spot, not too far out of town and we had plenty of wood. We now needed to wait for the next parcel to turn up.

There is always maintenance that needs to be done to the car and caravan when travelling. David needed to go to the hardware store to buy something. He parked outside the local men's shed and was approached by an indigenous man who asked him how long he was going to be there. They spoke for quite some time and he introduced himself as Jabal Jarri. He was involved with the men's shed and was an indigenous artist. He asked David how long he was going to be in town and David told him we were waiting for a part and not really sure how long it was going to be. It was coming by Australia Post.

Just as a side mention, the postal delivery in the middle of the Northern Territory had a strange way of getting to its destination. In our case, the parcel ended up on a truck up the Stuart Highway, through Tennant Creek to Darwin. Then from Darwin, it was put on the Greyhound bus and taken back down to Tennant Creek.

When David told Jabal Jarri our story, he told David he was offering free and safe accommodation to travellers in his own yard. He was remarkably close to the Main Street of Tennant Creek. He wanted to set up vacant land beside his house and have guests stay for free. Jabal Jarri had a studio at his house, where he did all his paintings. We left Tennant Creek station and went to Jabal's house until our parcel arrived on the Greyhound bus.

He had a white Australian wife and a couple of dogs. We camped with him for a couple of days. They were a lovely couple. He let me ask him a few questions about his life which was very interesting. His mother was full-blooded Aboriginal, and his father was white. He told me he had been a stolen generation child and sent down to Adelaide for school. He and his brother ran away and returned home. Then they were sent to Queensland to be with his father's family. He told me he said to his brother, "These aren't our people" and they returned to Tennant Creek once again.

He also talked a lot about the trouble that occurred in Tennant Creek, the violence and sexual abuse and the alcohol problems. He told me as a young man; Tennant Creek was a gold mining town. It had many pubs and drinking places and there was never any trouble. Then other indigenous communities came into the area and that was where the trouble started. One community did not necessarily get on with the next.

We looked through his studio, and he taught us what the signs on the paintings meant. We bought a piece with turtles on it and it is in our caravan to this day. I also bought indigenous art bookmarks. It was a thoroughly enjoyable experience.

Whilst we were still in Tennant Creek, I had my hair done by the only hairdresser in town. She and her husband had moved there for that reason. Her husband's job as a carpenter was a one only as well. We chatted away as usual about different things. I told her we were staying with Jabal and, of course, the conversation about indigenous local people came up. We talked about a lot of relevant subjects, and both expressed a need to find some solution to the ongoing social problems in these towns.

She told me of a visit by the prime minister about a year prior. When a prime minister, even our current prime minister, visited a town in the Northern Territory, there was an enormous cover up of our indigenous problems. Two weeks prior, the surrounding communities get a clean-up job. The indigenous that sat around the street during the day, were moved on or sent home. The rubbish was removed from the streets, and everything was cleaned up.

The prime minister arrived in a plane and did a quick tour of the town and then returned to Canberra. It was a farce. He spent 10 times more time in the air than he did in a town and did not see how it really was.

Our parcel arrived on the Greyhound bus at around midnight, and we set off the next day towards Darwin. We arrived in Darwin on 15th September and stayed at a place called Bees Creek. For my birthday on 16th September, David and I went out for lunch after we had explored the WW2 tunnels in Darwin. Another worthwhile activity to do whilst visiting Darwin. A couple of other places to visit are the Darwin Museum and the war museum.

The planned stay with our friends, unfortunately, fell through, so we headed back down the highway towards Alice Springs. Along the way, we stopped for a look at Barrow Creek pub. There was a lot of information about the disappearance of Peter Falconio, a back packer who mysteriously disappeared in July 2001. We had a beer and read up on the news information all over the pub's walls.

Another memorable time on this visit to Barrow Creek was having a beer with three indigenous guys in Geelong football club colours. Being a Geelong Cat's fan, I couldn't help myself but struck up a conversation with them. It was also the year Geelong was in the grand final and it was due to be played the following weekend. We took photos of the guys with their permission. They were delightful. I told them I would send them the photos to their phones and would put a post on Facebook.

When we left, I put their photo on social media and, in the end, I had over five hundred hits. I kept sending them the updates for a few days after. Geelong football club won the grand final that year.

We headed through Alice Springs and did the basic shopping as usual and got out of there. Alice Springs was a very scary place these days. The gangs in the streets were rough, and you always had to be on guard. We never left the car and caravan without one of us staying with it. We now no longer stayed at Alice Springs in our caravan and never would again. From Alice Springs, we stayed at Stuarts Well. It was a safe campground for travellers, and you could leave your caravan there safely to explore some of the hidden wonders close by.

*Rainbow Valley Northern Territory outback*

During our stay at Stuarts Well, we visited one of the most beautiful places I have seen in Australia. It was about 50 or so kilometres south of

Alice Springs and called Rainbow Valley. David and I drove from camp one afternoon to watch the sun go down. It was an incredibly special indigenous place where they could freely hunt and gather resources. The landscape was breathtakingly beautiful, and the colours of the rocks were absolutely stunning and unique.

We headed south to a camp at Owens Valley reserve and set up to stay for a couple of weeks. We wanted to watch the AFL grand final and just stay in the warmer weather a bit longer. After the first week David went back into Alice Springs to get some more water and food.

The trip through the Northern Territory had played on my mind a great deal this time. We had seen a lot of heartache when it came to indigenous people. It was so sad to know what had been going on for so long and nobody had ever had any success in fixing it. Unless you have travelled in the Northern Territory and stopped and experienced the towns, you have no idea what goes on.

It was because of the way I was feeling, and that was extremely sad, that I contacted my oldest son. My children's father has a small splash of indigenous blood in him. His great-great-grandmother had had a fling with an indigenous man who was shearing at their property in New South Wales many years ago. My children were only 3.5 percent Aboriginal but identified as indigenous to this country.

I decided to strike up a conversation on Messenger with my son. I was expressing how sad it was that I had seen awful problems in Tennant Creek, Darwin, and Alice Springs. We conversed for quite a while, but it became obvious he was stewing on events that had occurred in the past. All of a sudden, he totally blew me out of the water, with the following final message:

*It's not a discussion; it's you speaking your opinions without any consideration for the implications they have. You only send these articles to force your opinion. You're not an indigenous person; you've not had to endure what your kids have in terms of racism and the impact these opinions have on self-efficacy.*

*You claim to be understanding yet don't take the time to acknowledge the opinion of others, this goes for many other topics i.e. climate change.*

*This is why I don't enjoy our engagements; it's always a force of opinion for the sake of what? Being right about something?*

*But at what cost? All you do is make me resent talking to you.*

*I would appreciate if you don't contact me further on these issues. I have expressed this before, so for once, please respect my opinion.*

*Still up in the air whether I'll make time to come and see you when you are down.*

I was shattered to say the least. I had been talking about what I had seen and also the lacklustre of any politician regarding the hopelessness of our indigenous in the centre of this country. I was defending indigenous people, and I was extremely sad about the way that they were and are still being treated.

I started questioning myself. What had I done wrong? Was I a terrible mother? Was I a terrible person? Did I abandon my children? Only one of my children had ever told me about any racial vilification and that was my second son. And that had certainly been successfully dealt with.

I would have listened if I had been told. It either never happened with my older son or it was never mentioned. I find it extremely hard to believe, because my older son always came to me when there was something wrong. In other words, he respected my opinions and advice. Clearly not written in the above piece of his writing.

# CHAPTER 50

## *SOUTH AUSTRALIA AND KANGAROOS*

We headed south after a couple of weeks of staying at Owens Springs Reserve. On 14th October 2022, we went down the old Ghan track from Finke and continued towards the South Australian border. We camped on a station for the night, had a lovely fire, and took in more of the beautiful outback.

The next morning, we were due to go into Mt Dare to catch up with friends from Mansfield who had lived there years ago. Getting ready to leave, David was levelling up the caravan. I heard air hissing as he was pumping up the airbags with the compressor. I said I thought we might have a tyre going down. In fact, we had been driving through rocky country the day before and a rock had wedged itself up in one of the new airbags and worn a hole in it. Far out! We only had about 50 kilometres to the Mt Dare Hotel, so David put extra air in the front airbag, and we drove slowly into South Australia to the pub.

We arrived safely and set up in the campground. David called the suspension place in Queensland and ordered a new airbag. Interestingly, the bloke on the phone said, "This has never happened before."

Sounded a bit like Murphy's law to me.

We settled in and caught up with Graeme, Sandra, and Shaynee Scott. Mt Dare was the northern most pub in South Australia and was the start and finish of the trip across the Simpson Desert. Birdsville was at the other end. It had accommodation for weary drivers and a large campground too. Mt Dare was set up to do desert rescues, had fuel, qualified mechanics, a shop, restaurant, and bar. There were several staff who worked there and stayed for the season when the desert is open. It is an extremely popular place in the winter and extremely hot in the summer months.

*Remote pub in outback*

During our first week at Mt Dare, we stayed in the campground. In the first few days of our stay, a group that specialised in dirt and sand buggies had come in with Can-Am logos on their vehicles and set up at the other end of the campground with tents and above ground beds. Temporary accommodation for these guests who would be driving dune buggies on and around the outback tracks during the day. They had their own caterer, and the pub was providing them space to stay, with showers and toilets. Of course, alcohol was available to buy at the bar.

A crew came in the day before to set up part of the campground for guests. The afternoon after they had set up, we had a strip storm come through the campground. We sat and watched it tear out tents, small marquees, and up end beds. It totally trashed the setup, right in front of our eyes.

The next morning, David and I started to tidy up the site. Whilst we were tidying up, we noticed the Can-Am organisers had put a few pallets of wood out for campfires. Interestingly, there were quite a few green pieces of red mulga on the pallets. Red mulga is quite a rare tree and apparently had indigenous spiritual significance which we found out later from an indigenous woman from Finke. The group came in and left after about four days. David and I helped in the kitchen and bar.

The Can-Am event was an immense success after all. The buggies returned home most days with people covered from top to toe in red dirt and mud. When the group had gone, a group of indigenous came down from Finke. The woman, mentioned above, was an artist and had paintings for sale in the pub. After they had chatted for a while, the indigenous woman asked Shaynee if she could have a look at some of the wood on the pallets that had been left over from the Can-Am stay. When she returned from outside, she had two long pieces of red mulga in her arms. Being nosey, I asked her what she was going to do with them.

She told me they were sacred Aboriginal wood. Sacred for women because of their red colour and synonymous with menstruation. She told me she was going to make women's protection clubs. These indigenous weapons of protection are called nulla nullas. They are made by removing all the red curly bark and then sanding the wood down until it was smooth. Interestingly, another thing she happened to mention was, any white man who cut down a red mulga tree would be cursed. Maybe that was what had happened in the campground. David then made us some nulla nullas out of red mulga to keep in the car and caravan. Just for protection.

David and I invited to stay and help until we needed to return to Mansfield for Christmas. We took up the offer and moved our caravan out of the campground into a better area. Because of my experience from my cleaning business, I decided to earn my keep by spring cleaning all the accommodation, as well as tidying up and revamping the shop. My Target days were also well used.

For my constitutional walk, I went up and down the airstrip every day. On returning, I would set to the chores. We all caught up at night for a beer, and it was a terrific way to spend time there. On a couple of occasions, we needed to drive to Alice Springs to get supplies. The Scotts had a flat in there and we stayed the night once, before returning to the pub the following day.

Another attraction at Mt Dare was, Shaynee had a pet Joey. He was given to her by some of the indigenous in Finke. Much to my horror, they had killed his mother so they could eat her tail and then realised there was a joey in her pouch. His name was Jackie Longlegs. Shaynee was amazing with this joey, pretty much like she was with any animal. Her dog, Gemma, was also the luckiest dog in the world. Together we did a little bit of research into raising kangaroos and how their bodies worked. I had never really thought about it and finding out about their anatomy was amazing.

Kangaroos have a cloaca which serves as the exit for both the digestive and reproductive systems. It is the opening where faeces are expelled and where the penis is inserted for mating. They also have an embryonic diapause where a female can temporarily halt the development of a fertilised embryo. Jackie Longlegs ate dirt and gravel to enhance his gut flora. It was very interesting to learn a bit about kangaroos together. We tend to take our wildlife for granted. Yet they are extremely complex beings.

During the time we were at Mt Dare, I was also contacted by the victims register regarding Fred Smith. Fred Smith had applied for parole and was going to be granted an earlier release date in April 2023. One of the reasons for early release included a COVID clause. Obviously, it was a hard life in prison when there was a pandemic on. I was invited to do a written submission to the parole board to view my case and my daughter's case.

My submission included the following. Please note that names have been changed to protect privacy and security.

*In my opinion and in reading through the court transcript, I don't believe the time of imprisonment has been as long as it should be for Fred Smith. Fred Smith has had a criminal history for quite some time and has offended over many years. Understanding that they weren't all sexual offences, but he clearly has poor judgment and is affected by substance abuse.*

*He also has a history of substance abuse. What is there to say that he won't continue to use illicit drugs in the future and commit more of this type of crime?*

*For the safety of other members of the community, I feel he couldn't possibly be rehabilitated into society at this early stage. His crime, as the judge described it, was outrageous.*

*He was stalking my daughter long before he took any drug and was openly bragging about what his actions were going to be. It was premeditated. He planned the entire assault and even made the mistake of telling someone what his actions would be.*

Fortunately, I did not hear back from the victims register. I was informed by my friend, Petrina, that if I did not hear anything then Smith would have had his parole application rejected.

During our stay at Mt Dare, we managed to do a few days of exploration. We visited the Dalhousie Springs. Dalhousie Springs is a large upside-down shower rose discharging water from the Great Artesian Basin through approximately 80 holes called mound springs. The hot temperature of the earth's core heats the waters of the artesian basin.

Some of the water in Dalhousie Springs comes from Queensland and the Northern Territory. It takes water up to 3 million years to escape to the surface through rock faults as springs.

In the main pool where you can swim, the water temperature 34-38 degrees Celsius and up to 14 metres deep. West of the main pool the water is around 43 degrees Celsius. I dipped my feet in only. The water was too hot for me.

We also took one of the work vehicles out to the Old Andado homestead. Another destination to visit if you are in the area. We spent a couple of hours looking through the buildings. There were many relics and knick-knacks from a bygone era.

Molly Clark, the station owner's wife, who had taken over the running of the station, was buried out there and had a head stone in the cemetery at the homestead. Another Australian story of hardship and strength found in the outback and desert country.

Another highlight at Mt Dare was the Christmas party. It was held on 19th November and involved people from far and wide. It was a great party and, for the first time in a long time for me, it felt like Christmas. Children were given presents around the Christmas tree and the food and beverages were fantastic. We also had a great fireworks display put on by one of the Christmas guests. It was a fantastic way to finish off the party.

After about eight weeks at Mt Dare, we headed south through South Australia. Apart from trouble with the car at Pimba, it was smooth sailing. It was quite strange to be stuck at Pimba and not for the first time either. It brought back memories of the school excursion to Ayers Rock when I was at Bostock House in the seventies. We never made it to the rock and were bogged at Pimba. In those days, the roads weren't sealed and would turn to thick mud with the slightest drop of rain.

After two days when the part turned up, David fixed the car and we moved on. Our next scheduled stop was at an old friend, Spud's house at Mylor in the Adelaide Hills. About an hour before we arrived, we blew a water coolant hose on a large ascent on one of the main roads up into the area. David pulled over. Because we couldn't get right off the road, I walked down the road to warn the traffic there was a vehicle stuck in the left hand lane. We had lost most of the coolant out of the car and David needed to replace the hose and refill the liquid.

After about 15 minutes, a policeman turned up. He asked me what was going on and I said we were just having a cup of tea. Then I told him what had happened. He had his lights flashing which meant I could return to the car and help David fix the problem. We used our drinking water to refill the radiator after the hose was replaced. Another drama on the road but easily fixed.

We arrived at Spud's a little later and spent a couple of days there. We went for a drive down to Tailem Bend on the Murray River to have a look at the extent of its flooding and see the preparations put in place to save houses and a great deal of the town. Sadly, there were houses already under water, on the other side of the river.

The next couple of days were spent hanging out and catching up. We went out for lunch in a lovely town called Hahndorf, which is full of original German style architecture. The meal at the pub was enormous but thoroughly enjoyable. Another town worth visiting in South Australia.

On leaving Spud's place, we were asked if we would like to come back in 2023 in January to house sit. We accepted and then headed towards Mansfield, visiting David's sister and family in Harrow on the way.

We spent Christmas in Mansfield and had a Boxing Day get-together with two of my kids and David's daughter, Nichola. My older son, as stated in his Messenger text, didn't turn up. It was disappointing but this was his problem to deal with.

On 27th December, David and I packed up the Ford, armed with tarps and a mattress in the back, and headed up into the Wonnangatta for a week in the lead up to the new year. I had always wanted to go out there and see the history of the place. It was a working farm many years ago and had a pioneer history to it. The Wonnangatta also had some interesting, recent history in relation to strange murders that happened there. There was a book written about the Wonnangatta murders, *The Wonnangatta Mystery: An Inquiry Into the Unsolved Murders*, which was a good read.

*Howitt Plains in the Wonnangatta*

# CHAPTER 51

## *2023*

Apart from catching up with family and friends, we didn't spend too much time in Mansfield and headed back towards South Australia for our housesitting in January. The 10 days we were in Mylor were spent mowing, fixing gates, spring cleaning and tending to horses and a lovely dog.

Our next house sit was really a farm sit at Kadathinni. We had promised Michael we would come back in early February for shearing and stay until the weather got too cold.

We stocked up with enough food to make it across to Norseman. There is not much to offer fresh food wise from Ceduna. We also bought some prawns at Streaky Bay. We were on the Nullarbor on 4th February. Along the Nullarbor, we spent about a couple of nights at Bunda Cliffs, which looks out on the Southern Ocean. When we first chose our spot, we were about 10 metres from the cliffs edge. Because of my fear of heights, I stayed away from the edge. My walks were refreshing, taking in the ocean and surrounding countryside.

Crossing the border at Eucla, we made sure we had done the right thing quarantine-wise. The Western Australian and South Australian borders were very strict about fruit and vegetables and plants crossing over. The quarantine people accepted the food for the bin. When we were asked if we had any seafood, we said we had frozen green prawns. The woman at the quarantine told us to go back to the South Australian side, cook the prawns and eat them. We were told to give the quarantine people the empty shells and we could be on our way.

*Farm at Kadathinni*

I was always intrigued about what the prawns do in the Southern Ocean when they reach the border. Just a little traveller's tip. We have also now acquired a handbook of what is permitted and what isn't permitted when crossing the state borders of Australia. Driving into Western Australia, the first thing I noticed was the state of the roads. They were excellent compared the Victorian and South Australian roads.

We had a lovely stop and explored at Karalee Rocks. This was a water catchment area for a water reserve used by people travelling between areas of gold mining when gold was discovered in the area in the 1860s. The large expanses of granite rock had walls built around the bottom that guided water along aqueducts to a holding dam and wells. There was, incidentally, a great area to free camp away from the highway.

Another place we stayed on the way to Kadathinni, was Lake Indoon. We had a night stopover there. During the night, the dingoes came in and stole our thongs. Well, to be honest, both of our two left foot thongs. The mozzies were as big as March flies as well. Not a bad spot but put your shoes inside and cover up at night.

We arrived at Kadathinni on 19th February 2023. Michael was in the throes of shearing. There wasn't much we could do with the shearers because they had their own team who fed them and there wasn't the normal farmer involvement we had been used to.

The first morning, Michael asked David and myself to go for a drive and see what needed doing with bore water and the troughs. I replied, I had my own agenda and I stayed at the house and started spring cleaning. Up until this time, I was writing this book but things seemed to go on hold now for nearly six months.

Farm life was busy and it was amazing to be back on a working farm with sheep again. The days rolled into weeks and months. We would get up around 8.30am and I would go for a 6-8 kilometre walk, either on the farm or up Kangaroo Road. Then it would be home for breakfast and then out checking and cleaning troughs etc.

One other little task I had set myself, was to get the vegetable garden up and running. Weather in the area during summer was very hot at 45 degree Celsius heat. Most vegetables at the farm had no problem growing as long as they had enough water. Michael's father, Jamie, set up a water timer on the vegetable garden and it worked perfectly. On the extreme heat days, I would water in the evening as well. Some days I needed to put bed sheets over the garden to protect plants from the scorching sun. We did end up with our own fresh produce from March onwards.

*David shearing rams at Kadathinni at 73 years of age*

David and I did some fencing for Michael and David fixed a lot of gates that had been hit by machinery over the years. The gates were damaged mainly by backpackers who had stayed at the farm during seeding and harvest. We stayed at the farm until the end of March and headed into Geraldton to do a house sit for Michael's parents. It was a nice break for three weeks. Michael's parents previously ran a station northeast of Carnarvon and had retired to Geraldton. They loved the outback in the same way we did. Every year they had a trip away to remote areas just to have an outback fix.

It was during this house sit, I was contacted by Geelong Grammar School to get involved with another survivor and help her get the right help and advice in order to proceed with her mediation. This was one of many people I had facilitated healing with. For obvious reasons, I won't mention any names. Her abuser had been a science teacher at the school. He had, on a number of occasions, groped her in class. The problem was she couldn't remember his name. Between Kate Parsons and myself, we managed to get a photo of this man and she identified him that way. I was in contact with her, mainly for support, off and on during this year. I later found out this man had also raped his own daughter on numerous occasions. His daughter was a student in my school year at Corio.

I started writing again whilst we were in Geraldton. It helped me process the thoughts I was still having about Geelong Grammar's heinous past. The contact with other survivors also helped me believe more about the person I was now and how I could help others to survive.

We returned to the farm at the end of April. Every time we returned to the farm, I would have emotions about the freedom and sense of belonging to a rural place. It was home to me. We fed lambs, checked troughs and David, despite being a contract shearer for many years, started, at age 73, shearing rams.

When we first visited the farm in 2022, we had met a neighbour of Michael's. His name was Phil. Phil loved a beer and was a general shit stirrer. I was a little sceptical of him to start with and a little paranoid. Most likely a feeling developed from my past. But now I felt comfortable and enjoyed his company.

Michael had some merino rams that had been missed by the shearers in February. David had piped up and said he would shear them. Being a shearer for many years, it wouldn't be a drama. Phil couldn't believe he would do it. There weren't any bets but shearing gear was organised and a date set. Phil came to attend the procedure with his six pack in hand.

It was quite entertaining. Firstly, we needed to sedate the rams a little so they weren't hard to handle. Michael, who was a big strong man, held the rams and David sheared them one by one with a break after the first two and then sheared two more. Phil gave a running commentary and I videoed the footage on my phone. David managed to shear the 18 rams over a few days.

Because we were coming into lambing season and foxes and wild dogs were prolific at Kadathinni, David and I spent two days baiting the entire boundary with 1080. Every 100 metres we laid a bait and put a marker on the fence. For just an idea of how many foxes there were in the area, on my walks, I started checking for baits. The first day, I checked one of the fence lines and it was already bait less. It was a good feeling to know this would prevent a lot of deaths. At the time, Michael had about 4000 ewes to lamb down. And everyone needed a chance in farming.

The other big farming issue at the time was the attempt to ban the live export in Western Australia. Our own ABC was putting six-year-old footage of sheep in boats, that were going down and being smothered on the overfilled ships.

I drove a farm vehicle into Three Springs once a week to pick up stores and other items for the farm. I was in Michael's car one trip and heard a vet talking about the live export industry. He was onboard one of these export ships. His words were, there was one vet per thousand sheep on each ship. The sheep had fans and good ventilation; water and feed were easily obtainable without smothering and they, on average, lost one in a thousand sheep. The figures of death are much higher on a farm. Just one of the many issues farmers were dealing with in this day and age.

June came and so did the lambs. The weather was cold and the fire in the house had to be lit most days. My walks in the morning involved checking ewes lambing. Some days I would have to deliver a lamb on the way home. Because it was a particularly bad year for feed, the sheep had a few problems lambing.

There were a few other situations where I would have to dive towards a ewe and grab a leg so I could pull her down and pull out a lamb. I did do one dive out of the Toyota on one occasion. I think I forgot how old I was, momentarily. On most days, David and I were checking sheep and driving through the enormous paddocks, checking under every tree and around all the fences. There was one thing with sheep that never ceased to amaze me either and that was, a ewe would choose the coldest, wettest day to have a lamb on the top of a hill.

Some ewes who had twins, would often leave the weakest lamb. This abandonment sometimes happened when we had to with lambing. The ewe took off and didn't mother up. So, we came up with an idea that would prevent this from happening. We made a cage we could put a ewe and a lamb in. So, when the ewe had cleaned and fed the lamb some hours later and hopefully bonded, we would take the cage away.

On one occasion, we found a ewe having difficulty and set the cage up around her. To our amazement, a few hours later, she had produced another lamb. All three were doing well.

We left the farm on 21st June and headed for warmer weather. We did a crayfish tour out of Kalbarri and visited the world standard Kalbarri skywalk. The crayfish tour promised us two crayfish to take home with us when we left the boat. The tour was okay but I wouldn't rush out and do it again.

The Kalbarri Skywalk was magnificent. A very worthwhile

excursion. There was only one thing that was difficult to get and that was a photograph of the window in the rock formation. When we arrived at the window, there were hardly any other people around. But sitting in there, was a Japanese girl. For at least 15 minutes, she sat there posing for her boyfriend. She was glasses on and then glasses off, changed sides and flicked hair. Smile, smooch. The photoshoot seemed to go on for an eternity. I was starting get a little annoyed. All I wanted to do was get a photo of the window with nobody in it. In the meantime, there were also other people turning up to get photos.

Finally, she stopped. But then she grabbed the camera from her male partner and swapped places. Well, of course I piped up.

"Excuse me, but we have all been waiting over 15 minutes for a photo of the window, without you or your boyfriend in it. Would you please mind doing your photoshoot later?"

We all then took it in turns to get our photos. This was not the first time this had happened. And I was sure it wouldn't be the last.

By 3rd July, we were back in the warm country and on the red dirt. For our trip north this year, we didn't head to Broome as usual or Barn Hill outstation. Instead, we headed into the Pilbara and visited Mansfield friends who were based in Newman. We stayed in a park outside town but caught up with these friends for dinner. We also did some washing at their house on the day we arrived. Always a necessity when you head into a town, especially when you have been on the red dirt.

We did a fantastic tour which was organised by our friend, Brendan, who happened to be the superintendent at the East Newman mine, owned by BHP. We met quite early at the front entrance of the mine and were issued a hard hat and fluorescent vest to put on. Then Brendan escorted us all over the mine. We went into areas where there were autonomous trucks. All being operated from an office in Perth. It was fascinating and a once in a lifetime experience. It was definitely not what you knew but who you knew.

We headed about 60 kilometres out of Newman and set up in a spot about 400 metres from the road. When we camp anywhere, the first thing we look for is a quiet spot with plenty of wood. We certainly had it there. We stayed for over two weeks in the same spot and David went back into Newman to stock up with food and water.

After leaving the Pilbara area, we headed down through the wildflowers and then down to Casuarina in Perth for a house sit we had organised. We spent about a month there and did our usual tidying up in the garden etc. I also had to have surgery to get my veins in my legs stripped.

Another major event that happened when we were house sitting in Casuarina, was my old friend, Tony Dawson, had died of a heart attack in Bali, at the age of 59. His sister, Penny, rang me and it was a hell of a shock to us. I had known Tony since I was a little girl.

Because Tony had wanted to be cremated in Bali, the funeral and ceremony was held over there. For Tony's Australian service, Penny was going to have a memorial at her house in Wallington. The same house Tony was brought up in and also the same house Cam, her father, had his memorial service. In Penny's words, she said she was bringing him home. I told Penny we would be in Victoria for my nephew's wedding in November and would love it if she could organise a memorial for when we were there.

We flew into Melbourne in early November and caught the bus to Mansfield. We stayed at Lisa's place prior to and after the wedding. The wedding was lovely, however, because of my family situation and my estrangement by my older son, we didn't stay long into the reception. I didn't have much to drink and I kept myself busy chatting to other guests on our table.

The previous day, Lisa and I had organised dips and pre dinner nibbles to have whilst the bride and groom were doing photos. On arriving at the wedding, my three children walked up to me. My older son had said, "Hello Mum."

I responded, "Hello," and just walked away.

I needed to start getting nibbles set up etc. It was a good excuse as it wasn't the time or place to have any conversation. He watched me on and off the entire night. I didn't look at him once. My daughter and other son came up and gave me a hug and we had a chat and took a couple of photos together. As a family. It was uncomfortable but I am sure it was more uncomfortable for my older son than me. It was his choice to have sent me that letter and then not see me until then.

My daughter drove us back to Lisa's house and David went off to bed. I had a couple of glasses of red, talked to Shez for a while and then did the same thing.

The following day, the bride and groom were off overseas. Because they both had a car, the bride, Julia, kindly lent us her car to visit friends outside the Mansfield area. On our way down to Tony's memorial, we stayed with some good friends in Geelong. The owners of Bill's Farm, that fabulous delicatessen in the Victorian market in Melbourne.

Each year for the last few years, our friends from Geelong, Mal and Anna, had planned and done self-drive safaris in Africa. On the first night we stayed, David told them we were booked on a Trip-A-Deal tour of Vietnam and Cambodia in August 2024. Mal and Anna then invited us to do a trip with them to Africa in November 2024. By the time Mal had shown us their photos and videos of their safaris, we had made up our mind. Yes, we were going to Africa. This had been David's dream for years. We had been booked to go to Africa in 2021, but the COVID pandemic had fixed that.

We arrived a day or two earlier at Penny's place to help set up and have a catch-up. There were a few odd jobs we could do to help Penny and her long-term partner, Lee. On the day of the memorial, I helped Anna and Mal set up the grazing table of delicious foods from, of course, Bill's Farm.

Tony's memorial was a wonderful day. The weather was perfect and the people, from my past, were incredible. A description of the congregation could have been like a Geelong Grammar Highton reunion. It was wonderful to catch up with so many people from a long time ago. This was the happy past I loved at Geelong Grammar School. My parents also attended, and it was nice to catch up with them outside of Mansfield.

We partied and danced into the night, as only Tony would have wanted us to. He was probably cross he couldn't make it.

We stayed around the area for a few days, and Kate Parsons organised for us, an Air B&B just across the way from their house. It was wonderful and we caught up each day. Penny also visited us after she finished work. From there, we did a bit more cruising around, visiting David's brother and also his sister. Then we headed back to Mansfield to drop the car off and bussed it down to Melbourne to fly back to Perth.

# CHAPTER 52

## *2024*

At the end of 2023, when we flew back to Perth, we stayed at a friend's place we had previously house sat for. We had left our caravan and car there whilst we were in Victoria. As payment, we spent a week or two helping them out around their property.

Our friends were in the process of finishing their dream house and we just did a little tidying up. Also, whilst we were there, we had made a date to meet a couple to do a house sit in a suburb in Perth, called Spearwood. We met our future house sit couple one afternoon during those two weeks.

This sort of meeting is now standard for us when we house sit for someone. Especially after the horror farm sit in New South Wales in 2020. Normally, if everyone feels comfortable with each other and it is ideal for our caravan and car, we will take a sit on. We weren't due to start our sit until Christmas Day.

So, because we had a bit of time, it was a good excuse to do some more exploring in the Perth area. We visited Kings Park and the botanical gardens. A beautifully set out park with lots of information, both botanical and cultural. There were many native Western Australia plants and trees exhibited. There were also information boards on our indigenous people and animals. Not to mention the beautiful views of Perth city and its coastline.

Another place we also wanted to visit was Rottnest Island. We caught the ferry over on 18th December. The trip over was rough and a few people were quite ill. We must have strong constitutions.

David and I hired bicycles from the ferry people instead of making our way around the island on buses. This meant we could see more and also have a little exercise. I don't think I had ridden a bike for over 20 years. It was a little unnerving going down hills to start with, but I got the hang of it. It was fantastic fun and highly recommended. We dined at a restaurant in the main town and were entertained by quokkas trying to sneak into food places to eat scraps.

Quokkas are marsupials that are herbivores and mostly nocturnal. They certainly were not sleeping the day we were at Rottnest Island. We spent the afternoon just lounging around after our exhausting morning of cycling on the island. Rottnest also offers a large and diverse range of overnight accommodation. Another highly recommended jaunt whilst staying in Perth.

We turned up to start our house sit on Christmas Day. We had a light Christmas lunch with Kate and Tony and then they departed to the airport to fly to New Zealand for their holiday. We had a lovely month in Spearwood looking after Bruni.

Bruni was an American Staffordshire terrier. An older, slightly overweight dog with a little arthritis. Of course, I put him on a diet. When Kate and Tony returned, they could see an incredibly positive difference in him. He had lost weight and had better movement. Kate told me the vet was delighted with his improvement too. I wrote a diet for them to give him that was not as inflammatory and also had less carbohydrates.

Whilst we were there, I did my fair share of walking. One day, when trying to get near the beach, I stumbled across a reserve called Davilak. When I had worked for the vet many years ago, he had named his farm in Mansfield, Davilak Pastoral Company. I texted him excitedly and he informed me; it was once where his parents had farmed. Another small world encounter.

Another day, we were asked to go out on a crayfish boat with the next-door neighbour, Pete. He kindly took us out with his extended family, and we all feasted on crayfish, fish cakes, and fish. All cooked and caught previously on the boat. We went out to some of the small islands off the coast of Perth and swam. One of the nearby islands was covered in sea lions. Again, it was great to do something with a local of the area.

Also, whilst we were at Spearwood, we answered a house sit ad in a nearby suburb. David and I rang and arranged to go around and meet the couple and see whether we could put the van there.

We met Kathleen and Gordon and their various animals to look after. They were a lovely Irish couple, and we liked them a lot. The only problem was, we could not fit our van at their house. The driveway was too steep and that would have been the only spot to put our caravan.

Kathleen was one of those people that I zoned into very quickly. She was employed in the mental health industry, and I found her very spiritual. We talked freely on the first day we met and she very disappointed that we wouldn't be able to do the housesitting. She invited me around to see her one afternoon and to maybe do some healing. I had told her I was writing this book and we spoke about the reasons for my writing and she was very encouraging.

The afternoon we decided on meeting, I was going to walk from Spearwood and then her husband, Gordon, would drop me home later. I walked around there and for some reason it wasn't a good time for her to do a healing. So, I stayed and we had a glass or two of bubbles, a chat and then I was dropped back to Spearwood. During our chat, she invited us around for dinner a few days later.

Because Gordon didn't drink alcohol at all, he suggested he pick us up from Spearwood and then drop us back after we had dinner. So, we could both enjoy a few drinks without worrying about driving. It was a hysterical night. We sat outside for a while and had drinks and nibbles. Then, because Gordon, a builder/carpenter, was on call and had to go to do a call-out, our meal was slightly delayed. Another Murphy's Law occurrence.

When he finally returned, we started organising the food. Kathleen had bought some fish for the meal. But instead of getting fillets, it was discovered, when it was unwrapped, that it was an entire fish. David suggested cooking it whole on the barbeque, which we did.

On serving the fish, there was absolute hysterics. Kathleen didn't have a sharp knife and the fish ended up in one hell of a mess. It was the sort of thing you would see in an episode of Fawlty Towers. Or a set with the Swedish chef from the Muppets. We all enjoyed our meal but, wow, we were so sore from belly laughing.

Kathleen and Gordon visited us at Spearwood for another night together. It was fabulous fun again and we invited Pete from next door over as well. House sitting could sometimes be a great way to meet new people in new places.

At the end of our house sit, we decided we would like to go and stay with a friend I had met years ago in Broome. We had kept in contact over the years and he had helped David and I out on a few occasions with items for the caravan and car.

I had also helped this friend out as well. He had gone through a marriage breakdown and was also a survivor of abuse as an altar boy. We had a lot in common. There had been nights on the phone from Mansfield to Perth with tears and discussions about all this. He was a lovely man but, unfortunately, he had all the emotional fracturing and clutter that goes with being sexually abused as a child.

We stayed at his rented property in Safety Bay for about three weeks. Safety Bay is a lovely suburb, south of Perth, near the more well-known and popular suburb of Rockingham. We busied ourselves whilst we were there. I did the washing etc and David helped him out, fixing and painting a camper trailer. We also got stuck into a bit of gardening and I did the windows. It was lovely to have a look around. Also nice to catch up with him and his son.

He told me he had finally gone to a redress scheme and was on a waiting list now for compensation. Compensation was never enough but it was worth having the crime recognised and an apology made. Most redress schemes now did apologise for the crime. It was a formal apology, and it really improved the mental state of the victim as well.

From Safety Bay, we decided to go down to the Margaret River region. I had always wanted to see the beaches there and go to the wineries. The friend at Safety Bay had recommended a winery tour called Bush Tucker Tours. And that is what we did. David contacted them and they said they would be there to pick us up at the Prevelly caravan park 2nd February.

We arrived at Prevelly on 31st January. Our campsite wasn't far from the beach, so, of course, I was there in a flash to go for a walk. The beaches were as beautiful as everyone raved about. It was quite windy as well, so on some days there were surf kites out on the ocean. Also, whilst we were there, there was an Australian championship event held.

The day of the Bush Tucker tour arrived. We were picked up, as promised, by our tour guide at the caravan park kiosk. There were about 10 of us all together, by the time we finished picking up the wine tourers. There were a few of young people and the rest of us were between 50 and 70.

I always found it interesting how these tour guides managed to connect us all with each other. The stop at the first tasting brought out the conversation amongst us. The guide went around and asked us to tell everyone a little bit about themselves. After the introductions, everyone became more comfortable with the new people around them. Not to mention, we were wine tasting by this time and with some wine in us, the guards came down a little.

David and I made sure we spat most of our wine until lunchtime. We did buy the odd bottle though. Not sure how many wineries we visited in the morning, but we had lunch at a winery in Wilyabrup, looking out over a man-made lake.

Before we were served our lunch, we did a tasting so we could select a wine to eat with our meal. There was a good selection of wines with less alcohol and I chose a lovely bottle of sparkling. The tour guide talked us through the different native foods we were going to consume for our lunch which was absolutely fabulous. We ate crocodile, emu, snake, kangaroo and then a collection of native berries and nuts and products that were made out of these ingredients. The food was delicious, and it was a first time for me for eating emu and crocodile.

After lunch, we hopped back into our van and had a guided tour to a chocolate factory. At the end of our tour, we visited a craft brewery. It was a fabulous day, and I would highly recommended Bush Tucker Tours for a day's outing.

On our way back to the park, it was quiet. The young couple were asleep in the back of the bus. I think there may have been too much wine not spat out. The rest of us were all tuckered up and pleasantly marinated. We met some lovely people to boot. I even met my editor for this book on the tour.

We stayed a few more days in the Margaret River region and then moved on back towards Geraldton. On our way up, we stopped at a place called Eneabba. There was a great campground there which had a minimum charge per night. It was clean and well managed.

It was on this evening we started talking to a couple of backpackers, Janne and Jorn, who were from the Netherlands. They walked past and we invited them to have a beer with us. We asked where they were heading and they said they had a job at Dirk Hartog Island. It was a resort island off the west coast at Denham. They planned to stay in Geraldton and then go into Kalbarri to see the skywalk on a day trip. After Geraldton, they were going to head further north to the island.

On hearing they were going to Geraldton, I invited them to stay with us at our house sit in Woorree. They were going into the backpackers in town, and we hadn't heard good things about being in town. I knew Jamie and Di wouldn't mind.

Our house sit was for only about a week until we were to return to the farm. We arrived at Woorree on 17th February and Janne and Jorn drove in later that day. Because they had a few of our beers the night before, they thought they would repay the generosity. On their way to stay, they had gone to Dan Murphy's and purchased some of their own country's beer, so we could try some Netherlands and also German beers.

We had a lovely night in the back garden. Wow, some of those European beers were like a meal in the bottle. They also had a lot higher alcohol content.

The following day, we sat and watched the temperature gauge get to 48.2 degrees Celsius at 1.37pm. It was roasting. Janne and Jorn were going to go out to Kalbarri that morning but, because of the extreme heat, they hadn't gone. Also, very often on these extreme days, the skywalk was closed for obvious health reasons.

They spent the day with us in air-conditioned comfort and continued on their journey the following day. I had a great discussion with Janne. Her profession was in mental health and she dealt with people who had trauma. Very similar to my past situation, so you can imagine how I zoomed in to her.

We kept in contact with them while they were still in Australia. The job at Dirk Hartog Island, unfortunately, didn't work out well for them because of poor management. They returned to the Netherlands and hope to come back again one day.

Di and Jamie returned from their trip down south and we headed back to Kadathinni in early March. It was great to have that farm home feeling again. The first thing to tend to was my vegetable garden. To my absolute delight, it was replanted and looking edible when we arrived. A younger couple, Pete and Marissa, who had come to the farm just after we had left last year, looked after it beautifully. They were interested in keeping the garden going, so it looked amazing. I was back in fresh, home-grown veggie heaven.

We filled in our time at the farm with a few different projects. David fixed and reinvented the front entrance. Old iron was collected from the junk store in the shearing paddock and screwed onto new steel posts he had welded together. Then the tops of the fence were levelled with a grinder and a dog, made out of iron, was put on the right hand side. It was a vast improvement. We had a few fire incidents during that project but we always had the fire fighting vehicle full and at hand for when we were welding and grinding. The grass was very dry at this time of year.

Along with trough checking and fencing, there wasn't much else to do. To fill in our days and coincide it with things for the farm, we did a couple of stints of exploration. We did a visit out to Carnamah on one particular day to pick up some ring lock for a fence we were doing. At Carnamah there is a fantastic tractor museum to visit. The oldest ever John Deere tractors in Australia and another brand called Chamberlain. It was fascinating to see the evolution of tractors in this country.

The lovely gentleman who gave us an initial spiel also told us about the town getting an enormous tractor to put in the Main Street so there was a draw card to visit Carnamah. Some of these small towns in the area were surrounded by large wheat and sheep farms. Apart from the wildflowers in the spring, there needed to be a little more to draw the travelling public to these towns.

Another trip we did was to Ellendale Pool. This stunning waterhole was naturally formed on the Greenough river. It was surrounded by beautiful gum trees and a rocky gorge. We could swim in Ellendale pool but, at certain times of the year, it had blooms which could cause amoebic meningitis. Best not to put your head under the water because it usually entered the body through the nose.

*Giant tractor*

Our next trip up north, we headed for more places we haven't been in Western Australia. We visited the Quobba Blow Holes in May and headed to a few new campsites near Exmouth. Most of which were on the coast.

We did our usual stops at Yannarie and Miaree Pool and stayed in Port Hedland for a few nights. We ventured to more new places on the way to Broome. We stayed at Cape Keraudren, a working cattle station opened to the public for camping on the beach and the cliffs. Great spot to walk and fish. We also saw whales off the coast whilst there.

Another new place we visited was Port Smith which is on the coast and situated in the Bidyadanga community. Bidyadanga was the largest indigenous community in Western Australia. We met some friends of some of our friends there. Wendy and Geoff knew we were coming, so they introduced themselves when we had set up.

Wendy was supposed to be going out the next day to a lunch at Eco Beach Resort. She was in a dilemma because they were travelling with a dog who needed looking after. So, I offered to look after the dog for the day. Off she went for lunch and it was too easy. We caught up with them for a drink that night and they offered to show us around. The following day we were driven to beautiful beaches you wouldn't know existed. In the afternoon, David and Geoff went out to get some wood for a fire. When they returned, we headed out to a beach and watched the sun go down with friends. After a fabulous stay at Port Smith, we headed towards Broome.

We always preferred to stay out of Broome because it was great to visit but extremely busy. Most years we stayed at the Gateway Caravan Park. The sites were large and it was a well-maintained park and not too expensive. We stayed for a couple of weeks so we could catch up with friends, as well as do a little more exploring.

We took a drive up the Cape Leveque Road to Cygnet Bay. The road had been sealed all the way. Unfortunately, during COVID Cape Leveque beach was closed by the local people and had never reopened. It was very sad because it was such a beautiful beach, according to those who had visited there previously.

Our trip to Vietnam was scheduled for 2nd September, so after we left Broome, we made our way slowly down to Perth. We needed to stay in the north because it was still too cold, so we just stayed at some of our favourite places to camp until the last minute.

We arrived at friends in Perth late August and set up our caravan in their garden. Because we were going to Africa as well in November, the caravan had a new long term back yard for a few months.

Vietnam was amazing. What an experience to go to a country like that. Our visit to Ha Long Bay, with its beautiful limestone pillars creating small islands, was breath-taking. The lush green of the tropics, unforgettable. The traffic was noisy but the food delicious and the countryside with its mountains and lush green tropical rainforests will remain in my memory for years to come.

The history was very confronting, especially at the war museum in Ho Chi Min city, but a must do. David crawled through the tunnels in the jungle and I dropped down into a hatch in the ground. The Vietcong were extremely resourceful and very clever and it was very interesting to do a tour of the tunnels.

The second part of our tour was to visit Cambodia. We visited the Killing Field which is now a tourist attraction. Another confrontational day, but worth learning the history and heinous treatment by the Khmer Rouge and the dictatorship of Pol Pot. We also visited in the south of Cambodia, Angkor Wat. The largest religious building in the world. What an amazing experience. We flew out of Siem Reap on 16th September.

We had a few weeks in Perth before we flew to Africa to meet Mal and Anna for our three-week safari. Our trip started off quite badly. We were due to fly direct to Africa with South African Airways. Our plane was delayed for 24 hours but we weren't told until we had spent the entire night sitting in the airport. We were going to arrive in Africa a day before Anna and Mal but, in the end, we met them at customs in the airport the next day. Just as well because they were accustomed to the way things worked in Africa. And that way is very different.

The same day, we flew to Victoria Falls in Zimbabwe. We had a few days to get over flights etc and then picked up our vehicles in Botswana. David and I went to the falls whilst we were there. They were magnificent and what an amazing experience and a wonderful feeling we got when gazing at them. We felt enveloped by them.

Whilst we were there, we also went on a sunset cruise on the Zambezi River and saw our first elephants. It had been a lifelong dream for both of us and now we were there.

We collected our vehicles a few days later and then the animal seeking adventures really started. We had the most wonderful experience in the three weeks. We saw a lion kill, plenty of elephants, giraffes, zebras, a leopard, white rhinos, hippos, monkeys, exotic birds and more lions. It was one of the most memorable trips we had ever done.

Anna and Mal left to go home a couple of days before us. David and I decided to do a tour in South Africa for only a day. We visited the Johannesburg CBD but hardly left the car. We also visited the Apartheid Museum which was very confronting but educational. We visited Nelson Mandela House and then had a guided tour of the slums in Soweto. The last tour was incredible. It was amazing to us how well the people of the slums existed. They had power they tapped into the railway; they had a supply of fresh water and they also had enormous vegetable gardens. Interestingly, there was no violence in the slums. The lower class do get it right.

We flew back to Australia and because we both had a good, but unexpected sleep on the plane, David decided to get out of Perth and head towards Victoria. One job we needed to do in Victoria was get our caravan upgrade done. We scooted home in about five or six days. From Perth it was around 3400km.

Another reason for our trip home this year was my daughter's 21st birthday celebration. We did our normal trip out to the bush for a few days and stayed at Davons Flat in the Howqua Valley. The kids and David's grandkids came and joined us for a few days. Then we went back into Merrijig and camped on a friend's block on the Delatite River, so we could celebrate the 21st.

After catching up with family and Mansfield friends, we headed down to Geelong and stayed at Penny's place in Wallington. It was lovely to spend time with Penny's mum, Jill, and her Aunt Chirp. Very entertaining because they are both elderly ladies now and tend to forget things easily. I guess we all end up that way in the end.

It was also a bit of closure for me, seeing these older people. They were a big part of my younger life and I never knew when I would see them again. David and I also visited Shez's parents. Ken and Dawn were very good to me as that extremely troubled girl in my late teens and early twenties. It was nice for them to see that all their effort did pay off somehow. I was now a very different person.

David and I headed across Victoria catching up with more friends and family. Then we made our way through South Australia and headed slowly back across the Nullabor. We thoroughly enjoyed this area and always took a couple of weeks to go across. This was because there was so much to see if you wanted to. There were cliffs to visit, the great Australian Bight to view and lovely places to camp. This was my fourth or fifth crossing and I hadn't been bored yet.

Christmas Day was spent at a water storage facility at Goldfields Woodlands National Park. We spent a couple of days near Coolgardie to try out our new gold detector. Unfortunately, we didn't get any gold, but I found a few dollar coins.

# CHAPTER 53

## *2025*

Heading back slowly to the farm, we visited the monstrous new tractor at Carnamah again and then arrived back at the farm in time to do our sit.

This summer was a different start at the farm for us. Michael and his parents, for the last couple of years, had being talking about a wind farm being located on their property at Kadathinni. In January this year, a team of men were coming to the farm to build a wind metre tower. The meteorological mast measures wind speed, direction and other weather conditions at various heights.

Michael had offered for the team to stay at the farm in the cottage we normally parked next to. He had asked me if I could possibly prepare lunch and dinner for them for the days they were staying. Also, they needed the flat set up and beds made for their stay. I agreed and said it would be no problem.

Michael had done a sheep kill so there was plenty of lamb to eat. I decided I would like to feed them exactly what we liked to eat, so we needed a few other items of food. I also decided it would be nice to have a little Thai food and a couple of lasagne nights with garlic bread. Just for a little variety. David and I drove into Dongara the day before and loaded up the car with food.

The evening the boys turned up, we organised what would suit them and discussed being flexible if need be. Because of the extreme heat at this time of year, sometimes things would change with mealtimes. Some days they would finish early and head to the beach. Other days they would start work in the dark and have an earlier lunch.

The 14 days went exceptionally well. The guys loved all their food and often had seconds. There wasn't a hiccup at all. I felt like they were part of the family. Extremely appreciative and always commenting on the way they were treated. Apparently, they had stayed at other places and the treatment hadn't been as good.

The day they left, they all gave me a hug and thanked us both for being such wonderful hosts. The supervisor on the crew's name was Ryan. This was his message to David and me:

*Thank you for taking care of us, we definitely have not got treatment like that at work. I can say confidently the lads will never forget your cooking and hospitality. Thank you again and never know when we will see you and David again.*

*Stu, Nick and me just got to the airport for the red eye home time.*

*Thank you again from all the boys.*

I was extremely touched by this message. What a fantastic human experience. I had a few more texts over the following weeks from the boys. I actually really missed them for a while after they had gone.

Now, back to business at the farm. When we first returned, to my dismay, I found the vegetable garden had been totally neglected and was full of weeds. There was a capsicum tree that had been there from the year before and it was flowering. A few tomatoes were in the garden but bitter tasting. My rosemary bush was happy but everything else was ruined

On one of our visits to Dongara, I had bought some vegetable seedlings to plant. This was my next struggle because I had to try and keep the seedlings going in a summer where we had at least 30 days over 43 degrees Celsius. It was a scorching hot summer. Out came the king size bed sheets in the middle of the day to shade the garden and I even spot watered to keep everything going. Water was on every night and the timer came on in the morning. I took progressive photos and everything I planted survived and flourished.

We also made the three farm dogs a swimming pool to dip in on those hot days. It was a tank made of fibreglass, cut in half and a concrete plug was put in the bottom of it. It was placed just beside the dog kennels and near a water source. There was a tap on the side to change the water and a ramp to get in and out for the older dog, Angus. Choko and Chester just loved it. Angus decided it was too hard, so he just found a cool spot in the dirt.

We built a new boundary fence this year and did the usual trough checks and cleans. We also did a lot more sheep moving than usual. Moving sheep onto more grass. It was a better winter last year than the previous two years. We were also only looking after 600 ewes now. Michael had cut down his flock considerably.

After we finished at the farm, we did a small sit for Jamie and Di at Woorree and then spent the month of May at South Greenough. This farm sit was for a cousin of Michael's. We enjoyed it there and I did plenty of walks to the beach. We also did a little bit of fencing and feeding of horses.

We were now back in the north of Western Australia enjoying 30-degree heat in the outback. Living the outback dream.

# CHAPTER 54

## *WORDS OF WISDOM*

There are definite reasons for including this part of my journey in my story. I hope it may help survivors deal with how they have coped with their voids, as well as their triggers. And also, there is a discussion about drugs and alcohol abuse.

These are some of my deepest secrets and I have toiled many a time on whether to include these truths in my story. But because of my honesty, I want to be completely open. I want others to understand this was some of my normal behaviour. Even if it wasn't the preferred way to behave. It could possibly also be some other survivor's behaviour.

We all have an element of misunderstanding by the way we behave at times. We also question it too. We drink to block, we eat to block, we use drugs to block. Blocking is escaping the memories, escaping the flashbacks, dealing with the panic attacks, and fighting off the demons. Meanwhile, we are actually destroying ourselves more, whilst practicing these behaviours. Even though we don't acknowledge it.

When you get to the time where you are beginning to heal, it is time to reflect on some of your not so healthy behaviours. You need to forgive yourself for what you have done. It is okay, you are okay and there is no need to beat yourself up about it anymore. You cannot change the bad decisions you have made; you can simply make better choices from now on.

## COPING MECHANISMS: ALCOHOL AND DRUGS

Life was always in turmoil in the years of my early twenties, with one embarrassing memory coming to mind.

I was working at an insurance company in Melbourne and at Christmas time, normally Christmas Eve, we would organise with work to have a breakup lunch. After lunch, I had caught up with a male friend, and we decided to smoke a joint. We both had a complete green out. A green out is where you just can't do anything but lie down and sleep. This nearly always happens when you have had a lot to drink and then smoke dope. We both ended up sleeping on a park bench right outside the Queensland Tourist Bureau. This building happens to be in Collins Street in the middle of the Melbourne CBD.

When I woke up after an hour or so, the city noise and lights flashing made it extremely hard to get orientated. Finally, I managed to get on the right tram, and I went back to North Fitzroy, where I was staying with a couple of friends. I was supposed to be catching the train to Corio that evening for Christmas, but I was in no fit state to do that.

Another embarrassing time was when I was working at Target Geelong and also helping out with horse rides in Merrijig. I had been asked out to lunch in Melbourne by a guy I had met on one of the rides. I got so drunk in the restaurant, he just disappeared without a trace. It was no wonder, I was quite drunk and probably very loud. Whatever could he have thought?

Unfortunately, in my tormented time, I have had a few experiences like this.

I have memories of galloping and staggering home from a pub in Mansfield to my house. This happened just after I was separated from my husband. My children would be staying with their father, and I would go out with friends to the pub. And, as usual, have too much to drink.

A couple of times, I fell asleep in a garden on the way home. I would eventually wake up with the dry horrors and start drinking out of someone's garden tap. Just really disgusting behaviour.

Over the years, unfortunately, alcohol became my best friend. It blocked out all the misery. When I was in an uncomfortable situation, which was normally with my family, alcohol always came to the rescue. It was legal and affordable. During my marriage, it gave me a sense of being happy. If I was drinking, I wasn't feeling bored or unhappy with my situation. I also used alcohol to induce sleep.

I watched a movie once called Rachel's Getting Married with Anne Hathaway and another movie called 28 days with Sandra Bullock. Both of these actors' characters' behaviours, could have been identical to the way I had behaved when under the influence of alcohol. Always misbehaving at weddings and events. Drinking too much and making a fool out of myself.

Behaviour at weddings, for me was, I always ended up getting drunk. I was always the loud and revolting one who yelled out silly things during the speeches. I would always end up dancing on tables at the end of the night and quite often falling over.

A wedding was always a good chance to get smashed for free. That's, unfortunately, how I looked at it. At my own wedding, I had to be sober and was. But at Lisa's wedding reception, I was so drunk and, along with a girlfriend, I put her wedding dress on at the reception. My mother caught me and was furious.

Other inappropriate behaviour to mention was, I was really stoned at Lisa's wedding service. It was the best church service I had ever been to and Lisa did look wonderful. So did the flowers arrangements. I had smoked a joint with my ex-husband on the way into the church. We knew, because it was a Catholic service, it would be boring, unless we were in an altered state of mind.

Another sister's wedding was a blur, but I remembered it was held at Timbertop and, yes, it was another smashed night. The recovery was great too and was held at my parents' place in Merrijig. I helped cater with my best friend, Robbie. We helped ourselves to glasses of champagne and smoked joints for most of the afternoon.

At another sister's wedding, I was a single waif. Incredibly thin, due to my recent marriage breakdown. I drank too much again and, yes, I was dancing on the table and staggering by the end of it. I can clearly remember the hangover as well. It was an extremely big night.

On another occasion, I remember a younger sister saying to me one year, when we were planning our family Christmas Day, "It's not all about alcohol, you know, Joanna."

Well, for me at the time it was all about alcohol. Alcohol was extremely important part of my life. It helped me. It helped me block things out and it helped me have confidence to say, "What the fuck anyway?" It helped me sleep, it stopped me having panic attacks, it made me not give a fucking damn about anything. Alcohol was my saviour.

Another thing I can never understand, was the mentality of someone making the comment, that it was not all about alcohol, to a serious alcoholic. This sort of comment was definitely a trigger to drink more. I remembered, after her comment at my parents' house in Merrijig, I quickly bundled up my three children into my car and headed home in a hurry. It was more like a mini panic attack. A panic to get home, so I could have a drink and just blot the comment out. My sister did, however, manage to call me, when I was about to drive into our lane and she apologised. A little bit of too little, too late.

They say, when you drink you need to eat. Quite often, food is referred to as blotting paper. In my case, alcohol was the blotting paper because it just blotted everything out. It was a sad state of affairs really. But that was exactly what my life was like.

I now no longer mix alcohol with any of my family, except Lisa. Or

I chose to be the driver, so I had to only drink one or two, for the family event. This tended to keep me in control and if I am triggered, I can just leave the event altogether. The absolute best remedy is just do not mix alcohol with my family. Sad, but true.

I totally understand the merry-go-round of alcohol. I still drink but rarely use it as blotting paper. Only when triggered. Now I try and avoid most things and the people that trigger me.

Alcohol was an enormous aid during the royal commission years. But it also became a band aid that was hard to remove. I don't beat myself up over that now. But my best friend did eventually turn into my worst enemy.

## OTHER DRUGS

There was a time where I tried other stuff but never heroin. Phil, the fisherman, definitely saved me from that. Thank you, gorgeous Phil.

The one and only time I tried cocaine was with one of my bridesmaids. We were out on one of our jaunts at a pub and she knew a guy who had some cocaine. We had been playing pool and then this guy turned up, and we were invited for a snort. It was great at the time and we felt we were totally in control of ourselves. The only downside was felt the next morning. The feeling that a freight train had gone through my right nostril.

I have used a bit of speed (amphetamines) when my marriage was newly over. But didn't want to continue using it, because I didn't like the way that it made me feel in the end. I had been addicted to Medislims earlier and only had a couple of tastes of speed but never used needles. The entire needle thing was really not my scene.

I remember, all those years ago, when I was living on the poultry farm, a girl from Anglesea, came to visit. She was using speed and needles. I was mortified to see her injecting herself. It was actually the first time I ever tried speed. Because I didn't like the idea of needles, she suggested that I use an empty pen to sniff it. Incidentally, this poor girl was using drugs all the time. After a deep discussion between us, she actually realised she had been sexually assaulted as a child. She had also blocked it out up until then. Possibly the reason for using drugs in the first place. I didn't try many other drugs, because I loved my dope. It took the edge off everything, like a Xanax pill.

There was a time, when I was employed as a vet nurse, I would have a little pipe at lunchtime, so I could deal with a certain staff member coming in the afternoon. This person ruffled my feathers so I would take the edge off, and the rest of the day was calm and pleasant.

I could never bring myself to having mushrooms or any sort of hallucinogenic drugs. My horrific memories of hallucinations, with a feverish temperature when I was at Ballarat, had put me off that.

## RELATIONSHIPS OF THE SEXUALLY ABUSED AND SEX

There are always going to be muck ups in a person's life if they have been a victim of sexual abuse. Abuse victims have no sexual identity or understanding of the way in which normal relationships happen or how the sex fits in. Sex to the abused is love and acceptance, whether you like it or not. And sex always seems to come first. Hopefully love develops later. Sex can be smutty and dirty or simply a duty performed by zoning out and focusing on the wall, until it is finished. Sometimes it can be terrifying, as a flash back may occur.

It is also incredibly vivid in some dreams. Many times, I have woken, yelling out or screaming. I have even punched David in my dreams, trying to protect myself.

Another thing I have done in relationships, which is cruel and controlling, is I have used sex as a weapon. This has enabled me to take back control. The sick use of sex as blackmail. It is almost a confusion between being in control or being out of control. I have always said, if you are a control freak, then you are the one who is out of control.

As a result of this confusion about what sex is, most of my relationships have ended. This is because of my neediness for love(sex) and ruined because of my self-destructive ways: bulimia, drugs, and alcohol.

Another thing that has always intrigued me is, I must have some sort of look. The look that makes men feel they can approach me and tell me about their desire for me.

I remember at the vet surgery, I was referred to-as 'a girl that has that look about her'. What look? Like I've been abused, like I need a bit of sex. Do I look like I need a good fuck? I really don't understand just what that look is. I wish I didn't have it. I have even been looked up and down by lesbians and chased around by them in hotels. Obviously, I have some sort of look to lesbians as well.

Other men have just come up and told me; they really have longed to have sex with me. Or, like the night of my wedding, when that guy told me he wanted to fuck me, when my husband and I were saying our goodbyes. Another man told me he wanted to have sex with me just after his wife had had a baby and I had just had a child. And then the dirty doctor asking me if I was still screwing around with the boys in the bushes. I was only 14 years old and still a virgin. But did I look like that girl, even back then?

# CHAPTER 55

## *COMING OUT OF THE TUNNEL*

My life now is living on the road in a caravan, with my amazing and supportive husband. Travelling our country is an amazing experience and David and I are going to travel and find unexplored places for as long as we can lead this life.

David told me once; it was always his dream to own a great set up and just travel the country. So that is why in 2019, he said he didn't want me to work anymore. I slowly wound up my cleaning business and retired at the age of 53.

We have travelled through some amazing places and visited some wonderful cities and coastlines. Unfortunately, there are some places we will never visit again in Australia. This is because they are tainted with horror and racism. This horror is predominantly found in parts of the Northern Territory and some parts in Western Australia.

We have seen the social complexity and complications throughout the country. The struggles our indigenous people have with day-to-day issues. The toxic alcohol abuse, the deodorant sniffing and vaping in young kids. The pregnant teenagers and the incidence of Foetal Alcohol Syndrome.

I have interviewed people from the Stolen Generation and heard about their plights. We have experienced the child gangs in the streets of Alice Springs. Children walking around at night, not wanting to go home, because they do not want to be bashed, or raped, or both.

One year in Geraldton, we witnessed a brawl between two indigenous girls. I had never seen girls behave like this before. Then the boyfriend of one of the girls, chased the other girl, wielding a meat cleaver. This all happened in broad daylight. We sat in amazement and horror. Because I was so frightened witnessing these actions, I promptly locked the car doors.

In recent years, I met with a lady in Newman, Western Australia, who was very community minded and wanted to help our lost indigenous children. She told me a young indigenous girl had told her; it was better to wear more clothes at home. The child's excuse was because there was more chance of running away from being raped, because it took longer to get her clothes off. It is horrific that these poor children are exposed to this on a regular basis. Unfortunately, child sexual abuse is just part of their everyday life.

It is incredibly sad that this is going on and no one knows what to do about it, to make it improve. People in the eastern states, where there aren't many indigenous people, have no idea about some of the issues that are going on in the Northern Territory. It is never televised.

In the last five years we have spent most of our time in Western Australia. It has some of the most beautiful countryside we have ever seen. And because it is such an enormous state, there is just so much more to see. We have met some wonderful people and have new and old friends now to visit.

Because of our love for farming we have especially spent a great deal of time in and around Geraldton. We spend most of the hotter months around that area and travel north in the winter months. Life has become increasingly easy every day for me. I have become the Jojo I once was. The person called Jojo before my entire innocence and childhood was taken away from me.

I walk every day for my physical and mental wellbeing. Walking has particularly helped with overcoming a great deal of things that have been cluttering my thoughts for many years. Walking is a meditation for me and what better place to do it than out in the outback? The scenery is breathtaking.

Another cathartic treatment I have genuinely enjoyed is writing. It has helped me psychologically as well as keeping my brain active. To write is sometimes to erase bad thoughts and understand why they are harmful. Ink releases pain and guilt.

Now, 60 years old, my life is rewarding me with a strong inner peace. David has helped me immensely with my life transformation into a peaceful life. Finally, my nightmare early life is turning slowly into my Happy Ever After.

# CHAPTER 56

## *ANOTHER GEELONG GRAMMAR SCHOOL FALLOUT*

On Saturday 12th July 2025, I was contacted via text from Kate Parsons. She was warning me there was an article in the Victorian Herald Sun regarding Geelong Grammar School. It was headlined 'Grammars $100m Shame' then 'School's Lost Generation'.

Kate had also sent me through, with this warning, the school-appointed clinical psychologist's contact number and asked me to call her if I needed some help. I was very intrigued by this latest article. Because we were in Western Australia in the outback, I rang Lisa in Victoria and asked her to buy the paper for me. When she had it she could send me through the photographed article as a text.

As I read the newspaper article, I also noticed Dr David Mackey's name was also mentioned. This was only the second time ever that he had been shamed in the media with respects to his sexual conduct at Geelong Grammar School. I knew about most of the other abuse and covering up that was included in the article. This knowledge came from my reading of Case 32, which was our own Little House of Horrors volume.

My reaction to reading the article was I simply went numb. I felt quite zoned out. This numbness happened every time something like this was put out in the media. I am sure it was the same for everyone else who was affected from this era. It was interesting how quickly I had life like visual flashbacks, when I saw a predator's face or read about a predator.

I spoke to Kate later in the day briefly and we discussed the article. I also contacted another Mackey survivor, and we spoke briefly via text. Whilst we were talking, I asked her if she was going to attend the White Balloon Day this year.

The White Balloon Day has been conducted every year at Geelong Grammar School for the survivors of child sexual abuse. It was put in place to raise awareness about child sexual assault and abuse prevention. Every year I have received an invitation and every year I have declined. This is because, previously, I have never wanted to or haven't been ready to attend mentally or physically. I haven't even seen it on zoom, which has always been made available to me.

During the course of the afternoon, David and I had a discussion about the article. We also talked about White Balloon Day. Because of the positive journey I have now experienced from Geelong Grammar School and my association with Healing and Hope, we both felt it was now time. I was going to attend the 2025 White Balloon Day.

I booked a return flight from Geraldton to Melbourne, and my daughter would be joining me for moral support. Finally, after all these years, I was beginning to feel more comfortable about returning to Geelong Grammar School, Corio campus.

I was also delighted to be attending the 10-year anniversary gathering for the Royal Commission. I was looking forward to meeting the amazing people who had helped me to come so far on my journey.

After all the excitement and organising of my trip to Melbourne, I noticed the same newspaper article in the Herald Sun had appeared on Facebook. Then I realised the writer of the article was a woman I had contacted previously on Facebook. I also had a phone conversation with her at a camp we were staying at in Queensland in December 2022. The conversation was about the injustice that was felt for all the Mackey survivors. There was never any newspaper recognition before, that his sexual abuse against twenty plus students at the school, had ever occurred. At the time, I decided not to go ahead with reporting it to her, because it was still very raw to me and it also may have caused unnecessary litigation.

This time around I sent the lady a message on Messenger telling her I was authoring my book. And reminding her I was also a Mackey victim. Her reply to me was to give her a call the following week. And any time! I called her whilst we were still in Port Hedland. We spoke about the article a little and I made comment on the monetary figures she had quoted. I told her I didn't think the monetary information was entirely correct.

The other thing I had noticed in the article was, it was sexist. There was no mention at all about any sexual abuse of female students. It was all to do with the boys that had suffered. It came across like an Old Men's Club article, giving the impression females were not as important. This had irked me quite a bit.

As we were talking, I gave her more details about the book I was writing about my life. She offered to help me down the track with promotion. I said I would definitely take her up on the offer. I did assure her I thought I would have no problem selling my book. I was very sure many people would read it.

# CHAPTER 57
## *MY DIARY*

**4TH SEPTEMBER 2025**

I am sitting on an aeroplane on my way to Melbourne via Perth. I am going to be picked up from the airport by my daughter this afternoon and we will head down to Penny Dawson's for the next three nights.

Tomorrow is White Balloon Day at Geelong Grammar School. Wow, I am finally going to take another needed step in my healing.

In preparation for this special visit to Victoria, I spent the day yesterday having a 'knock yourself out Jojo indulgence day'. Hair, eyebrows, eye lashes, and a leg wax. Total pampering girl package. And very much needed. After all, I had been in the outback for the last two months.

Apart from the total care and treatment, it was also an incredibly interesting day. I met a young woman who was tending to me aesthetically and another woman completely by chance.

The first young woman was only 20 years old. She was intelligent, lovely-looking and had the world at her feet. We started talking about my book and my life experiences. She was extremely enthusiastic about what I would achieve by writing my life story. She was also very keen to buy a copy. She told me it had been an amazing experience to have met me and also thoroughly enjoyed our conversation.

There was another thing that struck me about this young woman and that was, I was once that young woman in so many ways. But unfortunately, I never ended up with the world at my feet. Someone had pulled a rug out from under me, and I had landed painfully on my bottom.

The second woman I met in the school car park. She had eased her way, with a large vehicle, into the park space beside me. We had wound down our windows after she had parked. Then we began chatting about the difficulty of parking large cars in these sorts of car parks. Our conversation then revolved around school pickup and cars getting scratched by children's school bags and car doors. Then she told me her children always came in through the rear door of the car, with all intentions of avoiding damage to any car in the vicinity.

We somehow managed to start talking about cleaning. She told me she was a Virgo and had just finished doing her housework before she came out to the school. I had been writing my cleaning book in the car while I waited for Michael's children. When I had told her I was writing a book about cleaning, we touched on how obsessive Virgos were with cleanliness. After a little more discussion, we talked about whose kids I was picking up. She actually knew one of my Michael's three children, his youngest daughter, Heti who I was waiting for.

We then got on to talking about children, divorce and I touched on my first marriage etc. We talked about my current situation and then she asked me how to bring her children up. She appreciated how hard the job was. I explained I just tried to set boundaries for my own children, be firm and also to try and bring them up to be wonderful and respectful humans.

On finishing our conversation, she asked me about leaving my first husband. I explained to her the difficulty of any relationship breakup and adding children was another wildcard. Before she left, she turned to me and said that I should be writing a book about that as well. I didn't reply to her comment. But, because of that comment, I found myself smiling from within.

On reflection, I later wrote about my encounters of the day.

*I came into contact today with women I have never met before. They actually gravitated towards me and suggested topics I had mentioned I should write about.*

*I have never seen myself as someone who can lead, in the way these people wanted me to. But now I am starting to believe I am a person who can facilitate and help people to look into their inner selves to recognise and realise their own self beauty.*

## WHITE BALLOON DAY
## SEPTEMBER 5TH 2025

After a lovely evening last night of plenty of enjoyable conversation, delicious food, washed down with sparkling wine, my daughter and I woke this morning to get ready for my first ever White Balloon Day at Geelong Grammar School. Penny had helped me out with a few clothing additions for warmth and also for a lovely outfit to match the standard of dress.

We arrived at the Corio campus boom gate and checked ourselves in as attendees for the morning. I had no idea what was going to happen, and I felt a little nervous, as well as excited.

Kate and Tanya were both there as we arrived and we chatted and walked to the pavilion together. There were a few familiar faces, and I saw a woman who looked very familiar but wasn't sure of her name or where I had seen her before. We were introduced by Kate and started chatting. Her job at Healing and Hope was to engage people in an equine healing experience. Another great initiative the school is offering for healing.

As we chatted further, we managed to work out how we knew each other. This was another one of those strange meetings under hugely different circumstances to when we had first met. After chatting about Timbertop, I realised I had done quite a large clean for this lady about 10 or so years ago. She was working at Timbertop with her husband, and they owned a rental property in Mansfield. On vacating the premises, the tenant had left the house in a very unacceptable condition. The house was completely trashed. I was sent there, by the real estate, to bring it back up to scratch so it could be re-leased.

Whilst cleaning the house, this lovely lady and her husband visited and we had met. They had tried to do as much as they could prior to my cleaning, but it was an extremely challenging time for them and they needed me. More small world stuff once again.

After a cup of coffee and a delicious sandwich, we made our way over to the Perry Oval. It was very strange to be walking through the school at 60 years of age. The route we took brought back good memories of the school, more than memories of my abuse. I tried very hard not to look towards my old day schoolhouse Allen and avoided any views of the medical centre.

During our walk, I chatted to my daughter and the lady mentioned previously. Conversation was about my family mostly and how I had estranged myself from some of my sisters and my mother. I was escorted arm in arm past the dining hall and out onto the road in front of the clock tower.

We arrived at the oval to see a sea of colour encompassing a heart and a ribbon. The colour was from the children and teenagers dressed in their house and school colours. It was very welcoming, and it felt extremely warm.

The proceedings began with the Principal, Rebecca Cody. Her speech was beautifully delivered, and it was very obvious the emotional ethos at Geelong Grammar School had come a long way since I attended school.

During her speech, apart from all the initiatives to do with child care and prevention, Rebecca started to say sorry. Sorry to all the survivors that had come today and all the survivors who had been affected by the historical sexual abuse at the school.

My feelings were extremely confused and I found myself on the verge of a panic attack. I started to cry quietly, and my daughter took hold of my hand. I managed to suppress my anxiety and my tears ceased. I began the conversation that I have now established, where I can talk myself out of a panic attack. I was safe. I was okay and I wasn't in any harm. There was amazing support around me, and I was being beautifully supported.

In reflection at my reaction to those sorry words, I found myself, once again, agonising and questioning why I was getting so upset when I was being openly apologised to. This beautiful, endearing woman was saying sorry to me with all her heart. She was apologising for something she had no control over, and she did it with incredible empathy.

I guess I was asking the same old question, "Why, in all of the years of my life, have my parents never apologised to me for what their friends had done to me? And also, never apologised for what it had done to me all of my life so far?"

On our walk back to the pavilion, I was supported by my daughter and a few other survivors. We chatted about our bad old days, and I met a lovely lady I had reached out to on a few occasions. We returned to the pavilion on foot to where we first started our day and had cups of tea and coffee and some lovely food to eat. There was plenty of chatter and support amongst the Healing and Hope staff and survivors during this time. We had survived!

Following a few speeches, I met Rebecca Cody and we embraced in an amazing hug. What an amazing woman and what an incredible job she has done since becoming head of Geelong Grammar School. I was honoured to meet her. Without her and the team at the school, I would never have been able to live the life I am living now.

There were also a number of introductions to people I had a great deal to do with but had never met. It is wonderful to put a face to a name and a voice on the phone.

My daughter and I went out to lunch on the way home and went for a walk along the beach later in the afternoon. On returning home, we lit the fire, and I had a lovely long chat with Penny's mother, Jill. It was lovely to talk positively about my day with an old friend. It was really a day about me, and I thanked my daughter for being there with me and supporting me.

## 6TH SEPTEMBER 2025

Today was the 10-year reunion of the Royal Commission into Institutional Child Sexual Abuse. The Healing and Hope team and some survivors were invited to a beautiful winery in the Geelong area, called Scotchman's Hill. I was privileged to be a part of this celebration. I was picked up from Penny's by another survivor, and we arrived to be welcomed again by Kate and Tanya.

Today was a lovely way to finish my experience with Healing and Hope and to tie off the White Balloon Day. We enjoyed fantastic conversations and delicious food. I was able to catch up with incredibly old friends from the Bostock days and also to meet that special GGS advisor I had been in contact with since my mediation. It was amazing because we both knew who we were when she entered the room, before we had even formally met. We had a great chat and a good laugh, as usual.

## SEPTEMBER 7TH 2025
## THE FLIGHT BACK TO WA.

Going to where I now call home.

My daughter and I talked a little last night about leaving early this morning to catch my flight back to Western Australia. She had even joked, if I was not ready, she would leave me behind if I didn't wake in time.

Last night was an earlier night than it has been for the last few nights. Catching up with Penny and family has involved lovely meals, enjoyable conversation, some lovely wine and good old family friend reminiscing. I made sure I was in bed by around 9pm. That's 7pm Perth time.

I woke this morning at 4.09am (that's 2.09am Perth time). I had slept well until then. I looked at my phone and knew I had at least an hour and twenty minutes left, before I needed to get up. We had organised to leave at 6.00am. I would have fallen sleep again, but I had a mosquito dive bombing my right ear. Bloody annoying really and I did try to get under the sheet but didn't sleep any more. So, at 5am I decided to just get up and start the day.

My daughter was up early too, and we left the house at 5.30am. The drive to the airport went without any hassle and I had plenty of time to board the plane. We waited on the tarmac for about an extra half an hour before we took off. There were some technical problems with the plane that were sorted eventually.

I was in a seat on the aisle and had two spare seats between myself and a younger girl. Younger meaning 30 years old. We didn't really acknowledge each other for quite some time but when there was a medical issue with one of the passengers near us, she started to gravitate towards me.

An announcement came over the PA asking for someone who was a nurse or a doctor to help out. My first reaction was to sit tight until someone put their hand up. I was in the throes of speaking up when a nurse did finally come on the scene. Because of my vet nursing experience and my interest in health and medicine, I was quite happy to help if needed.

The young woman beside me and I struck up a conversation. She was very anxious about the older gentleman who was extremely pale. When the flight attendants did attend to him, she came closer to me and wanted to chat. Her manner was a little stirred up by the events going on around us. I must admit I had a little frustration too because, in my case, I had wanted to help the gentleman.

As our conversation continued, I got the feeling this young woman felt she needed to engage with me. She opened up to me and her terror, related to the older gentleman, then unfolded. She told me she thought he had looked so ill and he was going to die. She started to avoid looking his way. The flight attendants were there constantly and the nurse who offered to help was there on a few occasions. By this time, the man was also wearing an aircraft oxygen mask. I reassured the young woman and told her the gentleman was looking better, and his colour was improving.

As we talked more, she opened up even more to me. This poor young woman had experienced a terrible experience with an earlier boyfriend. She told me she had seen her boyfriend die. I didn't ask why, of course, but reassured her she was safe and no one was going to die.

We began talking a little about our lives. I told her I was writing this book and it was based around what had happened to me as a younger person. She told me about her post traumatic stress disorder, and I told her I had suffered with the same disorder. Her disorder was caused by her boyfriend's death. We also talked about eating disorders because she had anorexia when she was a model. We had a lot of things in common when it came to psychological problems. I asked her about her treatments and asked her if she had ever experienced EMDR.

EMDR is the abbreviation for Eye Movement Desensitisation and Reprocessing. This therapy is a psychotherapy approach that helps individuals reprocess traumatic memories and reduced their associated stress. It is used widely on individuals who have PTSD and is extremely helpful in a lot of cases.

It briefly involves bilateral stimulation, such as eye movements or other movements like tapping or sounds, while focusing on the distressing memory. This process acts to resolve trauma by integrating memories in a healthier way. It is widely used to treat PTSD, anxiety, and other related conditions. She told me she had experienced EMDR and had found it greatly beneficial in treating her PTSD.

We chatted further about her engagement with a clinical psychologist who she really liked. I thought that was especially important to have a good clinical relationship with someone who was treating you. I shared the similar experience with my own clinical psychologist.

We thoroughly enjoyed the rest of our flight and chatted about other interesting topics. Princess Diana's name came up because of her bulimia nervosa, and I told her I had ached for Diana during the exposing of her eating disorder. She recommended I read Diana's book about her struggles. I recommended her to do a victim impact statement about her bad experiences. A victim impact statement helps you process what has happened as a result of a horrible experience. It helps you believe it was not your fault and to process your feelings about your reactions to that experience. I quite often recommend to people who have had trauma to write down their feelings about their experiences. It has helped me incredibly with my writing.

I am absolutely sure we were supposed to be together on our flight this morning.

After we had said our goodbyes, I needed to go to arrivals to be picked up by my lovely Irish couple, Gordon and Kathleen. They had driven to the airport to take me out for lunch. It is never a dull moment with this couple, and we began our meeting, as usual, in hysterics. They had arrived early and been sitting at the wrong domestic terminal looking out for me for over an hour. I rang so we could find each other. Kathleen described themselves as Dumber and Dumber because they had gone to the wrong place. Anyway, after about 15 minutes we did meet up and went to a lovely pub for lunch.

It was Father's Day, so everyone was out for lunch. We enjoyed a lovely meal and some bubbles and then I was dropped back to the airport.

I began writing my book again until I was ready to board the plane to Geraldton. The plane left on time, and we were served snacks and a glass of wine. I chatted to a woman next to me for a while and we talked about why we were on the flight. I told her a little about my weekend in Geelong. She then announced to me she was doing FIFO to Geraldton and she was a psychologist. I could not believe it. What a day and what a weekend I have had.

## 9TH SEPTEMBER 2025

I loved my weekend, and I have recovered from it now. It was very tiring, very emotional but I feel amazing as a result of an extremely positive experience.

# CHAPTER 58
## *HELPFUL READINGS*

There have been so many things that have inspired me to write over the years. Whether it was people or events that made me want to write. There were also times, where I had so much to say. But at the same time, I also thought there was nobody out there who would want to listen. People like my family, who thought I was a waste of space. Or people like my mother, who had once said, "Who would want to read a book about you?"

Because of my past, I had never really achieved any dreams I had. Never finished a degree at university, never had a job in my field of interest. For a while, I thought of myself as a complete loser. I have spent my entire life so far and since this happened, trying to learn how to believe in myself and accept me as the incredibly intelligent and amazing woman I am. It is still incredibly hard because I still don't have a certificate that says that.

As a career, I became a cleaner, a 'Madge' in some people's eyes, scum of the earth. I cleaned people's toilets.

I believe some of these failures will be with me for an eternity, but they will hopefully keep fading and help me to become the old JoJo. The JoJo that was put here to do what I was supposed to do and that was to help and nurture. To make people feel happy in their own skin and believe in themselves. Whether it be physically or mentally.

I now have the power of freedom in my life. The freedom of expression. Freedom of being a woman who has been sexually and mentally abused but now looks on life so differently. A woman who can be there for other people and hopefully make their lives so much better.

I hope my writing will enable people to be more empathetic to survivors of child sexual abuse. And, more importantly, realise it is an incredible struggle for anyone who has ever been sexually abused. It is also a trauma that is lived nearly every day. There is always a reminder, whether it is a headline or a newspaper article that raises the trauma thermometer. Another thing to be mindful of is, there is always someone out there who has had it a hell of a lot harder.

It is now 10 years since the Royal Commission into Institutional Sexual Abuse. Ten years of intensive healing coming to terms with what I experienced as an innocent young girl. Ten years of evolving into the woman I am now. I don't think I would have ever evolved if it had not been for the Royal Commission. Not only the Royal Commission but all the people I have been extremely lucky to meet through it. Including people from the new age Geelong Grammar School.

Maybe if I had experienced the necessary help when I was hopelessly screaming out for it as a teenager, my life may have evolved very differently. Hindsight is a wonderful thing. Life now is hugely different, and I have become free. Free to enjoy the things I want to enjoy. Free to travel to unusual places.

As we travel around the country, we have week-long stops in the same place to have a good look around and enjoy the scenery. In my spare time, when I am not writing, I do a great deal of reading. Some inspirational books that have helped me understand and helped me to deal with some of my own personal life experiences and hang ups are:

## THE SINS OF THE FATHER BY SHANEDA DALY

This incredible woman is now a grandmother and was abused by her own father for over a decade. She reported him years later to the police and he was jailed for his crimes of sexual abuse. Her story is definitely of survival. And a great read.

The one thing that struck me the most about this book was, Shaneda had a great deal of difficulty with her mother. Not dissimilar to my relationship with my own mother. And that is how she thinks, that if you just get on as usual, everything will work out. Some sort of denial that nothing is wrong. I am sure there will be other survivors that have the same experience with their mothers.

My father never touched me indecently but the friends of my parents did, and my mother reacted the same way Shaneda's mother did. It was as if this was just accepted as normal behaviour. Or just not dealing with it for the sake of saving face.

Shaneda lives in Ireland. Her book is available on Amazon and iBooks. She has also set up an amazing Facebook page for survivors. I have touched base with her and now I am involved, from time to time, helping survivors in Ireland. Hopefully this book may be of some help to other survivors of child sexual abuse.

## HELL ON THE WAY TO HEAVEN, BY CHRISSY FORSTER AND PAUL KENNEDY.

Another book, which I found incredibly confrontational, and it actually took me over five years to even pick it up.

A friend of mine, Merran, told me they were reading this book at book club a few years ago. And she encouraged me to read it.

I sent her a message recently and told her I had finally read the book. There was one comment I made, that really inspired me more to write this book. My comment was, I thought that I was remarkably similar to the real life character in Emma. I then told Merran I was writing my life story. Beautifully, she said it was definitely a great idea for me to be telling my story. In other words, she thought my story would be great to be told. And people would read it.

## UNHOLY TRINITY BY DENIS RYAN AND PETER HOYSTED

This is another horror abuse book and absolutely true. Based mainly in Victoria, it is to do with the priesthood but also includes the corruption of the Victorian police force and the government and the let down in our judicial system. A similar theme of corruption and misleading, familiar in the past of Geelong Grammar School.

My other amazing inspiration has been the alias, Miss Parsley, Kate Parsons. She has been fantastic all the way through from my court appearance and mediation to this day. She has driven me to write this life story. And I am thrilled that I have her in my life. Kate also has an incredible sensitivity to everyone she works with who has been a victim of child sexual abuse. She also acknowledges and sees how I have struggled and how so many other people have struggled. Kate always helps to keep me focused.

There are so many instances of child sexual abuse and the hopeless dealings with it. This has caused considerable damage and if only we had been able to speak up and be believed, some of this damage may have been prevented.

Over the last few years, I have been asked and recommended to apply for the Victorian Victims of Crime Consultative Committee. My life story and experience, in having multiple sexual assault cases within my own family, have earned me this opportunity. I was not required in the first year, because there were others in a similar position to me. There were a few with families having multiple cases applying for the position. I had thoughts it might also had a bit to do with a certain QC being involved with the process. She probably saw my name and said, "Oh no, that's the one who keeps writing me letters."

The next year, I was offered an opportunity to apply but I chose not to. We were too far away from Victoria and I had started on my own story.

One special thing that needs to be mentioned and has helped me find some inner peace is the creating of Healing and Hope by Geelong Grammar School. Healing and Hope was established in 2022. It was created to provide comfort and practical support to survivors of sexual abuse and victims of trauma within the Geelong Grammar School community.

I have become as involved as I can to be an aid in helping survivors. Because of my experience with Healing and Hope, I have also helped myself to gradually heal from my own child sexual abuse. I am now able to call myself a survivor.

Healing and Hope is an incredible initiative, and I highly recommend anyone, who is a survivor of historical sexual abuse at Geelong Grammar School, to touch base and begin to learn how to heal yourself. I am, to this day, still in touch with Healing and Hope. There is a website set up to do just this.

Geelong Grammar School is so incredibly sorry for its lack of acknowledgment and lack of response to the horrific incidents that happened in the seventies, eighties, and nineties. The current head of Geelong Grammar School is a beautifully compassionate, empathetic, and extremely understanding woman. If it had not been for this amazing woman, there are so many people who would never have found their inner peace. The peace that was ripped out of them by sexual predators who lurked and were part of the sexual occult at Geelong Grammar School.

I hope this book has been of help to you, if you are a survivor of child sexual abuse. Or, if you aren't a survivor, it may help you to understand what it is like to be a survivor and the difficulties we have to face on a daily basis.

Please let your children know that child sexual abuse is the most important unpleasant experience that needs to be reported. Please let them also know, they will be believed. Please also let them know, your best friends are capable of sexually abusing them too. Think about your friends' behaviour also. Are they creepy or sleazy? There are tell-tale signs. And because of this, sexual abuse is very rarely, the stranger danger issue we think it is.

When you find yourself asking what you should do, which is not uncommon, go and talk to the police. Talk to your doctor for a referral to a clinical psychologist who can help your child deal with the trauma in a professional manner. A general practitioner is not suitable for this sort of treatment. Believe me, I can vouch for that.

Writing this book, has helped me understand so much about how I have now evolved as a person.

Finally, I forgive myself.

# CREDITS

## EDITOR

Samantha Elley

## COVER DESIGNER

Elizabeth McCracken of Coven Press
Front image provided by the author
Back image sourced from Wikimedia Commons

## INTERNAL FORMATTING

Alana Lambert of Coven Press
Body: Adobe Jenson Pro/11pt/17pt Spacing
Headings: Arsenica Variable
Internal images provided by the author.